BLACK MUTINY

BLACK MUTINY

The Revolt on the Schooner Amistad

by
William A. Owens

With Introductions by
Derrick Bell *and* Michael E. Dyson

BLACK CLASSIC PRESS
BALTIMORE

Library of Congress Catalog Card Number: 97-74501
ISBN 1-57478-004-2

Founded in 1978, Black Classic Press specializes in bringing to light
obscure and significant works by and about people of African descent. If
our books are not available in your area, ask your local bookseller to order
them. Our current list of titles can be obtained by writing:

Black Classic Press
c/o List
P.O. Box 13414
Baltimore, MD 21203

A Young Press With Some Very Old Ideas
www.blackclassic.com

Distributed by Publishers Group West

BLACK MUTINY

The Enduring Racial Paradox

By Derrick Bell

> If then, these negroes are not slaves, but are kidnapped Africans, who, by the laws of Spain itself, are entitled to their freedom, and were kidnapped and illegally carried to Cuba, and illegally detained and restained on board the *Amistad*; there is no pretence to say, that they are pirates or robbers. We may lament the dreadful acts by which they asserted their liberty, and took possession of the *Amistad*, and endeavored to regain their native country; but they cannot be deemed pirates or robbers, in the sense of the law of nations, or the treaty with Spain, or the laws of Spain itself. . . .
>
> —*THE AMISTAD*, 40 U.S. 518, 593–94 (1841).

The *Amistad* case brought to dramatic life nineteenth century America's worse nightmare: a bloody slave revolt. Supreme Court Justice Joseph Story's carefully worded opinion could not erase the dire danger that underlayed arguments on both sides in the increasingly heated slavery debate.

The Court was a most reluctant participant in this debate. Its decision to free the Africans was intended more as a rebuke to President Martin Van Buren, who on behalf of Spain had tried to pressure the federal courts to return them to Cuba, than it was a manifestation of judicial distaste for slavery.

Indeed, it was one of the few times during the nineteenth century that the Court issued a favorable ruling for slaves—or free Blacks for that matter. The very next year Justice Story, again writing for the Court, invalidated a Pennsylvania law requiring a hearing for Blacks alleged by southern agents to be fugitive slaves. The law's purpose was to protect Blacks, escaped slaves and free Blacks alike, from harassment and kidnaping by slaveowner agents. The Court, though, struck down the statute as an interference with the federal Fugitive Slave Act of 1793. Seventeen years later, the Court's Chief Justice Roger Taney, seeking to settle the status of Blacks and the slavery controversy, found in the infamous *Dred Scott* case that Blacks, whether slave or free, had no rights that Whites were bound to respect. For a great many Black people, the statement, despite civil rights laws, remains both an accurate description of their life experience and an exemplar of the paradox of race in America.

In a nation created out of a revolution against oppression, Black challenges to racial oppression, violent and nonviolent, never fail to evoke a defensive response in Whites. Notice Justice Story's reluctance to acknowledge the Africans' violent resistance to enslavement that was at the heart of the *Amistad* case. He "laments the dreadful acts by which they asserted their liberty." But it was those very actions that saved the Africans from spending the rest of their lives on a brutal plantation in Cuba.

Even so, it is likely this fear of racial mutiny that leads this nation, then and now, to deal so harshly with any Black deemed to be "getting out of line." On the other hand, the dramatic risks the Africans on the *Amistad* took to free themselves spurred abolitionist supporters and lawyers—Dr. Richard Madden, Lewis Tappan, Roger Sherman Baldwin, and John Quincy Adams—to a commitment of conscience that was stronger than their fears of economic ruin, public ridicule, and mob violence.

The pride of resistance may be the most lasting effect of efforts to confront racial oppression. Viewed from this perspective, we can see the parallels in the Africans' struggle to return home with the subsequent efforts of American Blacks to gain their freedom from slavery, to end segregation, and presently to make their way against the headwinds of a still deeply racist country that as its chief response maintains that it is colorblind.

Ambushed on a trail in his Mendi village by rival tribesmen, Cinqué, son of a village chief, like uncounted millions of other Africans, was sold into slavery not as a prize of war, or a hostage for peace, but for the expected profit that, then as now, serves as its own corrupting justification for endless variations on man's inhumanity to man. Denied every human dignity, Cinqué was transported a world away from the land and the people he knew, the wife and children he loved. Many died in the horrors of the Middle Passage. By throwing themselves in the sea or in other ways, many found in death a release from the horrors of their lives. Only a relative few were able to risk the brutal beating and mutilation that awaited those who showed any sign of resistance.

Cinqué was one of these. Having survived the tortuous, transatlantic voyage to be bartered and sold in Cuba, he and forty or so other Africans were being shipped to a Cuban plantation aboard the schooner *Amistad*. Pushed to the limits of his endurance by the brutal crew and despairing of the fate that awaited him and his countrymen, Cinqué managed to free himself and the other Africans. Armed with sugar cane knives taken from the ship's cargo hold, they rushed the ship's deck, and in a brief, bloody fight, killed the ship's captain and his attending slave.

Rather than an act of the moment, the rebellion was the culmination of Cinqué's deep yearning for his freedom and that of those around him. He understood then what today we dare not contemplate: that life without freedom is not worth living. To regain his freedom, he risked death and put aside his culture's traditional opposition to murder. The rebellion over, Cinqué took charge. As William Owens dramatizes the rebellion's aftermath,

> Under [Cinqué's] directions they dragged the bodies of Captain Ferrer and Celestino to the rail. Cinqué felt no remorse at the dead bodies, at his breaking the laws of Poro. The Africans cursed at lifting the bodies, and laughed as they splashed into the water. After them they tossed the two blacks [Seme and Cu-bah] killed by Captain Ferrer, cast them into the water without chant or ritual, without tears or show of sorrow. They had seen too much of death and suffering. Then they washed down the decks to clear away the blood. (68)

Two seamen escaped during the melee, and Cinqué ordered the two surviving Spanish crewmen to sail the ship back to Africa. By day, they headed east but at night, using their superior navigational skills, the Spanish seamen sailed west toward the United States coast where the ship and its African crew were captured.

Arrested and jailed for the next two years, and often placed on display for the entertainment of local citizens who paid the jailers for the privilege of seeing the "cannibals," the Africans became pawns in a major struggle between those who viewed them as property to be exploited for financial and political ends, and those who saw them as valuable exemplars for the anti-slavery controversies that would lead to Civil War a decade later.

The Africans suffered a great deal in their captivity during the months between the court hearings. They adapted poorly to the cold, New England winters and some died. Language barriers made it difficult to discern friend from foe. Men who had risked their lives and killed their captors seeking freedom now had to practice forbearance in the face of insult and abuse.

On one occasion, the homesick men obtained a jug of rum from a pub near the jail and began singing and dancing, refusing to stop at the insistence of their angered jailer, Colonel Pendleton, who calling them "heathen niggers," hit Cinqué with his whip: "'Stop it you black devil,' he shouted."(201) As Owens reports it,

> The cut of the whip brought Cinqué to a quick halt. Again he faced a white man, and the white man held a lash. Again the Wuja was crying in his ears, "Kill the white man!" Don Pedro Blanco, Captain Ferrer, Colonel Pendleton — their faces merged in a whirling mass of hate. He raised his hands to strike, and then dropped them. He could not fight back, and his comrades would suffer because of him. But this was no time to flinch. Proudly he faced Colonel Pendleton and waited for his punishment. (201)

Finally, through effective lawyering and a moving argument to the Supreme Court by former President

John Quincy Adams, the Africans were freed only to become indentured to Christian missionary groups that held them for the better part of a year hoping to prepare them to help establish missions in Africa. But all but ten or so, including Cinqué, abandoned the project shortly after the ship docked in Sierra Leone.

Returning to his home, Cinqué found that the slave trade had taken his wife and family, destroyed his village, and set his beloved world on end. Heartsick, he became a trader of goods and people. Having learned the ways of profit, he prospered and in the process, abandoned the humane instincts for others that had been the source of his strength, the essence of his leadership.

There are elements of the *Amistad* mutiny saga that characterize American racial issues then and now. The similarities are both a source of enlightenment and cause for deep concern. The country's racial history is defined by the dominance of Whites based on power and their willingness to use it against Blacks without qualms of morality, law, or simple decency. Concurrently, there is the subordination in varying degrees of Blacks who, fearful of the retaliatory power of Whites, only rarely challenge directly the exploitation and subjugation that marks and mars their lives.

Then, as now, no one escapes this paradox of race. It influences official policy making and individual behavior. Its endurance and its subordinating effect can be measured by the racial gaps between Blacks and Whites in virtually every measure of well-being. The significance of these racial disparities should be obvious, but many Whites seem to hunger for any word, no matter how absurd, that Blacks as a group continue to lag in education and income because of innate inability or lack of drive, and not because of systematic patterns of discrimination that run the gamut from the blatant to the unconscious.

There are the occasional Blacks like Cinqué and his

few dozen comrades, including Burnah, Kimbo, Grabo, who throw off their fears in a bold challenge to their oppressors. Even when they gain some relief, they learn that society's resistance to true liberty for Blacks has many facets beyond chains and the other tools of slavery. There are, as well, those Whites, always a tiny minority, who side with Blacks to fight racial discrimination. For them, identification is often with the anti-racist cause more than the victims of the evil they work to end. As a result, the hopes and aspirations of the Blacks are always at risk of being sacrificed for the cause.

The distinctions between slavery, segregation, and the current era of quasi-opportunity are real, but the paradoxes built on White dominance and Black subordinance are recognizable in each era. Those Blacks and Whites who challenge the racial status quo are seldom hailed as heroes in their own time. Their words and actions are too threatening to *what* is to allow either those they oppose or those they would help to comprehend when these bold individuals proclaim *what might be*.

In all times, the law is the handmaiden of those in power. Only in extraordinary instances will courts and legislatures break with this traditional role and reach out to the dispossessed, usually in ways that benefit those without power in small ways and in the short run. In large ways and in the long run, the seemingly remedial actions of law stabilize and legitimate even when, as is often the case, the powerful are most active in their opposition to these modest reforms.

Now, 150 years after his death, Cinqué and the few survivors of their tortuous experience in the Western world are being released from the confines of history and wheeled into a contemporary spotlight. One would hope that Cinqué's resurrected celebrity bestowed 150 years after his death will mean more than the profits from a top-grossing film. We do not need another Black hero sanitized and commercialized for public consumption.

Through the thick haze of modernity, we must see

beyond the promotional myths and come to know the man. For his life, fully revealed, offers lessons of value regarding our condition in America where the descendants of so many slaves continue to face the bias that differs from that Cinqué experienced in degree rather than in kind. We need not, as Cinqué had to, kill in order to win our oppressors' respect; but neither can we remain passive in hope, or active only in reliance on law. We must assert ourselves directly and firmly whenever we encounter barriers to human dignity.

It is time for us to face up to the significant similarities in our condition and that of the Africans on the *Amistad*. Despite our contributions and our faithfulness to this country, we remain today what they were then: a people presumed subordinate in entitlement to Whites and vulnerable to their exploitation and abuse. Overcoming that presumption remains our greatest challenge as individuals and as a group. The paradox is that our presence is both the problem and the promise for us and those Whites who still envision an America that actually lives, rather than simply asserts, its belief in equality.

The United States of Amnesia

By Michael Eric Dyson

Nearly a century and a half after its official death, the specter of slavery painfully haunts the American soul and psyche. The Great American Failure continues to color White perceptions of race and Black humanity. This is so even as this country denies its debt to Black ingenuity— of myriad, imaginative acts of sheer survival; of Blacks making their suffering at once spiritually sacred and usefully alien to the callous codes of American religion; of Blacks forging the hallowed destiny of American democracy in the crucible of fragmented languages, families, and cultures. The very fact of a thriving, though buffeted, Black existence after slavery—a literally unspeakable drama of human evil whose full impact remains virtually impossible to measure or mouth—is a testament to the great desire of Black Americans to, as William Faulkner phrased it, not simply endure but prevail.

Still, the process of Black prevalence has been hampered by America's torn conscience, and her equally torn will, as to what to make of her Black citizenry. The result is that Blacks are forced to carry their memories of oppression on their sleeves since America refuses to knit them *fully* into the tapestry of collective reckoning with either present traumas or past tragedies. For America to completely come to grips with race, it will take more than presidential apologies for genocidal scientific experiments, panels to lead a national conversation on the subject, or weak-willed attempts to salvage affirmative action, especially as welfare reform and crime reduction undertaken by the same president undermine Black social stability. It will take nothing less than the honest, pitiless examination of the consequences of selling human beings like animals at market for money— in order to deepen the rule of White supremacy—for us to heal our hurts. America has been remarkably consistent in avoiding such a step, but without it, the great march toward liberation from the ghosts of our past will be permanently stalled.

It is not overstating the case to suggest that, when it comes to race, we are living in the United States of Amnesia. America cannot solve its race problem because it cannot afford to remember what it has been through, or more accurately, what it has made its Black citizens endure: the horrible, cowardly, vicious legacy of racial domination stroked by religious belief and judicial mandate. The willed forgetfulness of our racial past continues to trap us. It makes Whites repeat harmful cycles of guilt, denial, hostility, and indifference. It makes Blacks cling desperately to victimization, White hatred, self-doubting, and self-loathing. It appears easier for most Whites, and for many Blacks, to reenact a pantomime of social civility through comfortable gestures of racial reconciliation than it is to tell each other the story of the colossal breach of humane behavior and democratic practice that slavery represented. What we need are stories that provide a window on the tangle of social and moral forces that drove the West's will to enslave Africans, and that reveal the equally strong heroism of Blacks and Whites who stepped out of their assigned roles of debasement or privilege to resist the fatal lie of White supremacy. No single narrative can completely comprehend the catastrophes that attended the West's trafficking in Black flesh for profit. But some stories about Black, and White, opposition to slavery are so singular that their dramatic retelling gives us a powerful sense of how the basic desire to live in dignity and freedom helped Blacks to achieve their liberation. The story of Black Africans fighting for their freedom on the *Amistad* is such a story.

The remarkable feature of the *Amistad* story is how well it holds up as a morality tale about the brutal effects of making an accidental feature of human identity like race the predicate for ill treatment or unjust benefit. The *Amistad* drama—particularly its bold, imaginative rehearsal in William Owens' colorful rhetoric—reminds us of just how absurd it is to treasure or trash human beings because of their color or country. Then too, the *Amistad* drama brilliantly captures the human element of slavery by revealing that behind the mask of inhumanity that White slavers doffed were the egregious manifestations of greed, fear, and envy. But even more powerfully, the *Amistad* gives us a thrilling character study of the irrepressible spirit of Africans, and their White allies, who were willing to risk their bodies in defending a belief in their essential equality with Whites. And as a glimpse into the fundamental conflicts between good and evil—especially as those poles were occasionally blended in Whites whose moral principles led them to abolish slavery even as their religion led them to practice paternalism and to suppress African religious and cultural practices, the *Amistad* is altogether compelling.

Perhaps, the most striking element of the *Amistad* story is how depressingly accurate it remains about the burdens that befall Black leadership, about how Whites and Blacks interact across a horizon of structural inequality, about the vile effect of oppression on Black psyches and bodies, and about the difficulties of supplanting Whiteness as a cultural norm and as a source of social privilege, even among Whites who side with Blacks against institutional racism. The story of Cinqué's brilliant leadership of the enslaved Africans reminds us of the continued need for bold Black leadership in our day, particularly as ethical imagination about racial justice fails, and as energy to resist its impact flags. And the obstacles Cinqué faced—the inherent fear of opposing Whites who outnumber Blacks, the limited material resources to effectively challenge oppression, the treachery of White divide-and-conquer strategies that undermine Black solidarity, the Black leader's temptation to exercise strict control over Blacks in punitive fashion, and the vast panoply of White means of control and corruption of Black life—continue to this day, even if in reduced scale and with diminished effect.

While it is undeniable that contemporary Blacks are in many ways light years from the conditions of slavery, they continue to face the brutal facts of social and economic inequality. One third of Black America is poor. These Americans, and the Black middle class, are bewitched by "consumer racism," and corporate bigotry as White businesses subject Blacks to pernicious practices such as seizing legally owned clothing and preventing promotion within the ranks of managerial elites because they are regarded, in the words of a corporate executive, as "black jelly beans." Characterized by the global crises of capitalism, the continued depression of Black working class wages, the Blackening of the poor working class, and the persistent problems of the so-called underclass, social and economic inequality are crushing blows to Black progress.

The *Amistad* story clarifies just how costly the systematic negation of a healthy Black self-image is to Black self-esteem. Despite his royal roots and regal bearing, Cinqué and his cohort were viewed by many Whites as savages without souls. Cinqué fought valiantly to remind his comrades that they were more than chattel and property. Such a reminder could surely be updated for the contemporary ghetto, especially among young Blacks who are viewed as the pathological agents of violence and destruction. While it is now fashionable to decry the therapeutic effect of enhanced awareness among Blacks of their cultural and racial origins, it is even more harmful, as James Baldwin argued, to believe the lies that Whites tell Blacks about their human worthlessness. Indeed, Baldwin suggested that their Whiteness itself was a lie, a hoax of artificial superiority perpetrated upon both Blacks and Whites who were the unequal victims of its myriad mendacities. The *Amistad* certifies Baldwin's insight, tracing over several continents the anatomy of White supremacist belief as it spread its terrible untruths in African societies, and in Spanish cultures and American colonies. Perhaps the most disappointing, though hardly unpredictable, feature of Whiteness is that even at its most edifying, it proves its solidarity with a dominant view of the inherent rightness of Whiteness—revealed in the *Amistad* story when Whites who had worked for the freedom of Cinqué and his fellow captives resented their minimal return to African practices and attempted to root them out by Christian catechism.

In the end, the story of the *Amistad* is a cautionary tale against American amnesia about the forces that shaped this country, indeed the entire West, and of how we must persist in remembering the dangerous stories of dangerous truths that were won in dangerous circumstances. Simply put, the truth is always struggled for, and the truth of Black life in America even more so. America will never be free unless it makes peace with its past, unless it faces head on the evil that it did to Blacks whose labor and love for this nation made it the global power it is today. The story of the *Amistad* reminds us of a value that we have too often forgotten even in Black communities: the value of strategic, principled defiance of White supremacy. It reminds us, too, that we have been heroic in the face of inhuman odds, a reminder we can certainly use now that informal drug economies and the social havoc to which they give rise threaten to devastate an entire generation. The *Amistad* story reminds us that we have been a great people, and that our greatness consisted precisely in our insistence on our dignity and freedom without qualification or compromise. Remembering that lesson is dangerous. But the greater danger is lethal amnesia, and the hostility to Blackness that it breeds, which beclouds our nation. The story of the *Amistad* is a powerful witness against forgetting about Black heroism and humanity. If we tell it in our generation, it is also a witness against the forces that still threaten our safe and sane existence. Since our nation has not fully learned the lesson of genuine Black equality, it must feel anew the fire of Black resistance. The story of the *Amistad* is a critical spark for that fire.

To

E. E. RHODES

with gratitude and appreciation

The African Chief

Chained in a foreign land he stood,
    A man of giant frame
Amid the gathering multitude
    That shrunk to hear his name—
All stern of look and strong of limb,
    His dark eyes on the ground—
And silently they gazed on him
    As on a *lion* bound.

Vainly, but well that chief had fought—
    He was a captive now;
Yet pride that fortune humbles not
    Was written on his brow.
The scars his dark broad bosom wore
    Showed warrior true and brave;
A prince among his tribe before,
    He could not be a slave.

            —William Cullen Bryant

FOREWORD

The story of the *Amistad* is one of those rare events when, by an extraordinary and mysterious combination of circumstances, human history converges, flows for a moment in a common stream, and then takes a new course. For one brief moment the attention of the major nations of the Western world was focused on thirty-five (or thirty-nine, or was it forty-one?) black people from an unknown tribe in equatorial Africa. The question before them was the nature of man. Slavery was the evil institution around which the moral storm was gathering, and the slave ship *Amistad* was in the eye of the storm. As in all such events when a great truth is incarnated, the people and things involved in the drama have a kind of scandalous particularity. Here were the bewildered and victimized people of the Mendi tribe who wanted only to return to their homeland. Here were the international murderers growing rich by acts of atrocity against defenseless people. Here were magistrates in the highest offices of the major capitals of the world betraying the principles of the governments they were sworn to uphold. Here were the partisan masses of the citizenry watching the drama through their partisan press. Here were the people who immortalized themselves by sacrificing everything for a great cause. It is in the sordid and glorious particulars of such an event as this that the social structure is broken open and for one brief moment the nature of man and the great issues of good and evil are exposed to history.

No institution in America has its origins in an event of such dramatic power as the American Missionary Association and the *Amistad* story. This is truly one of the great contemporary myths of the American folk. The myth of the *Amistad* would be much easier to live with if it were not historical, if it had its origins in primordial imagination. But it *is* historical and therefore we must live with its scandalous historicity. Its heroes are mortal men and its villains are not totally villainous.

The power of this drama lies in the symbolic representations of its leading characters and in the heroic dimensions of its staging. The first act is staged around that part of the Atlantic known as the Middle Passage, extending from the West Coast of equatorial Africa to the Greater Antilles of the Caribbean. Across this benign stretch of ocean lying, ironically, between the North Atlantic and the South Atlantic, there developed an international traffic in human beings enormously profitable in money and monstrously tragic in human suffering. In this act we are introduced to the Mendis themselves who provide the continuity in the drama. We meet the international criminals in the persons of the slave traders and we can discern in the background the African chiefs and tribal officials who were also profiting from the sale of their own people. How conveniently the crime of slavery was accommodated into the structures of social controls in the African tribes! On the Caribbean side of the Middle Passage the intrigue broadens and becomes more desperate as the African victims come closer to a lifetime incarceration in the legal institution of slavery.

The second act of the drama takes place on the ship whose name becomes the title of the myth: *La Amistad*. Again, no irony of history is more poignant than the name of this ship; a beautiful, low, black vessel designed for speed and maneuverability, whose decks were the scene of primitive combat between the abductors and the manacled desperate black people, and through whose scuppers ran the red blood of white men, down the black topsides and into the blue Caribbean. We cannot help but wonder what Mysterious Dramatist arranged to have *this* ship named *The Friendship*. Here in the death struggle of black and white the character of Cinqué begins to emerge as the leader of the Mendi people.

The third act is played in the courtrooms of our democracy—the courtrooms, where ultimately in any ordered society the great questions of morality and justice are decided. Here, with all the world looking on, the tangled moral strands were precariously unraveled and painfully reworked into an uncertain tapestry of approximate justice. The act begins in the lower courts of Connecticut and ends in the highest court of the land. It soon became apparent that this was not a fight over rival claims to a cargo of uncertain nationality but a national debate over the nature of man. In the Supreme Court of the United States the argument became "the trial of one president by another" with John Quincy Adams for the Mendis and President Martin Van Buren siding with the Southrons. It is in this act that the Christian abolitionists appear as a zealous and determined organization.

In the fourth act another ship appears and the stage is set for what should have been the denouement of the drama, but history at this point abandons the script and what should have been a denouement is more of an unmasking. The second ship is the *Gentleman,* procured by the *Amistad* Committee to take the Mendis and a few missionaries back to Africa, there to begin the "grand march toward the conversion of the world." The voyage of the *Gentleman* is as crucial to the myth as was the voyage of the *Amistad.* Here, on the long sea voyage, part of it through the same bloodstained Middle Passage, the loneliness of the sea stripped away the stereotypes and revealed the essential humanity of both black and white in a cruel nakedness which neither could tolerate. Cinqué assumed that his release and return to his homeland meant that he was again the leader. The white missionary

ix

assumed that *he* was in charge of this mission. The struggle for power on the *Gentleman* was not as bloody as the fight on the *Amistad* but it was just as cruel.

The voyage of the *Gentleman* with its human cargo of white and black, occurring as it did after the rights of the Mendis had been established in our courts, is comparable to the present post-civil-rights conflict in our country. Once the question of rights has been established and equality begins to emerge as a basic assumption, the struggle over political and economic power can take place in an impartial arena. The establishment of racial equality, instead of being the end of conflict is the beginning of a new conflict—or, more correctly, is the continuation of the age-old conflicts with the Negro in full participation.

When the *Gentleman* landed, after its voyage of self-discovery, the Mendis were so ecstatic at seeing their home-land that their thin veneer of white acculturation peeled off in one great burst of joy, and the white missionaries found themselves almost as lonely as the Mendis had been in New Haven. Cinqué found his tribe decimated by intertribal war-fare and in his disillusionment turned procurer for the slave trade.

In the present post-civil-rights phase, the black leadership's loss of nerve in the face of the threat of equality has been as disillusioning as the entrenched prejudice of white segrega-tionists. The white dilettantes in the movement have also lost their nerve and either have retreated to a safe distance or have followed the black racists, as far as their color will allow, into the apartheid jungle. There they present the tragically ridiculous, guilt-ridden figure of the white black-supremacist.

The only possible conclusion to this drama is an eschato-logical one and, with faith, its shadowy form can be seen backstage. Once the civil rights of all races have been estab-lished and the access to the institutions by which our democ-racy changes itself has been guaranteed to all, we can wage together the ancient fight against the enemies of man. War, poverty, ignorance, and disease are beyond race and creed and nationality, and in the great human coalition to fight them we will find our common humanity. Here is where the American Missionary Association is to be found, working quietly amidst the clamors of the "true believers," steering its precarious course through the turbulent Middle Passage from where we are to where we ought to be.

Wesley A. Hotchkiss
General Secretary
American Missionary Association
United Church Board for Homeland Ministries

CONTENTS

ILLUSTRATIONS

The Mysterious Schooner

For days a mysterious long low black schooner hovered on the New Jersey and Long Island coast. Her lines were sharp, her bearing proud, but time and storm had left their marks— her topsail yard gone, her sails blown to shreds, her copper bottom fouled with barnacles and seaweed. Sometimes she flew a Spanish flag, more often none at all. By day she stood east, pointing her gilt-eagle prow into the sunrise; by night she drifted like a derelict, or boxed lamely to the north and west. Men along the beach saw her and cocked their muskets against the pirates about to land. Sailors on passing vessels hailed her, then fearfully increased sail when they saw her decks lined with fierce and famished blacks brandishing muskets and cutlasses. Ships that approached too close were raked by badly aimed musket fire.

Rumors raced along the coast, growing from mouth to mouth, added to by every teller, spread by newspapermen whose imagination had been kindled by the sound of mystery and danger. Some said she was a pirate schooner bent on looting lonely coastal vessels and towns. Some swore she was the *Flying Dutchman* beating her way through the seven seas. Others identified her correctly as the Spanish slaver whose cargo had risen and killed the captain and crew. Word of such a mutiny had come from Nuevitas in the Island of Cuba —word that twenty-six whites had perished at the hands of the black cannibals on board.

3

Cries of "Pirates!," "Mutineers!," "Murderers!" echoed in every coastal town and hamlet from Boston to Baltimore. Men, stirred by fright and excited by rumor, demanded protection from the renegades on the schooner. They sent frantic messages to the Brooklyn Navy Yard, to the customs officials up and down the coast. They waited on President Van Buren in the White House and flooded his office with demands for capture of the pirate blacks.

Patrol vessels put out from points all along the coast. The cutter *Gallatin* from Bombay Hook, the *Wave* from New York, the *Vigilant* from Newport, the *Rush* from New London. The experimental steam frigate *Fulton* fired up and went in a pursuit that was hopeless, for she could carry only enough fuel for a forty-hour cruise. With a dozen vessels searching for her, the mysterious schooner still came and went like a ghost ship, appearing off Sandy Hook, Fire Island, Montauk Point.

Her master was an African named Cinqué and her destination the Slave Coast, from which he had lately been sold . . . but the wanderings of both master and schooner were stranger than mind could imagine, their effect on the institution of slavery greater than words could measure. Soon the name of Cinqué was on every tongue: Cinqué the pirate, Cinqué the mutineer, Cinqué the African chief, Cinqué the pawn of factions headed relentlessly toward the war of brothers. . . . Around the world friends of black men were retelling the story of Cinqué's journey from freedom to freedom, a journey beginning and ending in the village of Mani, in the land of the Mendis, on the West Coast of Africa. . . .

4

I

AFRICAN SLAVE FACTORY

The captives lay like a black mat before the door of the warehouse. There were shackles on their ankles, iron collars around their necks. A chain padlocked to each iron collar threaded them together . . . men and chains, chains and men—the warp and woof of human slavery. Black guards stood over them armed with muskets and whips made of manatee skins. Farther away, at the edge of the yellow lagoon, a black prince in blue robes turned his back on them and examined with interest the islands and buildings of Don Pedro Blanco's slave factory.

Except for one, the captives lay stretched on the moist earth, resting from their trek through the jungles. It was an hour now since they had been brought across the lagoon to the island on which the warehouse stood, an hour since they had lifted their weary, chained bodies out of unsteady native canoes, an hour since Prince Birmaja had sent Kroo to tell Don Pedro that he, the son of King Shiarka, had brought more captives to fulfill his bargain.

Except for Cinqué, the captives lay inert, all fight gone out of them. He had raised himself to a sitting position, his body braced against the flank of another captive. He still had the will to bargain, to plead, to promise if only Birmaja would take the chains off and allow him to return to his father's village.

"Prince Birmaja," Cinqué called to the blue-robed back.

5

Birmaja did not turn. Cinqué could remember times when Birmaja had been glad to heed his call—in the days when he and Birmaja had traded together, when he had brought rice and fruits to trade for cotton cloth and tobacco.

"Prince Birmaja," he said again, "the debt I owe you—"

He spoke slowly, for Birmaja had little facility with the Mendi language, being himself of the Vey people. Birmaja did not heed, but the guards uncurled their whips.

Cinqué dared again, as he had dared so often during the days of his captivity, to settle the debt. It had been an honorable trade in the beginning, and he had paid two-thirds of the total. The other he could pay as soon as rice was harvested. Fivefold he would pay to escape slavery, to escape ending his life on a Cuban sugar cane plantation far from wife, children, home.

"I will pay you fivefold—"

This time a guard let the tips of his whip sear Cinqué's shoulder. Birmaja did not turn. He was looking at Don Pedro approaching in a native canoe.

It struck mud at the edge of the island and Don Pedro, dressed in the white cottons and broadbrimmed hat of a planter, stepped ashore. At his heels was a dog, snarling and growling at the strange black men, the kind of dog that Cinqué had often wished for in his own village. But Cinqué was looking steadily at Don Pedro, the first white man he had ever seen, studying the slender body, the swarthy face made darker by a tropical sun, sensing the cruelty behind the dark eyes, the cunning that made his name feared by tribes back to the mountains of the interior.

The Krooman paddling his canoe sprang ashore after him. He was one of those who had brought the captives to the island.

"Prince Birmaja," the Krooman said to Don Pedro.

"Prince Birmaja," the Spaniard repeated, showing the proper condescension of a white slaver to a native prince and fellow trader.

"Don Pedro," Birmaja acknowledged the greeting.

6

The two men, the immaculate Spaniard and the polished black prince, advanced toward each other and cracked fingers, in the African fashion. This introduction was pure formality. For months Don Pedro had furnished King Shiarka and Prince Birmaja the guns and powder with which they had put down all rival tribes—made themselves the strongest people between the Gallinas and the interior, tribute takers from rival tribesmen.

"Twelve black fellow," Birmaja was saying to Don Pedro in broken English.

Don Pedro looked at the blacks with the eye of a trader. He let his gaze linger on Cinqué's body—young, strong, erect from his tribe's custom of carrying baskets on their heads. He looked at the bronze skin, the flashing eyes, sure marks of the submerged strain of Berber blood in his ancestry. He would make a fine house servant for some Spanish Don in Cuba. He should bring a thousand dollars on the Havana market. In New Orleans—more.

"A chief?" Don Pedro asked.

"Son of village headman—village of Mani," Birmaja answered. "I took him for the debt he owed me."

Mani. The word called to Cinqué's mind the cone-hutted village, the rice fields from which he had been kidnapped. For the first time he doubted the fetish placed in the fields by the medicine man to protect the workers from evil. The medicine man had promised a fetish so strong that any invader who approached it would shrivel and die. Cinqué, looking at Birmaja, fat, black and healthy, knew he would never be withered by a fetish.

"How much?" Don Pedro was asking.

Before waiting for an answer, he signalled to the Krooman, who brought rum and glasses from the warehouse, good rum of the quality Don Pedro drank himself, not the watered rum from the big casks reserved for slave trade. He knew that Birmaja, like any other black trader, despised the white man who was niggardly with his drams. He took two wine cups from the black boy, passed one to Birmaja, and himself filled

7

them with rum. He was pleased with the strong healthy bodies of these new captives. They would bring good sums from any trader, especially now that the English made slaving so hazardous. With such a good buy before him, he could afford to be generous with Birmaja.

The time was late; a sudden rain threatened. Neither Don Pedro nor Birmaja was in a mind to haggle over prices. The bargain was soon struck, and Cinqué watched Don Pedro counting out cowrie shells to Birmaja, he watched black boys roll out a cask of rum and a bale of tobacco, he watched Birmaja's look of pleasure at the bolts of red and blue cloth. It was a good day. He had received as much as his guards could carry on their backs to King Shiarka—for each captive tenfold more than the debt Cinqué owed him.

The dealings over, Cinqué and his fellows, by the laws of African slave trading, belonged to Don Pedro. No one asked by what right Birmaja had owned them. Don Pedro gave an order to his Kroomen. The guards flicked their whips again, and the captives slowly dragged themselves into the canoe. It was large enough for all of them, hewn as it was from the log of a large cotton-silk tree. With skilled strokes the Kroomen shot the canoe toward an island washed on one side by the Gallinas, on the other by the surf of the Atlantic. In their journey the captives saw most of the slave factory of Don Pedro Blanco.

The Gallinas River—so named by the Spanish traders in honor of the flocks of chickens in and around the native huts —idles sluggishly through coastal swamps and broadens into a lagoon before it meets the ocean surf. In its short course it catches up silt, turns it to yellow mud, and pours it into the sea. The tide casts the mud back to form a sandbar protecting the mouth of the lagoon, making entrance from the sea dangerous, providing security for outlawed slavers. The silt catches on mangrove roots, forming hundreds of little reed-covered islands in the lagoon.

At this place, called Lomboko, Don Pedro set up his trade

and established lines to Boston, Havana, Rio. When he bought Cinqué, in April 1839, he had been fifteen years at this spot—building his barracoons, warehouses, dwellings, making friends with native chiefs and traders, inspiring native warfare so that he might buy captives from both sides to supply the slavers putting in at his factory; using his keen intelligence to make himself a fortune in the black traffic, baffling the world with the question of why a cultured white man should elect to spend his life among blacks in a jungle. He increased his trade to nearly a million dollars a year, and his bond was as good as gold in Havana, London, Madrid, Paris. . . .

On a large island near the mouth of the lagoon he had his warehouses, where he stored rum from Boston, tobacco from Havana, cotton goods from Manchester, guns and powder of finest English make, slave irons—chains, shackles, padlocks—imported circuitously from England. Farther in on another island stood a single dwelling, the residence of his sister, a cultured Spanish lady who had forsaken their native Malaga to live with her brother in equatorial Africa. Blacks rarely saw her, except the women who served her, but stories of her fair skin and the God she worshiped reached far inland, creating mystery and suspicion. They swore the gilded figure she worshiped in her room protected Don Pedro from the *gris-gris* of African medicine men.

A little farther up the river, in a secluded spot, Don Pedro had his seraglio—an island covered with little huts in which lived comely black women, fair as human ebony, and their mestizo children, Don Pedro's legacy to Africa. Fortunate indeed was the damsel he kept for himself from among all those he sent to Havana. Like an African chief, he maintained his women richly and guarded them jealously. Once a black man, caught intruding, was shot dead by Don Pedro.

Nearer the ocean, some of them swept by the surf itself, were the islands on which Don Pedro had his barracoons, filled now with captives waiting for slavers from Havana, slavers who must rush in and out again before the storms of

9

the wet season could break, taking their chances with the British slave patrol.

High above the factory, on posts and trees, lookouts sat like ospreys, each in his little nest, sheltered from sun and rain, with spyglasses always busy, ready to cry "Sail ho!" if a vessel appeared on the horizon, ready to answer the musket fire of slave caravans arriving through the jungle.

Over all Lomboko was the smell of sluggish water, of rotting jungles, and the unwholesome smell of mangroves. . . .

The Kroomen brought their canoe to an island where the tall walls of a barracoon reached almost to the water's edge. At one side a fire flamed under huge cauldrons. Black boys, looking like evil medicine men, stirred the pots with long sticks. It was a "devil place" in spite of the sweet smell of rice cooking in palm oil.

Cinqué and the others were hustled out of the canoe and slipped through a narrowly opened door into a large room where near a hundred blacks milled about or lay chained on the dirt floor. At the order of a Spanish guard, the boatman took off their chains. They had to go back to Birmaja to serve again when he had fresh slaves to drive through the jungle.

When the captives were unchained, black boys brought them rice and palm oil on banana leaves. They ate hungrily, letting oil drip from fingers and chins. Then they tossed their banana leaves to the rubbish-covered floor.

After he had eaten, Cinqué walked among the captives, speaking to them, asking where they had come from, how long they had been captives. Many to whom he spoke had the Mendi tribe mark—a blue line of cuts half an inch broad from forehead scalp to nosetip. None of these were from Mani, but they were closely related and spoke a language he could understand. Their stories were the age-old stories of slavery. Don Pedro had sent word to native traders that he needed slaves to fill ships while it was still the dry season. Black traders had answered him with these men, kidnapped, like Cinqué, on the road, stolen from their villages at night, bartered away by greedy relatives, or otherwise treacherously taken. They were a miserable, disheartened lot, waiting in the barracoon for the day when they would be taken on a slave ship.

To one side Cinqué saw an old man, the age of his father, who alternately talked, prayed Mohammedan prayers, sang; at times he held up his chains to show his shame.

"Too old, too old," he said to Cinqué's question.

He had been overlooked in the last trading, being too old for the traders. He would be overlooked again and again until Don Pedro was convinced there was no profit in him. Then he would be cracked on the skull and dropped out of sight in the Gallinas.

"*La-Elaha Ella Allah—Mohammed Rasoul Allah,*" the old man prayed, bowing to the east.

His prayers were loud, but no louder than those of the pagan Mendis, who called on Ngil-li, the fetish of their people. But Cinqué did not pray. He had placed his faith in the fetish, and the fetish had failed him. Had the fetish been good, he would now be at home in Mani.

Cinqué, despairing without praying, sought a way of escape. Conscious of the guards watching him, he went around the walls trying to find some weak spot through which he might creep. But the barracoon had been built for prisoners like him. Its walls were of logs driven deep into the mushy earth—too deep for Cinqué to hope he could dig his way out. They extended high into the air, presenting a polished surface too slick for him to climb. They were lost in a thatched roof that kept out sun and rain. Cinqué could not help thinking that this was a stronger, better house than he had at home, and not too uncomfortable except that it was crowded with slaves and stinking from their filthy bodies.

Cinqué overheard the talk of two captives who squatted to one side. Their eyes were fierce, their manner defiant. They spoke in disgust of the captives who fawned on Kroo guards for extra food. Cinqué talked to them and found they felt as he did—determined to escape the horrors of life on a Cuban sugar cane plantation, determined to choose death rather than a life of bondage. They were Kimbo and Grabo, from different tribes but both Mendis. Kimbo, too fierce for his name "Cricket," was Cinqué's age and size, but he had mustaches and a few long hairs curling into a beard, a rare sight among Mendis. Beside them Grabo was a dwarf, not quite five feet tall, but the flat nose, high cheekbones, yellow eyes, and chalky-white teeth, pointed like a shark's, made him appear the fiercest of all.

"How are you here?" they asked each other.

Night came down like a cap and the barracoon was a void of blackness except for flashes of lightning from the growing storm. Rain came in a downpour, cooling the barracoon with the chill of the rainy season.

Most of the captives sprawled to the ground and slept. Cinqué and his new companions crawled every inch of the distance around the barracoon, feeling the logs, digging in the earth with their hands, trying to find some weakness in the wall. They began near the entrance, and before they came to the entrance again night was half past. At the entrance stood the Kroomen of Don Pedro, armed with rifles, ready to shoot any captive who made a dash for the water.

"Somebody go out, somebody die," the guard warned Cinqué.

These Kroomen were useful to Don Pedro, and loyal to him as long as he provided them with food, rum, and tobacco. They and their people escaped slavery by serving the slavers, by making themselves an indispensable part of traffic on the Slave Coast. They were strong men, good at bullying bush Negroes into submission. And when the slave ships stood outside the Gallinas, they could be trusted to take the slaves in their canoes through the rough surf.

Giving up hope for that night, Cinqué lay beside the other two, his head toward the entrance. He tried to sleep, but his thoughts, going back to his wife and children, were like humming flies. If he had only known, only taken more precaution, only ignored the words of the medicine man. . . .

He had risen early one morning and left his wife asleep on their bamboo bed, their three children beside her. He tied on a loincloth and threw a blue cotton robe about his shoulders. The oldest son of his father, trained in *Poro* to be the next headman, he had to lead the workers to the fields, to coax them and cajole them. The rainy season, the season for planting rice, would soon be upon them, and the ground had to be ready. For half a moon the days had been overcast, and there had been sudden storms to drive the workers to shelter. In a short time the heavy rains of May would be lashing field and jungle. With a knife at his waist and a spear in his hand, Cinqué crept out of his house into the half-light of morning.

Tall and erect, he walked through the cluster of grass-thatched huts, now alive with morning sounds. His mind was on the debt he owed Birmaja. On his fingers he counted the bags of rice, the chickens and guinea fowl he would need to satisfy it and buy more goods for trading.

With his mind full of planting and trading, Cinqué came to the house of his father in the center of the village, with the others set like haystacks around it. The old man was still asleep, but his women were busy cooking over an open fire in an outdoor kitchen. Ignoring the women, Cinqué took a ball of rice and a boiled plantain from the kettles.

"Bato," he called.

Bato, second son of the headman, came from the house, where he lived with his father, being yet unmarried. He took food from the kettles and hurried to overtake Cinqué, who had already set out along a trail for the fields. At the edge of the village Bato caught up with Cinqué. The two brothers cracked fingers in greeting and walked along together, talking of the rice they would have to grow to repay Birmaja. Behind them followed groups of workers, men and women wearing loincloths, carrying knives and sticks and spears for digging the earth. With them came the medicine man, with his bundles of fetishes. They crossed the fields planted the year before and came to new areas they had burned off during the dry season. There they set to turning the black earth with their

13

crude tools, while Cinqué walked among them to see that no one shirked his work, and to see that the ground was dug and furrowed. On posts about the field the medicine man, with the air of one convinced of his calling, hung his bundles of fetishes.

It was a happy season for the workers. The women looked forward to the time when they would walk ankle-deep in water setting rice plants in the rich new earth. The men looked to the end of planting time, to the long days of leisure for hunting and trading. All of them thought of the days of planting and the nights of singing and dancing the planting festival. If the season was prosperous enough, they would enliven their celebrations with tobacco and rum from Gallinas.

When it was time for his father to be abroad, Cinqué left the workers in the fields and started again along the path to the village to report to his father the progress of their labor. The old man was bent with years—too feeble to go often to plantings and harvests. But he was still of strong mind, firm and just in palavers, the village court of justice. The distance was no more than three miles, and Cinqué set out at an easy lope.

On a wooded part of the road three men sprang from the bush and threw him to the ground. From their tattoos and words, he knew they were of the Vey people. Cinqué fought back and yelled for Bato to help him. But the three men held him to the ground, took away his knife, and bound his hands with bamboo withes.

He knew what that meant. Birmaja had lost patience on the debt, or had a chance for better profits by selling him for rum and tobacco. By signs they indicated that he was to go with them into the forests away from the road. He knew that if he did, his own people would be unable to rescue him, and he would soon be in a caravan bound for the slave factories. Desperately he fought back, desperately he screamed to warn his people, but the leader threw his weight against the bamboo thongs and Cinqué fell with his face in the dirt. The leader tugged him to his feet and toward the bush, with the other two behind striking and pushing him. Soon they had him hidden in dense jungle; only a few marks on the road, only a few broken fern fronds, showed the fierceness of his struggle. When the jungle closed around them, Cinqué knew that fighting was futile, that escape was impossible, that he could never warn his people. There was nothing to do but submit and be led to the village of Birmaja.

Two days they followed dim paths, at first skirting fields and villages and then through dark jungle where palm fronds shut out the sky. At nightfall they came to Geduma, which Cinqué had once visited as a free and welcomed trader. This time he was not allowed to enter the village. Instead, he was taken to the visitor's house, a hut on the fringe where any passer-by might stop for the night. Here there were others, chained and shackled, waiting for the trek to Gallinas. The men cut Cinqué's bamboo thongs away, took his blue robe for themselves, and put an iron collar about his neck. Then they padlocked him to the group of waiting captives.

From the village of Birmaja to the coast was a journey of two days, if one walked fast and took little rest. Birmaja and his guards, free to choose their footing, set a pace at nearly a trot—a pace hard for the chained men to keep. They stumbled along, at times unable to see the sticks and stones that bruised their feet. Neither Birmaja nor the guides showed mercy. Soon there would be no trade for slaves, for the slavers rarely came to that part of the African coast during the rainy season. Slave factors were careful not to get caught with their barracoons overloaded.

Cinqué watched the terrain change from uplands where crops grew to coastal forest interlaced with marshes. At the end of the second day they came to the shore of the Gallinas, where they were welcomed by Don Pedro's lookouts. . . .

"Sail ho! Sail ho!"
Cinqué was awakened by the shouts of a lookout. He was quickly echoed by other watchers and soon they made such a din as Cinqué had never heard before, even at dances in cele-

bration of circumcision. He crowded to the entrance and edged outside the posted walls as far as the guards would let him. Down the muddy lagoon, past the breakers, far to the horizon he could see a schooner in full sail, the noontime tropical sun glaring on her white sails.

A captive beside Cinqué spoke to the Kroomen in Mendi. They did not understand him. He tried again in broken English. The guards answered him quickly. Cinqué, baffled at their words, pushed his way close to this man who spoke Mendi and could make the guards understand him in English.

"Massa slaver?" the man asked.

The Kroomen shrugged. She might be a slaver; she might be a British vessel patrolling for slavers.

"Massa Portuguese? Spanish? American?"

How could they know? She was still too far away for them to see her ensign.

Cinqué spoke to the man, asked him his name.

"Burnah."

How had he learned English?

Burnah replied that he had been a boy for English traders on the coast from Liberia to Sierra Leone, where there were English houses ten times the size of Don Pedro's warehouses. The English had taught him their language that he might better serve them. But the English had no slaves. All black men in Sierra Leone were free. Burnah had returned to his village to spend the wet season and had been caught by traders.

Cinqué sized him up. He was shorter than Cinqué, and a few years older. He had the broad flat nose of a tribe not closely related to Cinqué's. He was ugly of face and squint-eyed. But he was Mendi and knew English. He could be lips and ears for Cinqué . . . and teacher as well. He also had strength . . . if ever a fight should come.

Within an hour the ship was near enough for her colors to be seen.

"Portuguese massa," the guard told Burnah.

"Portuguese massa!" That could mean only one thing to Cinqué. They would be sold to the slaver. They would be on their way to Cuba. He looked at the lagoon, where Kroomen were pulling canoes together with speedy strokes, squatting low till they seemed to be treading water, forming a little fleet to transport the captives to the schooner.

More black boys came with shears and razors. They clipped the captives bald, showering the barracoon floor with crinkly black wool. Without soap or lather, they scraped the faces of the scraggly-bearded men.

By the middle of the afternoon the slaver was anchored just outside the line of surf, looking like a wonderfully free bird to the blacks in the barracoon. A boat put out from her, a broad flat boat, heavy in comparison with the native canoes. It passed near enough for Cinqué to see a white man being rowed by six white sailors. Seeing them, Cinqué thought all white men looked like Don Pedro.

"Massa Spaniard," the Kroomen said to Burnah, pointing to the man standing proudly in the boat. "Him come before."

Kroomen in long native canoes followed him through the lagoon, laughing and chanting, anticipating the extra rum and tobacco that would be theirs when Don Pedro had sold the slaves that packed his barracoons.

The boat passed on toward the island on which Don Pedro had his warehouses. Cinqué could no longer see it, but he could hear the excited cries of the Kroomen. The captives were no less excited than the Kroomen; but theirs was the excitement of fear, dread, anger, hatred for slave traders, white and black alike. They were captives; they were to be sold for slaves; they were to be sent beyond the wide waters. What lay beyond they could only guess. They expected hard work, misery, death in a strange land . . . if they survived the middle passage.

Yet some of them, urged by Kroomen, managed a *"Viva Havana"* when Don Pedro came to the barracoon with the Spaniard from the schooner. "Don Pablo Álvarez," he called him. Don Pablo Álvarez, agent for the House of Martínez,

17

dealer in slaves in Cadiz and Havana—known equally in Boston, New Orleans, Galveston as a dealer in rum, molasses, and black people.

"Don't take time over prices," Don Pablo was saying. "We must get loaded and away, ahead of the prowling British."

"Are Martínez' losses so great then?" Don Pedro asked.

"Indeed. Of four ships that sail for Havana, three are lost or taken by the British. Every month they put more cruisers in the African patrol. Sierra Leone is overrun with slaves released by the Mixed Commission. . . ."

"It is true," Burnah said to Cinqué. He himself had seen many a slaver brought by British cruisers as prizes to Sierra Leone. He had talked to blacks freed from the slavers. Many had settled in Sierra Leone to learn the ways and language of the English. Others had set out to their homes in the interior.

At this word of British ships that freed blacks and sent them back home again Cinqué began to dream of another way to freedom. If he could not escape being sold—that now seemed unlikely—he might be recaptured. Gratefully he yearned toward these strange people, the English, setting things right for black men.

A Krooman preceded the two Spaniards through the barracoon. With his bare foot he prodded dejected captives into standing for Don Pablo's inspection. The captives stood and stretched out their arms and legs. While Don Pedro stood back, Don Pablo examined the captives, running his hands quickly over their bodies, testing them for infirmities, for fever, for the bloating that sometimes showed when a sick slave had been doped to make a good sale. Cinqué, slinking to the rear of the barracoon, wondered at the readiness with which some of the captives submitted to the Spaniard's inspection. Questions rose in his mind. Did they look forward to slavery? Had they no feeling for freedom? Did they count the things they would see on the other side worth the price they would pay?

When the Spaniards came to Cinqué, he turned his face

Fig. 1 Painting of the *Amistad*, anchored in Long Island Sound. (Collection of the New Haven Colony Historical Society.)

Fig. 2   Mendi Huts.

Death of Capt. Ferrer, the Captain of the Amistad, July, 1839.

Don Jose Ruiz and Don Pedro Montez, of the Island of Cuba, having purchased fifty-three slaves at Havana, recently imported from Africa, put them on board the Amistad, Capt. Ferrer, in order to transport them to Principe, another port on the Island of Cuba. After being out from Havana about four days, the African captives on board, in order to obtain their freedom, and return to Africa, armed themselves with cane knives, and rose upon the Captain and crew of the vessel. Capt. Ferrer and the cook of the vessel were killed; two of the crew escaped; Ruiz and Montez were made prisoners.

Fig. 3

Old prints from John W. Barber, *A History of the Amistad Captives.*
(New Haven, Conn.: E. L. and J. W. Barber, Publishers, 1840.)
(Courtesy of the Massachusetts State Library.)

away in disdain and, scorning to look at them, refused to stand when the Krooman prodded him with his toes. His strong body and bold, stern aspect appealed to both buyer and seller of slaves. Don Pedro expected a good sale. But Cinqué refused to stand for inspection. The two white men shouted at him in Spanish, the Krooman in broken English. They kicked and prodded. He still refused to stand.

White with anger, Don Pedro turned to a Krooman standing near and jerked a manatee strap from his hand. With all his strength he struck Cinqué across the shoulders. Determined not to show weakness before these white men or his own people, Cinqué braced himself and bore the blow unflinchingly, still refusing to look at the Spaniards or to obey their commands. Don Pedro, stung by his contempt, struck again and again until gashes opened up on Cinqué's shoulders and blood dripped down to his loincloth. Still Cinqué did not yield. He knew that Don Pedro was angry enough to kill him, but would not, for dead men brought no money.

Cinqué bore the cuts of the thongs, shrinking only a little; but in spite of his fortitude the tears came to his eyes. He tried to hide them with his hands, ashamed to have the white men see how much he suffered.

After an interminable time Don Pedro stopped beating him and handed the strap back to the Krooman. Cinqué still refused to stand up. Don Pablo leaned over to him and touched briefly his skin, his muscles, his pulse. Apparently satisfied, he spoke to Don Pedro. Cinqué heard but could not comprehend the words that transferred him from the ownership of one Spaniard to another.

After the Spaniards had gone to other barracoons, Cinqué lay on the ground and held his face to the cool earth. In his own village murder was the worst crime, and he, as son of the headman, had sworn in *Poro* to oppose it. But now his pulse beat to new words: "Kill, kill, kill the white man."

Burnah and Grabo and Kimbo squatted on their haunches beside him and tried to ease his suffering. They brought him rice and water, begged from the guards. Burnah talked about the English, tried to make him hope the English would still rescue them. Darkness came to find the slaver still riding at anchor near the mouth of the lagoon, and the captives huddled together under Kroo guards, awaiting they knew not what horrors on board the slaver.

With the coming of daylight the Kroo boatmen were again at the barracoon. This time they had iron collars and chains. Quickly they snapped iron collars around the necks of the captives. Then they fastened them in groups of five with chains. Cinqué and Grabo, Kimbo and Burnah, all huddling together, were locked to a chain, with the fifth a boy Cinqué had not seen before. Burnah talked to the guards, but they could tell him little, only that the captives would receive double rations before they were taken on board the slaver. While they talked, black boys brought pots of rice by and the captives dipped their hands in as they passed.

After sunrise a guard led Cinqué's group from the barracoon to a native canoe waiting at the marshy edge of the island. Two Kroomen waited in the canoe. Ten captives were forced to climb in and sit facing out to sea. Cinqué held the chain away from his lacerated shoulders, but he could not hold back the sun that burned into his wounds.

The Kroomen pulled on their oars and the canoe shot out across the lagoon toward the surf and the slaver, now riding high on a calm sea. There were other boats about them. Cinqué counted twenty . . . all laden with captives bound for the schooner. The first boats were loaded with men, the last with women and children. Behind them came the ship's boat with Don Pablo, fresh and cool in clean white cottons.

Well out of the lagoon and cutting through the choppy surf, they were startled by frantic yells from the lookouts of Don Pedro. The new cry of "Sail ho! Sail ho!" made them look far to the horizon. There they could see the sails and outlines of a cruiser. Don Pablo screamed at the Kroomen. It was not necessary. They had already stopped pulling. Now they let the boats drift while all eyes looked seaward.

Don Pablo cupped his hands to his mouth and shouted orders to the slaver, still too far out for his men on board to hear him. Like monkeys they raced the decks and climbed the rigging. Soon the schooner was in full sail and Don Pablo watched as she pulled anchor.

"English massa! English massa!" the Kroomen shouted to each other when the cruiser was nearer.

"English massa!" The words ran like fire through Cinqué's brain. Here was hope—the hope he had almost lost. They would be captured by the English. They would be taken to Sierra Leone. Then he could go home . . . back to Mani. He looked at Burnah and shouted "English massa!" jubilantly.

The cruiser was now bearing steadily down on the slaver. The slaver, her sails now billowing, began moving away, leaving behind Don Pablo and his six boatmen, jabbering excitedly in Spanish, leaving behind two hundred blacks intended for cargo. Don Pablo shouted against the wind, knowing his shouting was futile, for his schooner could never escape the cruiser or repulse her in hand-to-hand fighting.

"The British!" Don Pablo shouted. "Mother of God . . . a malediction on their Wilberforces and Methodists. . . ."

A heavy roar came over the water, a roar louder than a thousand muskets, and Cinqué could see smoke rising from the cruiser. There was no answering fire from the slaver. The cruiser, now in hailing distance, fired again and the slaver began to take in sail. While Don Pablo watched a fortune slip from his grasp, the cruiser overhauled the slaver. A boat put out from her, loaded with British sailors ready to fight the Spaniards.

"The *Buzzard!*" the Spaniards shouted to each other. "It must be the *Buzzard!*"

H.M.S. *Buzzard* . . . most dreaded of all cruisers in Her Majesty's slave patrol. She had captured the slaver but missed her cargo.

Don Pablo gave an order to the Kroomen and they headed their canoes toward the lagoon, cutting through the surf, dodging the hated British, who had no right to enter the bar

21

racoons of Don Pedro, no right by the treaties of Spain and England.

Back in the barracoon, Cinqué stood staring out to sea, watching the two vessels become specks on the horizon in the direction of Sierra Leone. The cruiser had come too soon. Only a few minutes more and he would have been on the slaver. Then he would have been captured by the British. He too would have been on his way to Sierra Leone.

His chains were taken off again, but that did not lighten the burden of his heart. He was still a captive. One more chance for freedom had passed him by.

II

THE MIDDLE PASSAGE

Thunder and lashing rains, a night so chill the captives crowded together for warmth, naked skin against naked skin; then the sudden clearing of skies with the sun heating the jungle to a steam bath—the schooner with clean sails flying began to seem an escape from the barracoon.

When the cry of "Sail ho!" came again, the blacks, at their morning rice and water, took up the cries of the lookouts. Some of them laughed to the Kroo guards and said *"Viva Havana."*

"Portuguese massa," the Kroomen shouted when the schooner came to anchor outside the lagoon.

A boat full of white men put out from the schooner and was met in the lagoon by a fleet of Kroomen, chanting and laughing. This time there would surely be extra rations.

Before noon, the guards had put their prisoners in chains and herded them into canoes. Cinqué had managed to stay with Burnah—this time with three strangers. He did not know what happened to Kimbo and Grabo. He saw them being led away by two Kroo guards, one of whom was wearing a Friar's broadbrimmed hat.

The canoes crossed the lagoon and headed into the surf. The water was sickeningly rough. The Kroomen constantly bailed by kicking water out with their bare feet. Two boats loaded with Spaniards followed closely. Don Pablo stood in one of these, shouting orders at the men handling the oars.

A third boat, rowed by Kroomen, carried Don Pedro Blanco, his cottons white, his speech fouled with oaths tossed at his Kroomen. Like a hundred black arrows the canoes shot through the surf, many of them loaded with women and children. Cinqué and Burnah guessed there were more than seven hundred blacks altogether, more than the whole village of Mani.

The canoes came near each other, separated, came near again as the Kroomen fought to keep them afloat.

As he studied the faces in a canoe coming near him, Cinqué suddenly shouted "Bato!"

"Cinqué!" Bato yelled back at him. They strained toward each other, shouting their lungs out, begging for news of each other, of home, but their words were lost in the roar of the surf. Waves jerked their canoes apart again.

Bato had been taken too. New fears raced through Cinqué's mind. Now there was no one at home to look after his father, or to protect his wife and children. Pain forced a cry from his lips. His wife and children might have been taken—might be in a canoe near him. Hysterically he called their names until a Krooman thumped him on the skull with a paddle. He kept his mouth shut and his eyes open as they approached the slaver.

The schooner was two-masted, of sharp slaver build, designed for great speed—for running away from British cruisers. A Baltimore type she was called, a type built and outfitted for the slave trade in Baltimore. Cinqué saw the name painted on her side and heard Spaniards and Kroomen saying *Tecora*. He saw the flag flying from her mast.

"Portuguese massa," Burnah assured him.

Her bow was lined with white men, all slender and swarthy like Don Pedro. Standing amidships, his large body lounged against the rail, his red hair and red face bare to the sun, was the Captain, looking to Cinqué like a devil of a white man.

"Americano," the Spaniards said.

Don Pablo's boat came alongside and he shouted orders

24

in Spanish to her Captain and crew. Portuguese vessel, American Captain, Spanish crew. The sharpest British judge on the Mixed Commission might not be able to place national responsibility.

Cinqué was at one end of the chain; Burnah next to him. When the canoe was pulled under the rope ladder, there was nothing for him to do but lay his hands on the strands. Slowly, painfully he climbed the swaying ropes, tugged at from behind by the weight of men climbing after him, laden in his own spirit by sadness and fear. Where had his dream of freedom vanished?

On deck they were herded toward a group of other captives—men, women, children—who were being splashed all over with salt water from the hose pipe of the pump. A Spanish sailor ripped their loincloths from them with a sharp knife and tossed them overboard. Disease could breed in so small a covering. Cinqué stood naked with all the others. Like them, he tried to shield his nakedness with his hands. Black slaves belonging to the ship pushed him forward and he felt salt water splashing over his shoulders, stinging the sores left by Don Pedro's lash.

On the after deck great pots of rice were boiling over wood fires, watched over by black cooks who, like the ship's guards, had been long in the slave trade. Each captive was marched by and given a handful of soft cooked rice. Cinqué tried to eat his, but could not push it past the anger lump in his throat.

The schooner, longer than the palaver hall in Mani, was black with humanity. The decks fore and aft were crowded to over-flowing. Cinqué could see the captives brought on before him, all naked—men and women alike—all bound two by two, wrist to wrist, and ankle to ankle. Some were crying, some moaning, some lying dejectedly with their mouths and eyes open to the sun. Spanish sailors walked among them with no more concern than if they had been pigs or cattle.

A guard pushed Cinqué toward a hatchway. Looking back before plunging into the black night below him, he caught

25

one fleeting glimpse of Africa, the Gallinas River, the slave factory of Don Pedro. Then he stepped into the overpowering stench of a slave hold already overcrowded with black men.

Cinqué and those following on the chain after him had to crouch low, for this hold was no more than four feet high. The other captives were already lying down, side by side. A Spanish sailor, lantern in hand, motioned the five men to a spot and signalled them to lie down. Shifting the iron collars on their necks, they crouched on their knees and then eased themselves to the deck. The sailor kicked them on the feet, fitting them into a row of men already lying there. Cinqué's head pressed against the thigh of another man. Burnah lay against him on one side; on the other was a boy no more than fifteen. There the sailor left him, berthed for the voyage, lying on his back with his legs drawn close together and his arms at his side.

"Where massa take me?" Burnah asked the sailor.

The sailor did not reply. He went about his work, bringing more slaves to the deck and crowding them in. But the captives uttered "Cuba!" in a despairing wail. It rose above the weeping, the chanting of sorrow. Behind them was Africa: home, freedom. Before them? Cuba, or worse.

The only light and air came from a grating with slits too narrow for a hand to go through. Through it Cinqué could distinguish daylight and dark, but he could not see the color of the sky. The men around him were blacker shadows in a black gloom.

"How can they treat men so?" he asked Burnah.

"We are not men," Burnah said. "We are animals—to them we are no more than a dog-faced monkey."

For a moment Cinqué fancied he saw Birmaja, wasting and withering from the power of the fetish. But it can not be so, he thought. Birmaja, safe in Geduma, is enjoying rum and tobacco.

"We have no hope if ship goes down," Burnah said.

26

"It is better to go down than to be a slave on a sugar cane plantation," Cinqué said bitterly.

Soon they heard a creaking of timbers and knew the slaver was under way. Cinqué and Burnah and the men around them—some Mendis, some from tribes far inland—talked of homes and friends left in Africa.

Cinqué listened for the booming of British guns, hoping the cruiser that had come once might come again. . . .

Half-light and darkness, half-light and darkness—the days came and went, each worse than the one before. Cinqué counted ten days on his fingers and then lost count, being faint with hunger. Twice each day a Spanish sailor, accompanied by a black boy, came to the slave deck, lighting their way with a bull's eye and bringing boilers of rice without oil. A boiler contained enough for ten men. When it was placed before them, the captives worked their way to a half sitting position and, forgetting the Mendi etiquette of eating with thumb and forefinger, greedily fought for their portions. After they had eaten, the black boy held a tin cup of water for each to drink. Once when Burnah accidentally knocked the cup aside and spilled the water, the sailor lashed him across the shoulders with a cat-o'-nine-tails.

"Do you want to die of thirst in passage?" he demanded angrily.

As the voyage dragged on, food was cut to stomach-shrinking portions—cut so much that the captives began finding it difficult to force food down at all. The stench from their bodies overcame desire for food. Sometimes a man would reach his hand in and begin retching. Some became too ill to touch food at all. When they refused, the Spanish sailor lashed them and forced them to eat, in some cases until they vomited on themselves and their fellows.

At night, when there was no longer a grate to fix his eyes on, Cinqué let his mind wander to Mani, let his memories of food blot out all others. Seasickness of the first days had given way to a constant pain in his vitals. To lull the hunger

27

pains, he thought of feasts in Mani. There was one that came back like a vision—the feast for his initiation in *Poro*. . . .

He was thirteen, the age when tribal and sexual secrets were revealed to the elected boys of the village. It was a great day for the tribe when Cinqué, the eldest son of the headman, went to the *Poro* bush for his test in endurance. It was the rainy season and the two groups of boys—one taking religious, the other civil training—lived with their teachers, old and respected men, in a roofless pen in the bush, far enough from the village for their secrets not to be overheard by women.

In the group Cinqué was supposed to excel in memorizing tribal laws and systems of rewards and punishments as well as in all the feats of games and acrobatics. Being the serious son of a serious father, he applied himself well. He had been allowed to sit with his father in a palaver. He had listened to his father recite the laws. Now the time had come for him to memorize the laws. He felt the need to equal his father in meting out justice to their people.

Through the long weeks the initiates were exposed to chill nights, to wet skins, to hunger. Then came the dry season, the time for initiation of those who had stood the test. The religious group, those to whom the secrets of fetish and magic potion had been revealed, were examined first. Then the civil, with all the boys assembled while Cinqué recited without faltering the laws of his people.

The last test was for them to gather food and make a feast for themselves. Then they could leave the *Poro* bush and go to the *Poro* house for initiation. For this feast they could bring animals and fruits from the jungle; they could also steal from the village if they could avoid being seen by the women. In the dark of night Cinqué led a group to the village. From hut to hut they went, stealing chickens until they had enough for a great feast. In high spirits they boiled the chickens and rice in earthen pots and then stuffed their

28

lean bellies. It was the first food after real hunger, and they ate themselves into stupefaction. . . .

After the feast the men of the *Poro*, those who had gone through the initiation and now led the village, waited in the *Poro* house for the introduction of new candidates. They waited to be amused by the fake oral examination, given by the *Wuja*, the craftily disguised keeper of the door of *Poro*, to applaud when the candidate overcame the *Wuja* in exaggerated wrestling.

When Cinqué approached the entrance, carrying in his hands leaves of tobacco for payment, he heard a din of tom-toms, shouting, chanting of *Poro* songs. The *Wuja* met him, his weird mask leering.

"Who is there?" he demanded.

"Cinqué."

"Could you bring water in a basket?"

"Yes."

The drumming came faster and the chant rose to a wail.

"Could you carry a mountain on your shoulders?"

"Yes."

Faster went the tom-toms, louder the wailing. Cinqué became frightened. This was not how it had happened in *Poro*. The *Wuja* reached fierce grappling arms toward him, menacing him. This was not the mock wrestling by which he was admitted.

With his arms outstretched and his mask contorted, the *Wuja* shouted,

"Could you kill the white men?"

Cinqué, in the slave deck, jerked at his chains and writhed against Burnah. What was this being asked of him? Could he murder? It was a mockery in the *Wuja*. Had he not sworn not to kill . . . and to decree justice in palaver for murder?

But the *Wuja* was coming closer.

"Could you kill the white men?"

The *Wuja* was no longer the *Wuja*. He had the face of

29

Don Pedro Blanco, and his hands held a cat-o'-nine-tails raised to strike him across the shoulders.

"Yes," Cinqué shrieked, and his hands tore at the iron collar restraining him. . . .

Cinqué awoke from his delirium in the midst of a storm. A gale forced the odor of the sea into the slavehold, reviving the hot, stinking captives.

"Two days," Burnah told him.

For two days the storm had been blowing, battering the ship back and forth, howling in the riggings, torturing its victims from Captain to slave child. The captives, lying crowded on the bare decks, unable to brace themselves, rolled from side to side, rubbing their emaciated bodies on the wood until sores came. The irons on their wrists and ankles cut into the flesh and left wounds to fester.

During the storm the Spanish sailors did not come to the slave deck. They were too busy battling the wind. Only the ship's slaves came, bringing food and water, carrying away wastes. The captives begged for help, calling on the brotherhood of color. But the blacks had been too long away from Africa . . . too long the boys for Spanish masters.

Then on the third day the storm was over and the captives lay still, grateful for rest for their bruised bodies.

The young boy next to Cinqué had been sick before the storm. Affected by the schooner's distress, he grew weaker and weaker; his voice came in a whisper. The foulness from his body soiled the deck and made an unbearable stench. The vessel moved forward easily, with the motion of a gently rocking cradle, but his pain was not eased.

At the morning feeding he refused to put his hand in the rice boiler. The black boy struck him. He barely cringed from the blow. The black boy held the bull's eye on the lower part of his body and suddenly shook with fright.

"Bloody flux," he whispered in a fearful voice, loud enough for Burnah and Cinqué to hear him.

Bloody flux. Dread disease of slave ships. The black boy

30

had sailed the middle passage enough to know what that meant to slaves on board, to profits at Havana. He knew that it sometimes spread to captain and crew. Leaving the rice boiler behind, he ran for the upper deck.

After he had gone, Cinqué touched the boy's body and knew breath had gone out of it. He whispered to Burnah. Word passed quickly from one to the other, and they set up a rending wailing and wild rattling of chains. Some of them beat the deck with their hands. Chained men fought each other to get closer to the bit of light coming through the grating.

Lights again, and Don Pablo Alvarez and the American Captain, accompanied by a Spanish sailor and the black boy, stooped along the low deck, the American sitting on his haunches. It was the first time Cinqué had seen them since the Gallinas. The only change was that they had covered their faces with kerchiefs.

The black boy pointed out the still body and Don Pablo flashed a light on his face. Seeing he was dead, Don Pablo moved his light back and forth, looking at the living captives, whose wet black faces and white eyes glared back out of the gloom. Don Pablo was like a farmer who has suddenly discovered a murrain in his cattle. He spoke to the sailor in words that cut like a knife.

"Sí, Señor," the sailor answered to all his orders.

Don Pablo and the Captain stooped their way from the slave deck. Then the sailor made signs that the captives were to be allowed in the open air. He unlocked Cinqué and Burnah and bade them bring the dead boy with them. Unaccustomed to standing, they half crawled as they carried the body, now emaciated and light, up the companionway and out on deck.

The Captain and Don Pablo waited near the main hatch. Spanish sailors lounged about in the warm sunlight. The ship's slaves eyed the dead captive suspiciously. Thankfully Cinqué looked at the sun, but he had to close his eyes against the brightness.

31

Directed by the sailor, Cinqué and Burnah carried the body to the bow of the ship and laid it on a bare plank. Without ceremony the sailor tipped the plank and the body slipped into the water. Cinqué envied him. Death, burial at sea—anything was preferable to life on a slave ship. He saw the Captain and Don Pablo chatting unconcernedly. "Kill the white men?" He drew his hands to his sides and turned away.

All the captives from Cinqué's deck were brought out into the sunlight, blinking and shading their eyes with their hands. Cinqué looked among them for Bato, but could not see him. He wondered if Bato too had been slid off the plank into the boiling waters—Bato the quiet, the gentle. Cinqué looked back where the boy had been dropped and saw shark fins cutting the surface. No peace—not even in death.

The captives were herded together and sprayed with salt water until they were clean again. Then Don Pablo, with his handkerchief over his mouth, walked among them, examining them for signs of fever or illness. He looked at the patches of skin rubbed raw on the deck, at the cuts made by chains on wrists and ankles. He held his nose at the smell of putrefying flesh. Stepping a safe distance from the blacks, he gave orders to the Spanish sailors.

A sailor brought a basin filled with vinegar and a horn of gunpowder. Don Pablo stirred powder in the vinegar and made a light paste. This the sailor rubbed into the raw wounds, using his lash to make the captives stand still and endure the savage burning.

Then the captives were marched past a boiling cauldron and each ladled out a cup of salty soup—the only cure on a slave ship for dysentery. Cinqué drank his, and then went as far forward as the white sailors would allow him. From there he could see the area where women and children had been brought for an airing. Most of the women were squatting on the deck, trying to hide their nakedness. Some of them crooned chanting melodies to their children, others talked in low tones, or sat staring silently out to sea, looking backward over the broad expanse they had crossed. Among them were some big with child, waiting to be delivered in the hold of a slave ship. But Cinqué's wife and children were not among them. Had they not been taken?

All day long the captives were allowed to lie in the sun. Their spirits revived, and they were soon talking in low voices. Cinqué listened to their stories of home, to their dark forecasts of the future, but he did not join them. He had all he could manage in the questions raised by the *Wuja*. He sat looking at the setting sun. The ship was sailing west— due west. Back of him lay Africa; ahead lay Cuba. He wondered where his feet would take him before he touched African soil again.

To fight the epidemic now raging in the slave holds, Don Pablo brought the captives on deck for all the daylight hours. Day after day Cinqué sat staring across the rolling green water, looking for a sail. One day Burnah sat with him teaching him the words, the ways of the English.

"Will the English come?" Cinqué asked.

"It is better if they will not."

"Why?" Cinqué asked in surprise.

Burnah had been talking to the ship's slaves. The Spanish sailors' orders were plain. If an English vessel appeared to be overtaking them, they were to herd the captives on deck and make them leap into the water. If they had time, they were to weight them with irons. If they did not—well, sharks would destroy evidences of slavery anyway, and destroy them before the English could come to the rescue. Cinqué thought of the sharks circling the ship and began hoping to reach Cuba. From Cuba he might escape; from sharks, never.

Burnah told him of an old black woman he had seen at Sierra Leone. As a little child she had been taken as a slave to Havana, and sold as a servant to a Spanish Doña. For forty years her body was in Cuba, her heart in Africa. For forty years she worked and saved to buy her freedom and passage to Africa. When she was old and bent she returned to Sierra Leone, patted African earth with her hands, blessed it in the name of the Christian God of her Doña. Then she went to the interior to pass the end of her life with her people.

Surely, Cinqué thought, he could be as faithful to Africa as this old woman. No matter how long it took, he could hope to find his wife and children. . . .

Day after day they sailed, through storm, through calm, through days so hot the decks blistered and the slave holds became burning hells. Cinqué no longer tried to account for time, though he guessed they had been sailing nearly two moons . . . enough time for the rice in Mani to be knee high and heading.

More captives died, and their bodies were slipped naked into the sea. Now a school of sharks followed the schooner day and night, their great fins cutting the water, their horrible mouths opening to gash castoff bodies.

Illness and hunger left the living dull and listless. Each body thrown overboard bequeathed its living room to the remainder, but most of them were too sick, too weary to be grateful. Don Pablo, alarmed over the deaths, the cut in profits, worked for the health of his cargo.

Cargo. *"Bultos de efectos"* the slaver's papers called them. "Bales of goods . . . bolts of cloth." Words to help Cuban officials delude the British. No cargo of cloth could bring Don Pablo the rich profits he expected from this cargo on the *Tecora*.

He increased the portions of food and water, he made the captives move their arms and legs to restore their use. He gave them cheap fish oil to anoint their skins, to make them bright and shiny. A shiny ebony was the fairest skin to a slave trader.

Cinqué was grateful for the hours on deck. He kept watching their direction. Day after day the sun was behind

them in the morning, ahead of them in the afternoon. West
. . . always sailing west. . . .

One morning the wind blew a new odor through the
grating—the sweet odor of land. When the captives were
brought on deck, Cinqué could see the difference in the
green of the water, feel the excitement on board ship. The
journey through the middle passage would soon be over.
Masters and captives alike felt the magic of land. For the
masters it meant full pockets and the delights of Havana;
for the captives, freedom from the nightmare of slave decks.

The sailors were excited but cautious. Who could tell what
British man-o'-war lay waiting for the slaver as she approached the safety of Cuba? Many a ship had been seized
when land was in sight—taken all the way back to Sierra
Leone, where the ship was confiscated and the captives set
free. Many a slave trader had seen wealth slip through his
fingers almost within sight of the Morro Castle.

Don Pablo made his rounds among the captives and came
to where the Captain waited amidships.

"Is all in readiness?" he asked.

"Aye. The men have an American flag ready to run up
if we need it. I have here blank ship's papers signed by Consul Trist. Proper cargo and destination can be added if there
is danger of boarding. I for one feel confident. . . ."

An apologist for slavery, Nicholas P. Trist, American Consul at Havana, married to Thomas Jefferson's granddaugh-
ter, had thus made it easy to shift from Portuguese to American registry. In case of trouble, a few spaces filled, old papers
weighted and tossed overboard, and all was well for the slave
traders. The United States had fought a war to protect her
ships from boarding by foreign vessels, and she guarded the
right jealously, though the ship carry a cargo of black captives. The Consul, educated in the precepts of human rights
in the law office of Thomas Jefferson, in Havana lent his
signature as a tool to unscrupulous sea captains.

"What about Spanish ships?" the Captain asked.

35

"No trouble there. Her Catholic Majesty will protect the House of Martínez for the sake of revenue. In Havana they say it is her most profitable investment. . . ."

In 1817 the British Government paid Spain 400,000 pounds to effect a treaty between the two countries to put down the slave trade—the treaty to become effective in 1820. Ferdinand VII had maintained the treaty with some honor, but, after his death, Queen Christina, a coquette he had married in Naples, became Regent. She made public protestations of faith in the treaty; she sent elaborate directions to the Governor General of Cuba for assisting in fighting the traffic. At the same time she privately sent an emissary to improve her fortunes in slave trade. Don Pablo knew how much per head—ten dollars in American silver—he had to pay the Governor General to land his captives in Cuba.

Don Pablo called a Spanish sailor.

"Lock the captives below. Keep them there until we are safe at Havana."

The captives, full of food, greasy with fish oil, spent the waiting time below talking and laughing and chanting songs. Already they were beginning to forget the middle passage. There must be strange sights awaiting them in Cuba. When the sailors above at last called out "Land ho!" captives on the slave deck burst out with *"Viva Havana!"*

They were fed at dusk that day. Then they were chained as they had been before, five men together. When the tropical darkness had fallen solidly around them, they were brought on deck, the easier to be disembarked as soon as the schooner docked.

Cinqué found himself on deck near the prow. Next to him were the ship's black boys; beyond them the white sailors. Beside him stood Burnah, exchanging comments with the ship's boys, who treated him with kindness now that the journey was over. Cinqué wished harder than ever that he could speak English, that he could grasp the words passing back and forth between Burnah and the black boys.

swered.

The *Tecora* approached Havana harbor, slipping like a ghost through the blackness, in waters forbidden to ships after nightfall. At the helm was the Captain, with Don **Pablo** beside him ready to answer if their passage should be challenged, ready to pay his tribute to the Governor General's collectors.

"Ahoy!" The call came from a harbor cutter, her outline dim between them and the lights of Havana. "Who goes there?"

"*La Tecora,*" Don Pablo answered. Then he explained that she was laden with "*bultos de efectos*" for the House of Martínez.

"*Bueno,*" the challenger replied. And then, "*Pase.*"

The sailors of the *Tecora* shouted among themselves when they passed the Morro Castle—its grim outlines dark against the stars. They performed their tasks with speed and laughter as the schooner slipped through the narrow passage and, still without a harbor pilot, entered the harbor that spread like a shamrock before them. They laughed when they glided past a British cruiser . . . and an American man-o'-war. Safe in Havana harbor, they forgot their anxiety of the open seas.

The *Tecora* glided on through the harbor and came to anchor before a village near Havana, at a dock long used by the slave trade. The Captain brought her in close and lowered a gangplank.

Still bound with iron collars and chains, the captives were led down the plank and marched through a dark village to a grass-thatched hut. It was much like the barracoon they had left at the mouth of the Gallinas River. Here there were oil flambeaux and many more Spaniards, guards armed with rifles and pistols.

"*Bozales,*" the Spaniards said to each other. *Bozales*— Negroes transported from Africa after the Treaty of 1820.

III

CUBAN SLAVE MART

Morning in Cuba . . . morning of bright sunlight and sweet-smelling air . . . restful morning after sleep on ground that did not rock and roll . . . morning of hope again, now that the middle passage was over.

Cinqué woke with morning and stretched himself; surprised that he touched no one else, pleased that the iron collar had been taken from his neck. He sat up and looked at the captives sprawled on the ground, sleeping where they dropped, sleeping in stupor after the heavy meal of the night before. He touched Burnah lightly.

"My brother," he said. "We will look for my brother."

The two men took a few steps and found they could manage the shackles on their ankles fairly well, though running away was impossible even without the drowsy guards at the entrance.

They walked among the bodies sprawled and curled on the ground. They were all men, the women and children having been taken elsewhere, quietly at the time of disembarcation.

He had looked at most of the two hundred men within the walls before he found Bato, lying weak and ill in a corner. When Cinqué saw his drawn and withered face, he wondered by what strength of spirit he had survived the bloody flux. He marveled that the tattooed designs on Bato's breast and back stood out more sharply now that the flesh had

38

fallen away. Bitterly he thought of Bato in Mani, fat and happy, spoiled by his father's women.

"Bato," Cinqué spoke to him, kneeling beside him, touching his face gently. "Bato . . . brother."

Bato sat up at the sound of a familiar voice.

"Cinqué," he cried. "Cinqué . . . we have come far from Mani."

He braced himself against Cinqué's knees and pulled himself to his feet. The two brothers then cracked fingers formally. It had been difficult for them to show affection at home in Mani, in a land where only weak men give way to emotions; it was much harder here in Cuba, surrounded by strangers and under Spanish guards.

Hearing that his brother had been too ill to drag himself to the rice boilers, Cinqué brought food left from the night before. Bato ate slowly at first, then greedily, his eyes still haunted by fear of starvation. After he had pushed the last bits of rice into his mouth, the two brothers sat on the ground and talked about Mani, their father and people, the rice they had been unable to plant, the harvest celebrations without them. Bitterly they talked of the treachery of Birmaja, and Bato told how he had been captured.

He had been on the road to the village with workers from the fields when they were set upon by Vey raiders. Being unarmed, the workers ran. Bato was taken, but not till word had been sent to Mani to guard against Birmaja.

"Our father?" Cinqué asked.

"He must be safe."

"My wife? My children?"

"They must be safe too. Birmaja would only take captives in ambush. He has not the courage to make war on villages."

Cinqué felt easier in mind, but more determined than ever to return to Mani. He wondered how long he would have to slave to get money for his freedom and passage—if there was no shorter way.

While they were talking, Creole slaves brought in boilers

of food—much food, more than they had ever seen except on feast days in the Mendi country. They brought rice, boiled beans, boiled potatoes. One carried a stalk of ripe bananas on his shoulder. They set the food down and left the barracoon. The captives crowded greedily around the boilers and packed food in their mouths with their hands. Cinqué watched them eat and studied the effect on the Spanish guards. The guards did not seem to care how much they stuffed themselves. When everyone had his fill there was still rice in the boilers. Banana skins lay on the ground, tossed there by those who a day earlier would have devoured them. Even Bato, softening the end of a banana with lips and tongue, had lost the look of hunger.

Then the slaves brought in casks of fresh, sweet water. Each captive could have enough to drink and wash himself. Gratefully they drank; sparingly they poured water on each other, remembering their thirst on the *Tecora*. Each man washed himself down carefully. A Creole brought a jar of new oil and poured each captive a handful. This they rubbed themselves with from head to foot, bringing back the polished luster of their ebony skins. Fed, bathed, anointed, they began to forget the horrors of the middle passage. They talked and laughed together—all except Cinqué, who reminded them sharply there must be a reason for this bounty from white men.

Creole slaves came and went among the captives with easy familiarity. Cinqué and Burnah tried to talk to them.

"Where you come from?" Burnah asked in Mendi.

They shook their heads that they did not understand; then they spoke to him in Spanish. Though most of them had been born in Africa, they had been a long time in Cuba —so long they affected the clothing of Cuban laborers and spoke Spanish. With difficulty they remembered African dialects, but none of them spoke Mendi. With broken English and signs Burnah asked them what it was like to be a slave in Cuba.

"*Bueno*," they replied, in the words of their Spanish masters, "*me gusta mucho.*"

40

Too long ago they had lost home and freedom. Eagerly they tried to tell these naked bushmen of the wonders to be seen in Havana.

Nights, warm black nights with the sound of guitars and singing in the village, with the Spanish guards and Creole slaves singing Spanish love songs. The captives, stuffed with food and rested, raised their own chant. In tuneless voices they sang songs from Mendi, keeping the rhythm by slow beat of their hands on the ground. Except for shackled ankles and guards near them, they could forget they were captives in the land of Cuba. As the Creole slaves said, it was a pleasant land, a fat land. . . .

The thought raised questions in their minds. Remembering their old fears that the white men were taking them to Cuba to eat them, they began to whisper that this was the fattening period. As soon as they were fat, the white men would kill them like pigs and eat them. The rumor ran like a shudder over the group. Their happy singing stopped. Eating human flesh was forbidden to their tribe, but they could all recall stories that drifted from the interior—stories of captives made fat and killed for a ritual and their flesh roasted for a feast of honor.

Some of them tried to keep from eating, but the temptation was too great after long starvation. Days passed quietly and soon they were eating heavily again and, in wry humor, feeling each other's flesh, making jokes about the fattest. Cinqué, hard and lean himself, patted Burnah's round belly.

"They eat you first," he said, and wondered at the hearty laughter.

The captives grew sleek and shiny black or soft dark brown. There was no longer a sign of flux among them. Bato, who had been among the weakest, scrambled for food with the others and joined them in acrobatics.

One morning Creole slaves came with a new loincloth for each man. They put them on, but, accustomed to nakedness so long, they suddenly felt self-conscious as they stared at their new coverings.

"Where you take us?" Burnah asked the Creole slaves.

41

They did not know, but they made jokes about the kind of work assigned to bush Negroes.

Then Spanish guards came and put iron collars about their necks and fastened them to chains—twenty to a group. They took the shackles from their ankles and marched them out of the barracoon in columns of two. They marched past the village and skirted the walls of Havana, the Africans chattering excitedly about the wonders spread before them, their fears forgot for the moment. Cinqué studied each house, each road branching away, each clump of tropical shrubs, seeking a means of escape. Many places seemed inviting, but he was always brought back to reality by the iron collar around his neck and the clank of chains as they marched forward like condemned convicts.

The columns turned on to a wide highway, the *Paseo Militar,* leading from Havana to the Governor General's country palace. General Tacón, who had publicly denounced the slave trade and privately pocketed a fortune from it, had just been removed from office. Governor General Espeleta, his successor, had just taken over, and the slave traders found another friend in him, one more publicly tolerant than General Tacón. They found they could now advertise a sale of slaves by authority "during the celebration of Mass, before the church door."

The *Paseo Militar* was crowded with carriages going to and from the Governor General's summer palace. One of these carriages was shiny black and drawn by big white horses. Inside were two Spanish ladies, richly dressed, their faces protected from the sun and the common gaze by black lace mantillas. Redcoated and goldbraided black footmen looked down at the chained captives trudging along. The captives stared back with open-mouthed admiration. They'd never seen such splendor in all the African kingdoms.

"When I'm a slave I'll be like that," the captives boasted to each other, forgetting for the moment that their lot might be among the slaves laboring in fields by the highway or in the newly made public parks.

When the palace was just ahead of them, dazzingly white above the mixed reds and blues of the common dwellings, they turned off the *Paseo* and were herded into another barracoon—this one much larger than anything they had seen before. It was like a feast day in an African village. Hundreds of Negroes—more women and children than men—milled about the great open area, or gathered around cooking fires set at one side.

This barracoon, so near the walls of Havana, under the windows of Quinta de Los Molinos, the Governor General's palace, was at a place called *Misericordia,* a familiar name in Cuban slave trade, a model mart designed to show the advantages Africans had in becoming Cuban slaves. It was a pen made of logs driven into the earth. The floor was dirt and there was no roof. It most resembled a corral for exhibiting cattle. There were even places for white spectators, where they could enjoy a drink and watch the antics of wild Africans.

The captives from the *Tecora* were herded among the others, who jabbered their welcomes in a dozen African dialects. Their collars and chains were removed and shackles placed on their ankles. The newcomers stood awed by the scene before them. Dumbly they waited for they knew not what—to live, to work, to be killed and eaten by white men? They did not know the name of this place to which they had been taken, nor feel the mercy it made a mockery. They took some comfort at seeing among the blacks women and children from the *Tecora.* Among them Cinqué found Kimbo, and they stopped to talk over all they had seen since they left the factory at Gallinas.

Among the Creole slaves who brought food and water, Cinqué saw an old man with traces of the Mendi mark on his forehead.

"Mendi?" Cinqué asked.

"Mendi," the old man answered, and they cracked fingers formally.

This old man was brought from Africa when he was a

boy, and most of his life had been spent in Cuba, a slave for the House of Martínez. For many years he had been at *Misericordia,* serving the slaves who stopped there on their way to Spanish *haciendas.* Proudly he spoke of Don Pedro Martínez, of his ships in the slave trade, of his barracoons at Havana, Matanzas, Santiago. He boasted of Don Pedro's wealth and power, repeating stories he had heard from whites and blacks in Havana. It was true that Don Pedro had more power than the Governor General—that the Queen Mother of Spain was his friend and patron.

Cinqué wondered that the old man could speak so proudly of the white man who had enslaved him.

"When will you go back to Mendi?" he asked.

"Never. I have a home here. I have nothing left in Mendi."

The old man went on, ladling out water to the Martínez captives, doing his job in supporting *Misericordia.*

This barracoon was the showplace of the Cuban slave trade. Placed intentionally on the broad new *Paseo Militar,* where many people—Spaniards, Creole slaves, *emancipados,* Negroes freed by the Mixed Commission and indentured to white men—passed daily, it was open to any white man who wanted to come in. The spectator stands were shaded and comfortable, and not too near the smells of the slave pit. The stands were liveliest at afternoon feedings, after which the guards contrived a performance by the captives.

The men wore loincloths, the women strips of bright-colored cottons draped around their bodies. Often the men were forced to box and wrestle for the sport of the spectators. When Cinqué's turn came, he bore the flick of the lash, wielded deftly to leave no marks, rather than make laughs for the Spaniards.

Don Pablo Álvarez, the captives' evil link between the slave factory of Gallinas and the slave deck of the *Tecora,* had not relinquished his hold on them at *Misericordia.* Affecting the dress of a Cuban planter, accompanied by a Creole slave in green livery, he supervised his majordomos, or chatted with the spectators, talking familiarly of tribes and customs on the Slave Coast. His assistants were Señor

44

Riera and Señor Grassi, both skilled in taming *bozales*—Negroes fresh from Africa.

"Show us a Mendi dance," Don Pablo ordered Señor Grassi.

While some of the blacks organized a tribal dance for the white spectators, Cinqué made the rounds of the barracoon walls, like a caged tiger testing the bars of his cage, searching for a place of escape. Escape into Cuba would be better than being sold to work his life out on a sugar cane plantation. If he could get free, he might pass as an *emancipado*, might work his way back to Africa on a slaver. But he could find no place, and when he came near the entrance, Spanish guards drove him back to the middle of the arena, where he was lost among the whirling dancers.

A hired *volante* rolled along the *Paseo Militar,* its high wheels rattling and bumping on stones. The Creole slave driver rode astride the pony, whacking him to a trot with a stick. The lone passenger was an Englishman, Dr. Richard Madden, a member of the Mixed Commission at Havana, a man who had seen slavery around the world, and had fought it with the zeal of a Wilberforce. That zeal had taken him to Freetown in Sierra Leone, and then to Havana, where the sickness of slavery most wanted healing.

His spirit was as jaded as that of the pony drawing him. For weeks he had argued with Governor General Espeleta, discussing with him the Treaty of 1820, showing him that the 400,000 pounds England had paid Spain had more than indemnified losses sustained by Spanish subjects. He brought to the attention of the Governor General the six barracoons in the vicinity of Havana, especially the one at *Misericordia,* and with what ease slavers discharged their cargoes in Havana harbor. Espeleta answered by showing him a directive from Her Majesty, the August Queen Regent, through her Ministry of Colonies, issued on complaint of the Government of Her Britannic Majesty that the clandestine introduction of black slaves had been made

"Her Majesty," Espeleta translated, "who takes the great-

45

est interest in the security and prosperity of the worthy inhabitants of that rich colony, and who is convinced of the urgent necessity of putting a stop to such an abuse, which may give rise to evils of greatest transcendancy, has been pleased to resolve that Your Excellency shall apply the strongest zeal in dictating the necessary measures for preventing this deplorable contraband, obliging the local authorities to prosecute with energy those who are engaged in it, and bring the perpetrators before the competent tribunals for their exemplary punishment."

The Spaniard studied the Englishman shrewdly.

"I can but obey the orders of Her August Majesty."

Dr. Madden knew that further protest to Governor General Espeleta was futile. There was too much duplicity in Havana and in the highest government in Madrid, too high profits in slave trading.

On this morning he had turned to another possible source of aid, Nicholas P. Trist, the United States Consul at Havana. He knew that Trist favored the annexation of Texas to the United States as an extension of slave territory, to be followed soon after by the annexation of Cuba. He knew that his chance for assistance was slight.

Consul Trist received him coolly, listened to him impatiently, and then denied that his Government had any responsibility in the matter.

"I know *bozal* Negroes arrive daily," Dr. Madden said. "But the Mixed Commission is powerless here. The Spaniards evade the issue. Unless our British vessels capture slavers on the high seas, we are without jurisdiction."

"Then let your ships be more vigilant," Consul Trist said. He rose, extended his hand, and said "Good morning."

"I shall appeal to President Van Buren—"

"The President is fully aware of our course of action."

Dr. Madden came away from the American Consulate heavy in heart. Now he was on his way to *Misericordia*, to see for himself again the horrors of human traffic, to renew his determination to fight for black men. How often he had made that journey in his months at Havana.

Señor Grassi saw Dr. Madden approaching the entrance. *"Don Escrúpulo,"* he said to Señor Riera. "The English conscience is here to meddle again. Why do they always have to have a conscience?"

"The old ones have. It may be from their own sins. But the young ones? I do not think so."

Dr. Madden spoke to Señor Riera and then to Señor Grassi, remembering their respective ranks and the appropriate words of Spanish courtesy. Then he took his place in the spectator stands, with the two Spaniards near him.

"I see you have more *bozales,"* Dr. Madden remarked.

"It may be a ship slipped through your blockade, Señor," Señor Riera responded. "It is true we have many slaves here. Would you like to witness a Mendi dance from the Slave Coast?"

"I have been to the Slave Coast," Dr. Madden said impatiently.

"Are the blacks not better here than in Africa? Here they have food, clothing, the blessings of Christianity. . . ."

"There they had freedom."

"Freedom is not much to exchange for the advantages of civilization."

"What advantages? On my way here I passed the building on the Alameda where the public whipping posts are. My ears are still filled with the piercing screams and piteous shrieks for mercy of slaves sent by their masters to be whipped. What advantages? This mart at *Misericordia* where they will be sold again to the hard life of field labor without wife or home. What advantages—"

"Señor," Señor Riera broke in lightly, "you English are all alike—wasting your feelings on black savages. . . . See, the Mendis are dancing."

In the arena half a hundred blacks danced half-heartedly with eyes downcast. They did not look up at the one white man with a will to help them.

Humiliated by the Spaniards, Dr. Madden took a last look at the corralled Africans, bowed to the Spaniards, and strode

47

to his *volante*. At home again, he carefully recorded the meeting in his diary.

On June 26, 1839, by the white man's count, Don Pablo came to the barracoon with a young Spaniard in the dress of a dandy. Señor Riera and Señor Grassi joined them. The Spanish guards bowed deferentially to the newcomer.

"Señor Ruiz," they called the stranger. Sometimes Don Pablo called him "Pepe" affectionately.

Cinqué sensed immediately that this man was a slave dealer. At last the time had come for the Africans to be sold to the master of a sugar cane plantation.

With the other Spaniards accompanying him, Ruiz walked up and down the barracoon among the Africans lying or squatting on the ground. He stirred their hatred with his insolent staring like a buyer in a mart of pigs and chickens. He stopped when he came to Cinqué, noting quickly his strong body, good teeth, intelligent face. He felt Cinqué's pulse. Remembering his beating from Don Pedro, Cinqué stood quiveringly still. Then Señor Ruiz chose Kimbo, Grabo, Bato, Burnah. After them he selected a stranger to Cinqué. He was named Konoma—a Congolese, fiercer appearing than any of the Mendis. His incisor teeth had been pressed outward like tusks and filed sharp; his lips were large, his mouth projecting; he had a primitive design tattooed on his forehead and diagonal slits in his nostrils. The Spaniards laughed heartily when Ruiz chose him.

Soon Señor Ruiz had selected sixty men. These he stood in a row, stripped of everything, including the new loincloths. Then like a dealer in horseflesh he went down the row of men, who in shame stood with their heads down and hands clutched tightly in their groins. He shouted orders to them in Spanish. Unable to understand more than the word "Señor," they looked at him dumbly. With his hands he forced their eyes open wider while he searched for evidences of ophthalmia or blindness. With his forefinger as a mallet he tapped their teeth to see if they were sound. He jerked their hands away from their bodies and made a minute search for marks of venereal diseases, caring nothing for the modesty he violated. He made them stoop away from him so that he could examine them from behind. With stiff thumb and forefinger he pinched and prodded, scrutinizing them for any defect that might hinder them from being good work animals. All the time he carried on a rapid and jocular conversation with Don Pablo and his majordomos.

From the sixty men he chose forty-nine, most of them young, none beyond middle life. The others he pushed aside. At a command from Señor Riera, guards came again with iron collars and chains. This time they were chained in groups of ten. Cinqué looked at the lines of bound men standing four abreast in the barracoon. Among them he saw Bato and Burnah, Kimbo and Grabo. "My brother! My friends," he said to them, taking what comfort he could from the thought that whatever journey lay before him, they would be going part of the way.

The chained men stood facing the door of the barracoon. The other Mendis from the *Tecora,* huddling as near them as they dared, began crying, the women and children whimpering first and then wailing.

Grabo, dry-eyed, restrained, raised a hand toward them. "My people," he said, "we have come from the same faraway country. It is a good country, the Mendi country in Africa. We have friends there. From them we have parted forever. Now it is time for us to part. I bid you farewell."

The voices took up a chant of sorrow. Kimbo, holding back his tears, spoke to them softly of the beautiful land in Africa. He tried to comfort them with memories of home.

Cinqué, seeing the tears among so many, wept with them and shouted in bitterness, "My brothers, we are sick and suffering because of the white man. Now we are torn asunder by him. What can we do—"

His words stirred the men to straining at their chains. Women and children rushed on them, begging to be taken with them. Voices joined in threatening mutterings. But the guards came close with their guns at ready.

49

Señor Ruiz signed papers and passed gold to Don Pablo, four hundred and fifty dollars for each African. Then he came to the captives with papers in his hand—a *traspaso* for forty-nine *ladino* Negroes bound for Puerto Principe in the Island of Cuba, bound for the mart of Don Saturnino Carrias, who would sell them to the highest bidders. Negroes who had been landed ten days before as *bozales* were now by the papers legally *ladinos,* Negroes domiciled in Cuba since before the Treaty of 1820. This change had been wrought at a cost of ten dollars each, the money having been paid to the Governor General and his deputies.

Señor Ruiz stood between the captives and the entrance. He had the other Mendis driven to the rear of the barracoon to silence their wailing. Cinqué was at the head of the first row. Burnah stood right behind him. Ruiz stepped to the head of the line.

"Joseph," he read from the passport. Cinqué did not understand. A Creole slave spoke to Burnah in English. Then Burnah explained to Cinqué. He was to have a new name—Joseph. Already the majordomos had been speaking of him as "Cinqué," the nearest they could come to his name in Mendi.

"Joseph Cinqué," Señor Riera laughed.

Then Señor Ruiz went down the line of men, renaming them "Manuel," "Estanislao," "Frederico," "Gabriel," and so on until the forty-nine names on the passport matched the forty-nine Negroes in chains. Thus were the passports made legal. The slaves were fully protected from meddlesome Englishmen.

With spectators looking on, the captives were given food and allowed to put on their loincloths. Then when darkness came they were led away from the wailing Africans in the barracoon and half-marched, half-dragged down the *Paseo Militar,* through the streets and plaza of old Havana, to the docks under the grim shadow of the Morro Castle. At times Cinqué looked into the faces of both whites and blacks along the dimly lighted streets. He looked at them, begging silently

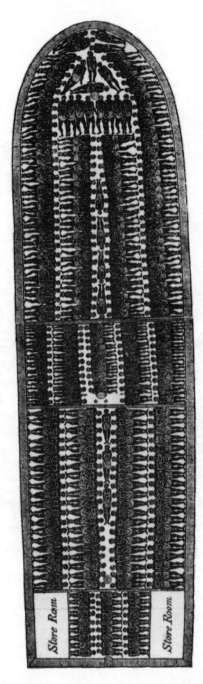

Fig. 4 Rows of slaves chained together in the hold of a ship, a photograph of an old print from *Abstract Evidence*. (Courtesy of the Boston Public Library.)

Fig. 5 Portrait of Cinqué, by Nathaniel Jocelyn. (Collection of the New Haven Colony Historical Society.)

for help, even for compassion. They only stared back, or stepped aside for the sad caravan to pass. The sight of chained men in the streets of Havana was too common for people to be affected by it. For the whites it was natural—for the blacks natural too, for so had most of them arrived in Havana.

From the docks they marched single file on board a schooner, and while they stood on deck Señor Ruiz reported to Captain Ramón Ferrer, master of the vessel. In the dim light of deck lanterns Cinqué could see that Captain Ferrer was like Don Pedro Blanco, only fatter and flabbier. Near Captain Ferrer was a mulatto youth. Cinqué and Burnah looked at the ugly hybrid of Spanish and African blood. Then they acknowledged to each other their distrust of him. On the African Coast one drop of white blood set a Negro apart from Negroes, gave him the superiority of white men. Never could a black man trust a mulatto. A Creole slave boy, black as he was but wise in the ways of Spaniards, stopped to talk with the mulatto.

By now a new group had arrived on deck—another Spaniard, an older man, with four other captives, three little girls and a boy.

"Señor Montes," the man introduced himself to Captain Ferrer and Señor Ruiz.

The captives were given little time on deck. If they had, they could not have read the name *Amistad* painted on her prow, or have understood the mockery of its meaning, *friendship*. It was too dark for them to discern the sharp lines of the vessel, or to marvel at the gilded eagle, symbol of freedom, she carried so proudly. If the mockery occurred to the Spaniards, they gave no sign, being much engrossed in securing their cargo.

Señor Ruiz and Señor Montes, with the manner of men afraid of their charges, hurried the captives to the slave deck below and locked the long chains to ringbolts on the deck. Then they placed additional irons on wrists and ankles and left Antonio, the Creole slave, to help them get settled for the night.

51

"Where you come from?" Burnah asked Antonio.

He had been kidnapped as a child in Sierra Leone, brought to Cuba on a slave ship, reared in the house of Don Saturnino Carrias. At first they thought he would help them, being like them from Africa, speaking Spanish, broken English, several African dialects. But they came quickly to distrust him when he showed his fondness for white men and his superiority to *bozales*. Might as well ask help of a white man.

The slave deck was no new experience. They were used to the low ceiling, crowding, foul air and smells. After the lanterns had been taken away, they eased themselves down, seeking comfortable positions on the bare deck.

When the deck was dark the children began crying. Not chained or manacled, they had been brought down last and were huddled near the ladder. Cinqué, remembering his children at home, spoke to them softly in Mendi. Three of them answered. With the help of others he made room for them to lie on deck beside him.

"What are you called?" he asked them.

"Marghru."

"Teme."

"Ka-le."

The last was the boy. They were all from Mendi and had been on the *Tecora*.

The third little girl was Kene, a Congolese, who could understand nothing they said to her.

As tenderly as a mother Cinqué talked to the children until their crying had stopped and they were sleeping.

Then in the darkness of the slave deck, safe from the prying eyes and ears of Antonio, Cinqué and Burnah talked of how they might yet escape bondage. If they were not chained, a quick leap overboard and they would be free. If there were weapons, they could fight their way free. There must be some way, and they searched for it with all their primitive cunning.

IV

"KILL THE WHITE MEN—"

Daylight shining through a narrow grate above the slave deck, harbor smells borne on a land breeze, the schooner buoying gently in sheltered waters. . . . Cinqué woke from his turn of sleep and saw that Kimbo and Grabo were keeping guard as they had agreed. On this voyage there must be constant watching for weakness among their captors.

"Have we sailed?" he asked.

They assured him that the schooner was still fast to the dock. The only sound that had disturbed them was the singing of drunken Spanish sailors returning from a night in Havana.

Now there was activity on deck, and the smell of food cooking. The captives roused themselves at the sound of voices, and stretched themselves to the sound of clinking metal.

The hatch to the slave deck opened and two white sailors descended the ladder, flashing lighted lanterns into the gloom. They spoke to each other in Spanish and shouted "Comida" to the captives. Not comprehending, the Africans remained silent. Then the sailors came down among them. They lifted the chain to which Cinqué's iron collar was padlocked. Counting aloud to each other, they unlocked the blacks until they had freed ten. These they herded up the ladder to the deck, urging them along as fast as the shackles on their ankles would permit them to go. They made Cinqué

53

lead, apparently marking him as the natural chief of the captives.

On deck the Africans gasped and stared at the view of Havana spread out before them, its white walls and red roofs gleaming in bright sunlight. Cinqué could see white men walking about the docks and streets—free. He could count fifty Negro dock workers—also free, or at least not in chains. They did not wear iron collars around their necks or shackles on their feet. He was suddenly envious. He glanced quickly over the side of the schooner, the thought strong in his mind that with one leap he might be as free as the others.

Before the thought could develop to action, the sailors pushed him and the others to a section of the deck where food was cooking in copper boilers set in a framework of brick. There the mulatto they had seen on deck the night before placed boilers of rice and boiled potatoes before them. "Celestino," the sailors called this mestizo. Celestino Ferrer, mulatto slave of the Captain. Cinqué searched his face and thought he had inherited more of the Captain's characteristics than his name. In him surely the worst features of white man and black woman were molded. . . .

The captives squatted on deck and ate from the vessels with their hands. After they had eaten the portions allotted them, the sailors marched them to another part of the deck where casks of water were lashed together. One of the sailors, the one called Vicente, drew water in tin cups and gave it to them. The other, Jacinto Verdagne, stood guard with a musket. He was a young man, little more than a boy, with the bluest eyes and ruddiest complexion the Africans had ever seen. *El Rojo,* the Spaniards called him, "The Red one"; red he was in contrast to the dark skin and black hair of his companion Vicente.

For half an hour the captives were marched back and forth on deck for exercise. Cinqué studied the ship as carefully as he had studied directions and sails on the *Tecora.* Though he knew nothing about ships, he could see that the *Amistad* was a trim schooner, well equipped for her task of transporting

54

slaves in the coastal trade of Cuba. Much smaller than the *Tecora,* she was a neat clipper, with her top painted black, her bottom green, and one white stripe at the waterline. In the sun's glare he could see the gilded eagle on her prow clearly outlined.

A shout of laughter came from the slave hatch, followed by the four children, with Antonio close behind them. Marghru and Ka-le led them, laughing with the freshness of morning, seemingly untouched by their night on the slave deck. When they saw Cinqué, Ka-le and Marghru ran to him and danced around him, calling him their good father. Antonio led them away, gave them food and water, and then allowed them to run free about the schooner.

"Take us to Havana," they begged Cinqué.

He laughed bitterly and pointed to his shackled ankles. Then the Spanish sailors took him below. Subdued, the children followed him out of the sunlight into the fetid air of the slave hold.

It was Cinqué's time to sleep again, but the excitement above penetrated to the slave deck. They heard the Captain shouting orders to his men. They heard snatches of sailor songs interrupted by replies to the Captain, and quick, hot cursing. Then the creaking timbers told them the schooner was moving.

Antonio came to the slave deck to see that all was quiet and in order.

"Where you take us?" Burnah asked him.

He shook his head with the air of one who knows much but chooses to say nothing. Cinqué more than ever distrusted this Creole slave, Antonio González. He mimicked too easily the manners of Spaniards; he spoke their language with too great a fluency. His heart and soul belonged to his masters.

"Cuban sun has not made your skin whiter," Cinqué told him. Antonio shrugged and went back to the Captain.

When the sun was slanted low from the west the captives were again brought on deck in groups of ten for food and

55

water. Cinqué could see that the schooner had changed her position considerably. They had sailed most of the harbor and were headed toward the narrow stem of the shamrock. While he was on deck they passed many ships—Spanish merchant vessels, an American man-o'-war, a British cruiser.

"English massa," Burnah said.

Cinqué yearned toward this English ship. If they only knew, they would help him. But he had no way of making known to them that he had just been brought from Africa—that he had a wife and children grieving for him.

For a moment Cinqué had hope as another ship came within hailing distance. But his hope passed quickly when he heard her master hail in Spanish. She was the guard vessel *Geraldino*. Her master came aboard the *Amistad*, where Captain Ferrer met him with papers. He examined the papers, barely glanced at the chained Negroes on deck, and stamped his approval on the passports. Everything was in order. The *Amistad* was bound for Puerto Principe with a cargo of goods and fifty-three *ladino* Negroes. He sent the schooner on, marking nothing unusual in either crew or cargo.

When they were near Morro Castle all the captives were brought on deck, the schooner being too far out for any of them to try escaping over the side. As they watched, a boat put out from under the cliff and came alongside. A ladder was thrown out and two Spanish officials came on board, important in bearing, insolent as a Vey chieftain. Captain Ferrer, José Ruiz, and Pedro Montes waited for them on deck. Hurriedly, perfunctorily, they examined the ship's papers. They looked at the *traspasos* issued for the captives.

"Forty-nine *ladinos*," one *traspaso* read. "Four *ladinos*," the other.

The *traspaso* for the little girls called them *ladino* women, a misstatement that caused no concern to the officials. It also called them passengers for the government—an added precaution should the schooner be spoken by a British cruiser.

Vicente lined the captives up on deck and one of the officials counted them, mumbling to himself the names written on the *traspaso*. Then he stamped the papers "Passed June 27, 1839" and returned them to Captain Ferrer. Everything was in order. Captain Ferrer handed them gold for their services and they climbed down the ladder again. The *Amistad* was entirely clear, free to resume her journey.

When they were past Morro Castle they dropped anchor for the night. The captives, below deck, well filled with food, lulled by the gentle rolling of the schooner, slept—except those who with Cinqué took turns at watching. The Captain and crew on deck were content, satiated by ten good days in Havana. In a month or two they would be back again for another cargo of slaves, another liberty in Havana. Morning would be soon enough to sail. The distance to Guanaja, port of Puerto Príncipe, was no more than three hundred miles—a distance Captain Ferrer expected to sail in two days and one night, in three days at most.

When Cinqué awoke the next morning the creaking timbers and roll of the schooner told him they were already under way. "Since daylight," Burnah told him.

Antonio hustled them on deck for food and exercise. They were already far from Havana, and the coast of Cuba lay like a low bank to their right. The schooner was sailing due east at the time, into the sun, in the direction of Africa. Cinqué took note of the direction and made a count of the Spaniards.

Captain Ferrer, middle-aged, soft, amiable in spite of his cutlass and pistol, was at the helm. Vicente and Jacinto worked about the deck, obeying commands of Captain Ferrer. Ruiz and Montes were taking a morning rest in their cabin. Those were the white men ranged against him. Of them all, Cinqué judged, only the two sailors would put up a hard fight if he could stir up a rising.

There were only two other crew members on board—Celestino and Antonio, neither a match for Cinqué. Celestino was busy cooking food, helped by Kimbo and Fuleh, whose shackles had been temporarily removed and hooked on the rail near the boilers. Antonio hovered near the Captain,

57

ready to run his errands. Who would fear these two? Cinqué thought.

Cinqué went below when his turn came and spread hope to Grabo and Burnah.

"We are forty-nine to seven," he told them. "Without chains we would be the stronger."

Without chains. . . . The thought set Cinqué in a fever.

Their rest was broken by the pitching schooner. In spite of their chains, they were rolled from side to side on the bare deck, rubbing against each other, wearing their skins raw on the boards. "Storm . . . wind," they said to each other.

When Antonio brought them on deck again in the late afternoon the sky was hot blue, and the schooner was bucking a strong headwind. She had already drifted out to sea, much farther than a coasting vessel was prepared to navigate. The coast of Cuba was no longer in sight; as far as eye could see there was nothing but whitecaps on rolling green water.

Cinqué could see worry on Captain Ferrer's face; he could see it in the way Ruiz and Montes hovered about the wheelhouse. Burnah caught Antonio apart and learned the extent of worry. At the rate they were going, the voyage might take four or five days, or more. Some vessels had been fifteen days from Havana to Guanaja. The *Amistad* did not carry enough food and water for her slave cargo for so long a voyage.

"You will see," he said to Burnah.

At mealtime the captives saw their rations had been cut. Instead of putting boilers of food before them, Celestino dipped two boiled potatoes into the hands of each. Then he gave each half a raw plantain. When they held their hands out for more, he shook his head and pointed toward the Captain. When they marched past the water casks, Vicente gave each half a cup of water—scarcely enough to wet a throat in the parching tropical sun.

Progress was slow and fighting against the headwind dull. The heat being fierce below, Captain Ferrer allowed all the captives to stay on deck and cool themselves as well as they could in a wind that blew hot out of a burning sky. Captain Ferrer kept in the shade of a sail and allowed the wind to blow directly on his body, bare to the waist. Celestino sweated over the pots boiling on deck. Vicente and Jacinto rested on boxes and bales of merchandise lashed to the deck, ready to jump at the Captain's bidding if the wind should slacken or change.

Antonio came on deck stripped to a pair of white pantaloons. Seeing him, Vicente and Jacinto sprang to the deck. They caught him and dragged him to the brick fireboxes.

"You forget you are a slave," they told him.

"No—"

"We will make you to remember."

He watched in horror while they heated Celestino's poker red hot. While Vicente held him, Jacinto, his blue eyes glinting, branded an "F" on his shoulder, branding him a slave of Captain Ferrer, in the manner of Cuban plantation owners.

When the iron touched his flesh, Antonio screamed and begged for help, but no help came. Captain Ferrer laughed as if he had witnessed a clever practical joke. Ruiz and Montes, who had come on deck at the sound of excitement, looked on indifferently. Celestino calmly took the poker from Jacinto and stirred the fire under a boiler of potatoes. The captives, fearing they would be next, drew as far away from the scene as they could. They hated Antonio, hated and distrusted him, but they would have helped him had they dared. He was black and in pain.

"*Ave Maria* . . . Holy Mother," Antonio prayed the Christian prayers his Spanish masters had taught him.

The sailors then rubbed his wounds with gunpowder, palm oil, and vinegar—to heal the flesh yet leave the scar vivid. Wherever Antonio went, the world could know he was a slave. When the sailors released him, he slunk down a hatchway.

Still pleased with their joke, the Spanish sailors returned the captives to the slave deck and locked them to the turnbolts.

Full of the thing that had happened to Antonio, more fearful than ever of what could happen to them, they huddled close together in the heat of the slave deck. Mendi or Congo, they were all black people, welded into one by the hard fortune that had thrown them together. They felt each other's misery, talked over their hardships, let their hatred of white men grow. Most of the night they spent whispering the cruelties they had seen since being sold into slavery. The leader in their talk was Cinqué. The savage anger he had felt toward Don Pedro Blanco had increased tenfold. With voice raised above their murmurings he promised death to the white men—if only the others would help him.

Morning again, with the wind still blowing strong out of a hot sky. With sullen looks the captives came on deck. Again Celestino handed to each two small boiled potatoes and half a raw plantain. Vicente dished out to each the amount of water that would fill the small half of a cow's horn. They begged for more food and water. Jacinto and Vicente raised their lashes and pointed to the angry "F" on Antonio's shoulder.

Fearful that he might lose some of his profits in the heat of the slave deck, Ruiz came and with Jacinto herded them to the pump and sprayed them with salt water. Some of them, half crazed with thirst, drank the water and became thirstier almost to madness—the appalling madness that comes from drinking sea water.

"I will have water," Fuleh said defiantly.

Stronger and bolder than any except Cinqué, he eluded the eyes of Celestino long enough to get to the water cask and steal a cupful for himself. But he was caught by Jacinto and Vicente. They called Celestino and Antonio to help hold him, and, while Ruiz and Captain Ferrer looked on, they beat him across the back with a cat-o'-nine-tails. The whip cut his skin in long gashes. He bore it with clenched jaws and burning eyes.

After they had beaten him till they were exhausted, the sailors treated his wounds by rubbing them with salt, gunpowder, and rum. After taking the beating without a whimper, he screamed in agony when the mixture touched his raw flesh. He kept screaming until they threw him below and chained him to a bulkhead.

The sun set like a fiery ball in a burning sea. Jacinto herded all the captives to the steaming, stinking hold. Fuleh talked of the pain he suffered. They had neither help nor comfort for him, except in the threats of revenge Cinqué led them in speaking. Somewhere their chains would be struck from them; sometime, fate willing, they would repay Fuleh's debt in full measure.

But the sailors were not through with their fun for that night, or with venting their frustration on Fuleh. Again and again—five times altogether—they dragged him on deck and repeated the flogging. At last he lay on deck unable to move, surrounded by primitive black men who had released all restraints in anger, who pounded the deck in impotent fury.

Another day of strong wind and rough water. Another day in which the whites, unable to vent their wrath on wind and waves, punished the helpless captives. With excuse or without they flogged Kimbo, Pieh, Moru, and Foone. The slave deck was a hell of suffocating heat, but the captives begged to stay below. There it was harder for Jacinto and Vicente to wield their lashes.

On the morning of the fourth day the wind was still against the schooner, though the Captain had, through force of will and muscles, maneuvered her closer to Cuba. Captain Ferrer, obviously tired and distressed, allowed Señor Montes to relieve him at the wheel. Montes, though he himself had been master of a vessel for years, and was skilled in the waters of the West Indies, took on the Captain's worry.

The captives took their portions of food and water and then lingered near the boilers to talk to Celestino. He was mulatto and not to be trusted, yet who else was there left to answer their questions? Talking with their fingers and Burnah's English, they made sure he understood them.

61

Then Burnah asked, "What will the white men do with us?"

Celestino laughed mockingly. Then, with his hands, he told them that when they arrived at Puerto Príncipe, they would have their throats cut, be chopped to pieces, and salted down for meat for the Spaniards. He pointed to some barrels of beef on deck, then to an empty barrel.

"You will fill that barrel," he told them.

Celestino drew a knife across his throat. "The white men will eat you when you get to Puerto Príncipe."

His joke was no joke to the Africans. Since the first day of their captivity they had feared being eaten by white men. Now their fears were to be realized. Surely Celestino had seen other Africans made into a feast for the Spaniards.

Cinqué, Burnah, and Kimbo pressed together on deck and talked of how they could prevent this terrible thing from happening to them.

"We must fight," they said.

They looked at the rough green water. It was better even to leap overboard and die in the water than to be eaten by white men. It was better still if they could make it to the low-lying shore of Cuba. There must be a way to take off their shackles. . . .

The sky, intense blue for four days, was now black with clouds made ragged by stronger winds. Rain fell in short bursts and then swept on across the rough water. The schooner, never built for such seas, was carried by wind and waves like driftwood.

The captives, on deck for their afternoon feeding, milled around the pitching deck, grateful for the cooling rain, feeling the slackened discipline. Captain Ferrer was at the helm, unwilling to trust others in the storm. Jacinto and Vicente worked at the sails. Celestino stirred his boilers. Antonio had taken food below to Ruiz and Montes.

In their milling Cinqué found a loose nail in a deck board. He worked it out with his fingers and quickly secreted it in his arm pit. He looked about furtively to see if he had been detected. Finding no one looking at him, he turned to the sea and breathed deep of the storm. . . .

Vicente returned the captives to the slave deck and locked them up for the night. Like subdued children they lay on the deck and let him lock chains to their iron collars. A sharper man than he might have detected the fierce smoldering under their submission.

The storm passed soon after darkness. The schooner rode at greater ease, somewhat protected by the Cuban shore, now not more than two leagues distant. Captain Ferrer seemed ahead in his struggle with the elements.

In the slave hold the children cried and begged for *yamyam*.

"Hush," Cinqué quieted them. "Soon we will eat. Soon there will be plenty *yamyam*."

He whispered his thoughts to Burnah, Kimbo, Bato, and Grabo, and touched them with the nail from his arm pit. His talk was of mutiny. He would escape from his chains. He would kill the Captain and the crew. They would take the ship and all the food on it. Somehow they would get home to Africa. These the strongest of the captives agreed with him, offered their own strength and cunning.

Then all the captives were made a part of the council, whispering in Mendi. All their discussions were open, even for the children to hear, but guarded lest any word should be understood by Antonio. White man's slave that he was, he would take their plans to Captain Ferrer. Then Jacinto and Vicente would come with their lashes and beat them into submission.

"We feel bad at what has happened to us," Kin-na said. Kin-na, who always before had held his counsel. Kin-na, who was young and strong and of a bright countenance.

His words stirred them. Their mumbling became excited jabbering. The children forgot to cry for *yamyam*.

"What will we do?" Kin-na asked.

63

"I will think," Cinqué answered to give himself time, "and then by and by I will tell you."

While they waited, Cinqué, with the nail and Grabo to help him, picked the locks and freed himself from the irons on his wrists and ankles, and from the iron collar about his neck. Feeling him move about among them, free from his chains, the others clung to him and begged him to lead them to freedom. With his help they threw themselves against the chains and broke the locks from the ringbolts. Then they crowded close around him in the darkness.

"Now I will tell you," Cinqué said. "If we do nothing, we will be killed. We may as well die trying to be free, as to be killed and eaten—by white men."

"What will we do?" they begged him.

"We will kill the Captain," he told them.

"And the cook!"

"And the sailors!"

"And Antonio!"

They added the words as fast as they could say them, letting their hatred burst the names out like explosions.

"We will kill them all," Cinqué agreed. "But first we must get free of our chains. Then we will find knives and muskets."

Feverishly, noiselessly, they worked in the blackness freeing themselves. Some arms and hands were so emaciated that Cinqué was able to strip the manacles from them. Their ankles he unlocked with nimble fingers. As they felt themselves freed, they worked their arms and legs to ready them for action. Quietly they moved, and the children hushed their whimpering.

Toward midnight the men were all free. From among them Cinqué selected those he thought best fitted for their dangerous fight. These he led to the cargo hold, where they broke open bales of goods till they came to some sugar cane knives, being shipped along with them for tools when they reached the plantations. These were knives with thirty-two inch blades and metal grips. Better weapons for their purposes could hardly have fallen into their hands.

Back on the slave deck again, they handed out the weapons and made a swift pact of mutiny, a pact which bound them in life and death together. Cinqué would be the leader in their attack on the Captain. He would be helped by Grabo, Kimbo, Faa, and Maum. Faquanah would protect Cinqué. Fuleh would protect their rear, with Seme and Cu-bah to help him in whatever fighting came handy. Sessi, the oldest of them, the only one who had held the wheel of a vessel, would navigate. Sessi, who had worked on British ships at Sierra Leone, was mirthful, quick to laugh. Cinqué could only hope he would not be foolish at the moment of fighting.

When they were ready to go, Marghru began crying with fright. Cinqué stopped to pat her head, holding up mutiny to comfort a child. He spoke sharply to Ka-le, telling him to keep quiet himself and see that no sounds came from the other children.

With Cinqué in the lead they crept up the companionway to the deck. The moon had broken through the clouds, and they were like weird shadows moving among the casks and equipment. Released from the storm, the schooner made full sail for Guanaja.

They found Captain Ferrer and Celestino sleeping side by side on a mattress on deck, where they had dropped exhausted after the storm. The moon made their faces strange masks of pallor and shadow. Cinqué was seeing the mask of the *Wuja*, the face of Don Pedro Blanco. Beatings and starvings and the horror of the slave deck distilled into wild hatred. "Kill the white man," his pulse beat. But it was not time to shout yet. It was better to kill these two while they slept. Cinqué and Kimbo crept forward carefully.

But the noise they had made in the forecastle had awakened José Ruiz. He rushed on deck in time to see two blacks creeping forward, their knives raised for slaughter.

"No! No!" Ruiz shouted at them. He grabbed an oar and shook it at them threateningly.

But Cinqué would not be stopped. All the hatred stored in him since the day he left Mani weighted his arm as he struck

65

at the Captain. His silence was broken and he was shouting "Kill the white man!"

The Captain, awakened by the noise and confusion, dodged the blow and threw Celestino between himself and Cinqué.

Yelling with rage, Cinqué struck again and almost severed Celestino's head from his body.

"Murder! Mutiny!" Vicente yelled from his place as helmsman. Then he and Jacinto ran aft to escape the onslaught—in cowardice ran and eluded the blacks, who wanted first the blood of the Captain.

The Captain, on his feet now, began calling for Antonio.

"Go get some bread and throw it to them," he shouted to Antonio, hoping yet to pacify them.

His words were meaningless to Cinqué and his companions; they would not have stopped had they understood. Bread could not still their wild anger. Revenge was better than a full belly. Ruiz, seeing how desperate the Africans were, darted past them and ran below, shouting for Montes to follow him on deck and help save the Captain.

With his rapier Captain Ferrer fought back desperately, slashing Seme and Cu-bah, who had rushed forward unguardedly. By now all the blacks were on deck, the children screaming, the others running around yelling like legions of devils. Seme and Cu-bah, angered by their wounds, rushed past Cinqué. The Captain ripped each bare belly with a thrust of his rapier.

The Captain fought savagely, but he was no match for Cinqué and his knife-wielding companions. Kimbo and Grabo slashed him three or four times. Then Cinqué stepped forward and, with a mighty blow, split his head open. The Captain fell forward; Cinqué grabbed his rapier by the time it touched the deck. "Kill the white men," he shouted again, the tension already breaking.

Then they rushed aft in pursuit of the Spanish sailors, but they were gone, and Fuleh was denied the revenge he had threatened.

"They cannot catch land—they must have swum to the bottom of the sea," they consoled each other at first. Then they discovered that the stern boat was missing. The sailors had escaped—with a boat and a calm sea they would soon be in Cuba.

They rushed forward again and ran into Ruiz and Montes. Cinqué shouted to Ruiz, that they would not hurt them and to stand still and he did so. Montes, who had armed himself with a stick and a knife, did not understand Cinqué and attacked him. Faquanah sprang at Montes and slashed him with a sugar cane knife. Montes, begging for help, ran below. He hid himself between two barrels, wrapped up in a sail. Fuleh went after him to kill him, but Kimbo ran between them. Montes would be valuable at the wheel of the vessel. Bleeding profusely and already weak from fright and the loss of blood, he was taken on deck and tied to the hand of Ruiz.

Antonio was the only one left free. After escaping the first onslaught, he had hidden away among the casks and bales on deck. There Cinqué found him and dragged him out for practice with the Captain's rapier.

"No, no," Dama intervened.

Antonio was the only language link they had. They must use him now. Then Cinqué could hack him to pieces if he liked.

The captives, victorious, boasting, savage from their first taste of blood, gathered on deck around Ruiz and Montes, eager to make their white victims suffer. The last clouds had passed and Sessi was wrestling the schooner along, farther and farther from land, in a bright moonlit sea.

Cinqué sent to the slave deck for shackles and manacles. When Ruiz and Montes saw them, they begged not to be locked in chains. Montes wept like a child in his pleadings. But Cinqué was firm, his words through Burnah direct.

"You say fetters good for nigger," he said. "If good for nigger, good for Spanish man too; you try them two days and see how you feel. You learn how it is to be slaves."

Montes begged them to spare his life. With signs, with the

English of Burnah and the Spanish of Antonio, Cinqué told Montes what they wanted—under what conditions they would let him live. They wanted him to steer for Sierra Leone, and put them out on the beach near home.

"I do not know the way," Montes told them.

Neither did Cinqué or the others, but they knew the direction. Cinqué remembered all the days of sailing away from the sun when they left Africa. To return, they had to sail into the sun.

"East—sail east," was the command Cinqué gave through Burnah and Antonio.

Again Montes shook his head. But when Cinqué held the Captain's rapier to his throat, Montes agreed to steer for Sierra Leone—if they would allow him to return peacefully to Havana. After they had bound the vessel so the drift would be easterly, they let Ruiz and Montes go below to recover. The Africans had work not needing the presence of white men.

The Africans had accomplished their purpose. They were free, and in command of a vessel that would take them back to Africa. Theirs was the *Amistad*. Theirs the forbidden barrels of beef on deck, the casks of water, the stores of food below for the Captain and crew. In the moonlight they wept and shouted and danced in their new freedom.

Cinqué knew this was no time to stop. He had to hold them together, make his authority sure. He shouted them to silence and ordered them to clean the deck.

Under his directions they dragged the bodies of Captain Ferrer and Celestino to the rail. Cinqué felt no remorse at the dead bodies, at his breaking the laws of *Poro*. The Africans cursed at lifting the bodies, and laughed as they splashed into the water. After them they tossed the two blacks killed by Captain Ferrer, cast them into the water without chant or ritual, without tears or show of sorrow. They had seen too much of death and suffering. Then they washed down the decks to clear away the blood.

After that, Cinqué allowed them to gorge themselves on

68

the food Celestino had left in the boilers, and to drink as much water as they wanted.

Cinqué needed a grip of steel to hold the blacks together—a grip he did not have. The command he had held during the mutiny gave way when danger was over. There were too many of them and it was too easy for them to scatter to dark places on the schooner. They had tasted blood and food; now they were tasting a new kind of freedom. With it they went into an orgy that lasted the remainder of the night.

In spite of Cinqué's protests they ransacked the cargoes, breaking open casks and strewing food and goods in the holds and on deck. Crockery and cloth and vermicelli they jumbled together. They were in search of food chiefly at first, but they grabbed for themselves clothing and trinkets. Trying to imitate white men, they put on garments, not caring if they were wrongside out and hind part before. They gorged themselves on food until, their shrunken stomachs rejecting it, they vomited wherever they were. They found cases of assorted medicines, as well as cases of wine and raisins. These they opened, and they drank the wines and medicines indiscriminately. Before daylight most of them were sick from too much food and medicine. Many were drunk. Still they would not heed Cinqué.

Their revolt lasted until the sun was bright again across calm green water. Then, with two more dead and a dozen unconscious on deck, they became quiet again. Alcohol and sickness had accomplished what Cinqué had lacked strength to do.

Cinqué called together those still able to walk. He stood before them with the rapier strapped to his side and a cat-o'-nine-tails in his hand—symbols of authority the Negroes understood. He had put on a pair of white pantaloons and tied a red kerchief around his neck. Carefully he explained his decisions, his plans.

The Captain's doubloons were in his possession and would be used for the benefit of all to get them back to Africa. The other spoils would be divided, with him receiving the smallest portion. He would take the four children under his special care, and protect their share of the goods. In all things his word was to be absolute law. He would not hesitate to use the lash on offenders. There was no other way to return to Africa.

What would they do in case of capture? They asked this question soberly.

With an earnestness born of deep suffering, he bared his heart before them.

"If the white man comes again," he said, "if there is danger of being taken, I will kill all of you to save you. Then I will kill myself. I would rather die than be taken in bondage again. If they kill me first, I beg you take this knife and avenge me. . . ."

V

EAST BY DAY

Sessi, bewildered by the gear and charts of the *Amistad*, used only to holding the rudder of a small English boat in sheltered waters, wrestled with the schooner in the early morning hours. He set his course toward the morning star, but in spite of him the schooner drifted before the wind, getting farther and farther away from the Island of Cuba, and approaching the entrance to the Old Bahama Channel.

Cinqué watched the coast of Cuba slip out of sight with relief. Gone was the threat of slavery, gone the Spaniards and all they stood for. He pointed to the sun and told Sessi to keep pointing toward it.

With Cinqué shouting orders, the Africans worked at clearing the decks and restoring order. They now cringed before him, fearing the cat-o'-nine-tails he had taken from the Spaniards. They had seen him use it mercilessly on those who disobeyed him. He knew that their only hope to return to Africa was through rigid discipline and close working together; most of the others agreed with him. The main effects of the mutiny had passed; their blood, aroused to the boiling point to kill the white men, cooled again and they were willing to trust Cinqué to bring them safe to Africa.

More like a village headman than a ship's captain, Cinqué appointed the men to their tasks. Sessi would continue as navigator, with Cinqué to help him and be his apprentice. Foone was made cook, with three others to help him. The

71

sick were all brought on deck; Bato and Dama were set to watch over them. Cinqué retained complete control of the four children.

Foone got the fires going and boiled rice and potatoes. He broke open the crates of crockery on deck searching for more food. Having no use for plates and cups and saucers, he let them spill from their straw packing and add to the wide-strewn rubbish. Cinqué inventoried the food and water on board and worked out a ration. Of food there was enough to get them to Africa if they ate sparingly. Water they would have to get on some lonely island.

Seeing that Sessi was unable to stay the drift of the schooner, Cinqué brought Ruiz and Montes on deck. Ruiz had regained some of his debonair manner in spite of his chains. Montes, looking old and pale from loss of blood, trembled before his captors who had so recently been slaves. He was suffering from the wounds on his head and arm, and his heavily furrowed cheeks showed signs of recent weeping.

With Burnah to help him, Cinqué made Montes understand he wanted the key to his trunk. When Montes refused, they searched his pockets and found it. Then they stripped his bloody clothes from him, brought fresh ones from his trunk, and made him put them on.

Ruiz and Montes begged to have their irons removed, but with the cold contempt of a haughty chieftain Cinqué refused, telling them it was better for them to learn how to be slaves.

Cinqué took Montes to the helm. There, with the help of Burnah and Antonio, he gave instructions again, with a hand pointing to the east and a rapier brandished near Montes' throat. There could be no doubt of what Cinqué meant. When he was sure Montes understood, Cinqué took the manacles from his wrists but left the shackles on his ankles. While Cinqué and Sessi watched, eager for learning, Montes righted the vessel and set her course east. He tried to explain to the Africans how to set the sails. They followed his directions as well as they could, but when they had finished the ropes were slack and the sails flapping. Though the sea was calm and the wind fair, they made little headway.

Cinqué took the wheel himself, and with the help of the sun kept the schooner pointing toward Africa. There was no other marker on the broad expanse of water. Montes he kept beside him, allowing him to sleep fitfully on deck, waking him at intervals to check course and set of sails. In spite of their reckonings and Cinqué's strong sense of direction, the schooner boxed back and forth in the Old Bahama Channel, with little more control than a derelict.

At night, much recovered from his wounds and fear, Montes took the wheel. While steering east he calculated the distance to Cuba and the chances of getting the *Amistad* back to Havana harbor without arousing Cinqué's suspicions. Because of the narrow channel, he would almost have to make an about-face. That he was afraid to do. His wounds were too painful a reminder of the vengeance of the blacks if they caught him deceiving them. The threat of Cinqué holding a rapier across his throat was too vivid in his memory. Then he thought of other harbors he had taken refuge in. Some island in the Bahamas, perhaps. But there they would have to take their chances with British patrol vessels.

Then he thought of the United States. If he could bring the schooner to the coast of Florida or Virginia or anywhere in the slave territory, he would be sure to get help. American slave holders would be quick to aid him. A plan began to form in his mind. When he had the opportunity, when Cinqué was unaware of directions, at night or under cloudy skies, he would sail north by west. Perhaps he could make the mainland by Hatteras, or even farther south. Then if luck was with him. . . .

Montes talked his plan over with Ruiz, who was ready to take any chance, no matter how desperate. But during the first night Montes was afraid to make an obvious change in course. He had to get out of the Channel first. Also, Cinqué slept but little, napping like a cat on deck and like a cat

73

creeping up beside Montes in the dark to keep reminding him of the agreement he had made.

At midnight a violent squall blew from land, blotting out the moon and driving the schooner through waves that splashed on deck. The Africans ran about the deck crying in fright. "We will drown," they said to each other.

"Suppose you lower that sail," Montes suggested.

They lowered sails until only the foretopsail was left. Then Montes tacked to the west out of the center of the squall. When the squall ceased altogether he bore away from the wind, happy in the chance that took them nearer the United States. Desperately he held the westward course, trying to get as many furlongs westward as possible.

Cinqué awoke at dawn and discovered the change of direction. He called Kimbo and Grabo to a consultation.

"Montes lie," he told them. "I do not trust him."

"What will we do?" they asked.

"I will kill him."

Holding a dagger in his hand, Cinqué led the other two to Montes. Montes fell on his knees and begged for his life. He reminded them that they were in dangerous waters. No one else could save the schooner if they came upon rocks.

The decision was difficult for Cinqué. He hated this white man who had fought him and lied to him, hated him more than he had hated Don Pedro Blanco. He looked at Sessi, who was grinning foolishly in the face of danger. He could not trust Sessi to bring the schooner to Africa. Slowly he put away his dagger and pointed east until Montes had set the course in that direction. Then Cinqué took the wheel, his mind clouded with distrust and anxiety.

Toward midday the shoals of Los Roques showed black and white across the green water. Kimbo, at the masthead, saw them and shouted. "Havana! I see the buildings of Havana."

Cinqué whipped out his dagger again and waved it at the Spaniard. Montes sank to his knees pleading in a broken voice. "I swear," he said, "they are not buildings but rocks. If I lie, you can cut my throat. . . ."

They allowed the schooner to continue her course until they could see that they were rocks indeed. Then Cinqué signalled Montes to steer around the small island. Montes had told the truth in one thing, but Cinqué hated him as intensely as ever.

The sun was high and the deck hot. Foone was ready with boiled rice and potatoes. With his own hands Cinqué apportioned the food, giving Montes and Ruiz the same amount he gave the Africans, adding to the ration only for the children. Then he dipped water for them, dealing it out to the Spaniards in the same little cup that had been used for the blacks. Ruiz and Montes complained bitterly of being thirsty.

Cinqué said to them, "You say little water enough for nigger; if little water do for him, a little do for you too."

Suddenly Montes returned to his task at the helm. At the rate they were going, they would never reach the United States. Water would certainly give out within another day. There was no hope of making better headway. The untrained Negroes were slight help in taking advantage of wind and current. Ruiz, with a dandy's attitude toward work, was no help at all. Montes saw the *Amistad* limping on and on till dry throats and swollen tongues were eased in burning death. He summoned Cinqué and Antonio.

"We have little water," he said. "Do you want to go to a land where there are no slaves?"

"Is there water?"

"Fresh cool streams flowing."

Cinqué called a group together and told them what Montes had said. He had been right about the rocks. He might be right about the water. White men had ways of knowing denied to black men. They agreed, and he steered toward Andros Island.

During the second day a heavy gale came up. For more than twenty-four hours it buffeted the schooner about, and

Montes was hard put to keep from going aground on some of the barren sandy keys they approached. Cinqué took all of Montes' chains off and gave him full control. In saving his own life, the Spaniard had to save them all.

After the gale had passed they found that the *Amistad* had suffered heavily. The topsail yard was gone, the sails were in shreds. Montes pointed the damage out to Cinqué and said they should try to make land as quickly as possible.

Their water supply was now so short that Cinqué drank none from the casks himself and forced the others to drink nothing but sea water. Carefully he dealt out half a cupful to each of the children and an equal amount to the Spaniards. Thirst seared the minds of all of them, and the black men were nearly crazy from sea water.

In the afternoon of the next day they came in sight of Andros Island. The Africans shouted at the sight of the cool green island. Montes anchored and Cinqué with five others went ashore in the boat. In a clear stream they drank their fill, bathed themselves, and began filling casks. Startled by the sound of musket fire, they ran out into the open. Farther along the shore smoke billowed above green palms. With only one cask of water they ran to their boat and rowed to the *Amistad*.

A number of black men came in boats along the shore and fired at them with muskets. Black slaves, Cinqué thought. This was slave country after all, and Montes had lied again. Cinqué ordered his men to return their fire and drive them away. Then he ordered Montes to make sail and escape as rapidly as possible. The Africans, never having fired before, sprayed bullets wildly across the water.

Safe from Andros Island, Cinqué demanded that Montes steer to some smaller island where there were no people.

The muskets had to be reloaded and there was no one among the blacks who had ever loaded one. Fearing to ask the Spaniards lest they get the upper hand, Cinqué decided they must load without help. When the question of how much powder to use came up, there was loud argument.

Konoma decided the argument by saying, "If little make little noise, much make big noise."

They then poured the barrel full of powder and packed wadding and bullet after it. Then with hands over their ears they stood back for Konoma to fire. His filed tusks exposed in a grinning smile, he pointed the barrel out to sea and pulled the trigger. A mighty blast shook the schooner and threw Konoma to the deck. Pieces of barrel splintered and whizzed through sails and rigging, while the blacks threw themselves down in fright.

Aghast at the strength of powder, they took a horn to Ruiz and asked him to measure out enough for each load.

Montes sighted Green Key and steered for it. It was small enough for Cinqué's liking, without signs of human habitation. He ordered Montes to steer close and anchor. Unmolested, they went ashore and filled their casks.

While they were getting water, Montes took bearings again. He knew they were not far from New Providence, and he felt that if he could bring the *Amistad* there he could surely get help. Capture by a British cruiser was better than sailing on and on with this fanatical African.

After they had taken on water and the fear of thirst no longer crazed the Africans, Montes worked their way along the Middle Bight.

While Cinqué slept, a group led by Kwong came to Montes. Antonio was with them as interpreter.

"We want women," Kwong said. "We want to go back to the island of the black men. We find black women."

Montes studied the men carefully. Was this revolt? Was Cinqué's hold breaking? He called Ruiz and the men repeated their request. Ruiz gave each black a pinch from his snuffbox and he and Montes talked in Spanish. Where was the best place to take them? New Providence was an answer blessed by the Virgin.

"There are women in New Providence," Montes told the blacks. "Many African women. You will each have a woman

77

if we go to New Providence . . . women . . . food . . . to-bacco . . . rum. . . ."

Eagerly they commanded him to set the course for New Providence, while Cinqué still slept in the cabin.

"How far?" they asked.

"Very near . . . an hour, perhaps two."

The Africans filled themselves with food and water and took up watch on deck. They boasted among themselves of how they would make love when they came to the women, and chanted love songs from Mendi. Then when the houses of New Providence were clear on the horizon, they began shouting and dancing.

Their noise woke Cinqué and brought him to the deck. When he saw the port in full view, he slapped Montes several times by way of correction and took the helm. He withdrew some distance from the harbor, but, hoping himself to fall in with some vessel that could sell him food, he anchored in sight of New Providence.

Then he sent for Kwong. When he had the full story, he took the cat-o'-nine-tails and made Kwong kneel on the deck before him. Then, in the presence of all the blacks, with the white buildings of New Providence still beckoning, he slowly, deliberately laid fifty lashes across his shoulders.

At sunrise Cinqué had Montes brought on deck again. He made the Spaniard kneel on deck before him. While Burnah and Antonio interpreted, he berated Montes for stirring up feeling against him. Then he turned to their future. They must sail for Africa without delay. They had enough water, enough food for the slenderest rations. If Montes did not obey orders, he would receive more stripes than Kwong had.

They raised anchor and Montes steered the schooner through Exuma Sound. Late in the afternoon they came to an island that separated the Sound from the Atlantic—the Long Island of the Bahamas. Here they remained for three days, anchored at a safe distance from shore but close enough for the men to bring water until every cask, tub, and boiler was filled. They saw no people and found no food except tropical plants which made a poor substitute for vegetables. Cinqué kept Ruiz and Montes below deck, his people separated from their beguiling tongues and snuffboxes.

When they were again ready to sail, Montes tried to persuade Cinqué to steer for the United States, "Negroes are free there," he insisted. Cinqué listened to him and then pointed east across the Atlantic. Then they set their course east, with Cinqué at the helm, his eyes calculating direction by the rising sun. But at night he had to turn the schooner over to Montes again.

In the open ocean, under a cloudy sky, Montes could at last take up his plan of steering to the northwest to the United States. He kept his reckoning all night without detection, and then, when light began to show, he headed east, and east they were sailing when Cinqué awoke from his sleep. All that day Cinqué steered to the east. Again at night Montes set his course north by west.

On the following day they came against a head wind that drifted them steadily north by east. Cinqué, with his eye on the sun, tried to keep the schooner due east, but was unable to do so. Finally he saw that the only thing to be done was to anchor until the wind died down.

"Throw out the anchor," he had Antonio command Montes.

"There is no bottom," Montes replied.

Cinqué would not believe him. He thought it was a trick to let the schooner get off her course.

"Throw it out anyway," he commanded.

There in mid ocean they lowered the anchor. The schooner continued to drift. Cinqué motioned for Montes to stand aside and told Sessi to take the wheel. He would find out for himself whether this Spaniard told the truth. He went to the rail, took off his white pantaloons and belt of doubloons, and dived overboard.

Swimming with skill learned in African rivers, he came to the cable. Then he went under water, walking along the cable with his hands as the water closed over him. Down,

down, down he went until his hands touched the anchor. There was no ground beneath, the deep below seemed bottomless. Montes was right again, as he had been right at Los Roques. Cinqué released the cable and with bursting lungs shot upward to the surface. The Africans at the rail greeted him with shouts of pleasure. They had thought he would never come up again, so long he had been out of sight. They lowered a rope and he climbed on deck.

"There is no bottom to be found," he said. Then he helped haul in the anchor.

Days sailing east, nights sailing north by west—the *Amistad* left a zigzag wake in the waters of the Atlantic. By day Cinqué steadfastly held her pointing to the east. By night, Montes, still hoping with a desperate hope to fall in with some man-o'-war or to make some port, set the course as near a westerly direction as he dared. Through sun and wind and storm the schooner roamed like a derelict, her sails rotted, her bottom fouled, while supplies grew shorter, while six of the Africans sickened and died, while the two Spaniards feared daily to find death on the blade of a knife or in the depths of the ocean. Still Cinqué held them in check, by the force of will, by the cat-o'-nine-tails always at hand.

Once they sighted a sail. Cinqué immediately sent Montes and Ruiz below and forbade them to come on deck on pain of death. But the vessel never came in speaking distance; the Africans, with eyes dulled and hopeless, watched her bear away toward the United States.

When Ruiz and Montes came on deck again, they brought a letter they had written giving their names and circumstances. They read it to Cinqué and begged him to give it to the master of the first vessel they spoke.

Cinqué took the letter. "Very well," he said. Then he sent the Spaniards below and called a council of Africans.

He showed them the letter and listened to their distrust of this thing of the white men. He joined them in expressing hatred of Montes. This letter might be a fetish of the Spaniards. Then Cinqué spoke.

"We have no letter in Mendi. I don't know what is in that letter—there may be death in it. So we will take some iron and string, bind them about the letter, and send it to the bottom of the sea."

The Africans cheered with relief when Cinqué plunged the weighted letter into the Atlantic. . . .

On a blistering August day the *Amistad* came in sight of Long Island. The smell of land, the sight of green shores, aroused the blacks to laughing and singing. It was six weeks since they had left Havana, a month since they had sighted land at all. The Spaniards walked among them confidently at times, sure that Montes' plan had worked. At times they were afraid to hope. Death stood too near them in the form of an African headman.

The blacks did not know what to think. They knew this land near them could not be Africa. Not enough moons had gone by. But they knew not what shores had been between them and Africa from the beginning. They suspected the Spaniards of having tricked them, but they could not be sure. They began to think that Montes should die, but they knew he was still their one hope of reaching Africa. Cinqué and Sessi knew too little of navigation to bring the schooner safe home. They lined the rail to stare at Long Island, the Spaniards hoping for rescue, the Africans for fresh water to relieve them from the salt water they were again being forced to drink.

But Cinqué was not ready to take shelter in this strange land. The shore would have to be reconnoitered, the muskets made ready to ward off attack.

During that day and the next, when they were no more than twenty miles from Egg Harbor, they sighted several vessels, but none came within hailing distance. Then on the morning of August 19 they sighted a schooner with the name *Eveline* on her prow. When Cinqué saw that the *Eveline* meant to come alongside, he sent Ruiz and Montes below and brought Burnah and Antonio to stand beside him. He stationed twenty of the African men on deck, armed with sugar cane knives, which they knew how to wield, and muskets, the use of which they were beginning to learn. When the *Eveline* was near enough, Burnah cried out "Water!" as clearly as he could.

A boat put out from the *Eveline* rowed by two white men and with a third standing erect and alert. They came alongside and Cinqué lowered a rope ladder. Hesitantly one man climbed aboard, doubtfully facing the fierce blacks staring at him.

"Captain Sears," he said. "From New Bedford. Philadelphia is my destination, by way of Wilmington."

This man did not look like a Spaniard, and he spoke English in a voice that heartened the Africans.

"Americano," Antonio whispered to Cinqué.

The word relieved tension among the Africans.

"Where is your captain?" Captain Sears asked.

His question took a long time to filter through the minds of Burnah and Antonio to Cinqué and return.

"Below," Burnah answered. "Sick," he added then, but nothing more. He needed Antonio's help.

"White man," Antonio added. "Too sick to talk."

Captain Sears showed his distrust of the blacks. Quickly he strode toward the main hatchway, but he found his way blocked by half a dozen blacks with muskets and sugar cane knives.

"Water," Burnah said again, and Cinqué held up a doubloon. "Plenty gold," Burnah added.

Captain Sears had his men haul up a demijohn of water, for which Cinqué gave him a doubloon and two pistareens. Captain Sears made them understand that he could tow them to where plenty of water could be found. "Can this white man be trusted?" they asked each other. He was American and spoke English, and their need was desperate. With some misgivings they agreed he could tow them.

Captain Sears went aboard the *Eveline* again and his men made her fast to the *Amistad*.

While they were in tow, Burnah and Kimbo took the *Amistad*'s boat and went alongside the *Eveline*, with five of the others to row them. Burnah and Kimbo went on board the *Eveline*, where they were surrounded by curious white sailors.

"What do you want?" Captain Sears asked.

"Food—for Captain," Burnah answered.

Captain Sears told them supper was being prepared and as soon as it was ready he would send some to their Captain. He would also send some for the four children he had seen on deck. Then he gave them apples, one for each of the children.

"Have you ship's papers?" Captain Sears asked.

They did not understand "papers," but they shook their heads in assent and returned to the *Amistad*. Cinqué met them for their report. All seemed well. The Captain of the *Eveline* seemed friendly. From him they might get enough food for their journey.

Unable himself to manage the schooner while in tow, Cinqué brought Montes to the helm. The appearance of a white man created a stir on board the *Eveline*. Captain Sears hailed him. "In the name of God, save us," Montes replied in Spanish, not having understood the words of the Captain. Back and forth the white men shouted questions. Cinqué began to get suspicious. What could these two white men have to say to each other? He sent Montes below and took the wheel again.

After dark a slight breeze blew up, enough for the *Amistad* to make good headway under her own sails. Quickly the blacks made another decision. They would get food and water from the *Eveline* and go on their way. They hoisted their boat. Then they hoisted their jib. Captain Sears hailed them again.

"You must not make sail," he shouted, "or I can't tow you."

They did not understand him and did not haul down the jib. Captain Sears demanded an explanation. All the answer he got was "Water!" and "Sails!" in the voice of Burnah.

The blacks crowded the side nearest the *Eveline* brandishing their knives and muskets. Shouting for his men to prepare for battle, Captain Sears cut the line. The two schooners drifted apart in the darkness, the *Eveline*'s lanterns dim across the water.

Cinqué tried to understand Captain Sears' action. They had meant no harm—only to buy food and water. But the *Eveline* was moving away from them. The Africans ran up an old mainsail and the two schooners drifted out of sight of each other.

When daylight came Cinqué saw the *Eveline* hovering about a mile to leeward. He ordered his men to get out their knives and muskets. They could expect harm from this strange vessel. The *Eveline* approached within hailing distance and Captain Sears hailed them again.

"Who is your captain? What is your destination?" he demanded.

Their reply was a blast from five muskets held in unsteady hands.

Captain Sears tacked, and they fired again. He tacked again and hailed them, telling them to lower their boat and come alongside for water. They answered with their muskets. Then Cinqué, fearing the strength of the *Eveline*, ordered the foresail hoisted and the *Amistad* stood north by east. Minus a water cask and part of a cable, Captain Sears continued on his way to Wilmington, to report to the *Columbian Sentinel* his encounter with this mysterious long low black schooner.

All that day Cinqué and Montes partly drifted, partly steered in the waters off Long Island. Late in the afternoon, some twenty-five miles off Fire Island, they fell in with the pilot boat *Blossom*. When they sighted her, Cinqué ordered his men to make ready for a fight. He and twenty-four of his companions took their places on deck with their weapons. Some of them wrapped themselves in blankets. Cinqué put on a white coat, tied a belt full of doubloons around his waist, and carried in his hand Captain Ferrer's gold watch. When the blacks saw it they shouted approval. It would be a fetish against the Captain's spirit.

When the *Blossom* was within hailing distance, Burnah and Antonio asked for bread and water. The master of the *Blossom* brought his vessel near and cast a line. He pointed to the *Amistad*'s ragged canvas.

"I will tow you to safety," he told them.

The Africans, not understanding him, gave a primitive battle cry and brandished their knives. Kin-na and Fuleh began trying to climb the line to the *Blossom*. The master ordered them to remain where they were, and then cut the line.

"Bread! Water!" Antonio and Burnah shouted.

The master of the *Blossom* heard them and came near again. The Africans watched as white sailors lowered a boat and put a bag of bread and a keg of water in it. Then five sailors rowed to the *Amistad*. Cinqué accepted the bread and water and gave the sailor in charge two doubloons.

The sailor came aboard and tried to talk to Antonio and Burnah, but was unable to understand their broken English. He asked to go below, but Cinqué kept him above with the threat of his rapier.

"Who is your captain?" he asked.

"White man . . . sick . . . below," Burnah answered. Those words had served before.

"What is your destination?"

Trying to get his meaning, the Africans surrounded him and pressed close. Suddenly the sailor burst through the ring and darted to the rail. He sprang to his boat shouting "Pirates! Mutineers! . . . The Havana slave ship. . . ."

The white sailors scrambled aboard the *Blossom*, glad to escape the cannibals. Another pilot boat, the *Lafayette,* approached the *Blossom* and stood by. "Pirates! Mutineers! Cannibals!" The words passed quickly from one white crew to the other. Cinqué, fearing the two vessels would try to capture him, commanded his men to fire their muskets.

There was no returning fire, and the pilot boats withdrew, every available canvas open to the breeze.

Cinqué took the helm and stood east; at sunset, when the sails of the pilot boats were specks on the horizon, he was still standing east. As he gazed across the darkening water, Africa seemed farther and farther away: The two Spaniards were against him, the Africans were ready to give up their dream of home for rest on strange shores, unfriendly ships lurked near.

But he held the schooner pointing east as long as he could hold the wheel. When Montes took over again that night, in desperation greater than fear of death he set the course north by west. A second day Cinqué steered east; a second night Montes steered north by west, aiming for the tip of Long Island. A sense of helplessness seemed to settle over the schooner. The Africans, despairing of setting foot on land, became openly rebellious. Ruiz and Montes, with the help of Antonio, spurred their revolt against Cinqué.

On August 23 they sighted another pilot boat, the *Gratitude*. Cinqué tried to sail away from her, but he could not get enough sail—the work of his men being slow and unsteady. The *Gratitude* came within hailing distance and the Africans danced excitedly on deck. Ruiz and Montes, braving Cinqué's wrath, ran from below and stood among the blacks.

"Captain Seaman of New York," the master of the *Gratitude* shouted. "I will bring your schooner in safely."

Cinqué looked at the Spaniards, then at the Africans. He could see how near his friends were to mutiny. His command could not hold much longer. If he let the *Amistad* be towed, let them talk to other white men, his grip might break altogether.

Then he caught Konoma secretly signalling to the crew of the *Gratitude*—Konoma playing him false and begging rescue by these white men. The time to fight had come again. He ordered his musketmen to fire on the *Gratitude*. They faltered, then obeyed. A few ragged shots raked the *Gratitude*—enough to frighten Captain Seaman into quick withdrawal.

86

Then Cinqué ordered his men to make as much sail as possible.

With Sessi at the wheel and the *Amistad* limping farther away from the *Gratitude,* Cinqué called a palaver on deck. With all the Africans to witness, he took a cat-o'-nine-tails and lashed Konoma across his shoulders till the blood ran. All eyes were fixed on Cinqué, but the sympathy was greatly with Konoma. Who among them would not beg rescue from this hellish voyage? this devil in the shape of their tribesman?

All that night Montes tried to bring the *Amistad* to the coast of Long Island, but Cinqué stood guard over him, with Kimbo and Grabo anxiously near. When daybreak came they were past but well within sight of Montauk Point—close enough in shore to see two houses gray against the morning sky.

Cinqué jerked Montes away from the wheel and slapped his face.

"White man lie," he said, using the English he had learned. Then he spoke in Mendi—spoke of how Montes had played him false all through the voyage. He had steered off course and brought the schooner to strange shores. In the same time they could have reached Sierra Leone. Except for this white man with whiskers he would be in Mani. "Kill the white man," the Wuja prompted in his brain. He slapped Montes again and had him dragged below.

Then, while the schooner tacked back and forth near the tip of Long Island, Cinqué held another palaver to map plans for their voyage. They would land, take on food and water from whatever source came to hand, and the next morning sail for Africa.

Though it was broad daylight, Cinqué did not trust himself to bring the *Amistad* to anchor. Again he had Montes brought on deck. Briefly he explained their plans.

With all the Africans on deck, and Ruiz beside him, Montes began bringing the schooner into Block Island Sound, explaining to Cinqué that there they would find safe anchorage out of sight of houses. He did not mention that

87

they would be in the course of vessels entering and leaving Sag Harbor.

Late in the afternoon they were sailing slowly past Montauk Point, the Africans happy with the prospect of safe landing. Suddenly a strong breeze blew from the ocean, hurrying the schooner along toward the dark green mass of Gardiner's Island. Montes asked for more sail, to bring the schooner to anchor before nightfall. The blacks gave him all the sail they had, and the schooner sped over the breaking whitecaps. Montes worked in close ashore. Then, with a quick signal to Ruiz, he turned the schooner sharp about, so quickly that she shook in every part and snapped the blacks sprawling on deck. But Cinqué was too alert for him. He jumped to the helm, shoved Montes aside, and brought the schooner about in time to save her from the white sandbar.

While he was wrestling with the schooner, Fuleh and Kimbo caught Montes and threw him to the deck. Then they stood over him with cutlasses raised, ready to sever his head from his body. But Cinqué ordered them to lower their weapons. He had other plans for dealing justice to his enemy —after he had been sentenced in a palaver after the custom of Mendis.

Again Cinqué brought the schooner about and anchored her off Culloden Point, where the waters of Fort Pond Bay offered some protection. He sent Montes and Ruiz to confinement below deck and had them bound with chains and shackles. Then he held a council, himself taking the place of headman in the manner he had learned in *Poro*. On one thing they were all agreed. Montes must die. He had tried to murder them all. Death was the penalty for murder in Mendi law. He might have taken them to Africa, but he did not. Now they could trust him no longer. Now they would have to depend on Cinqué and Sessi for the long journey to Sierra Leone.

From their talk a plan developed. On the following day they would put Montes to death. Then they would take on whatever provisions they could and sail for Africa. Ruiz they would take with them to use as a pawn in Sierra Leone. In all things they agreed, Montes' duplicity having restored Cinqué to leadership.

The following morning a boatload of blacks went ashore and brought back water and potatoes. They had tried to trade for pigs and chickens, but the whites, seeing them wandering naked on the roads, closed their doors against them.

At noon they made a feast of potatoes boiled in fresh water. Then they lay down and rested. After their rest, they brought Montes on deck again. He had been in the hold without food or water. He was a dried and broken old man as they led him on deck and placed him on his knees facing seaward. Then they made more palaver over him, delighting in every new kind of fear they could etch on his face. They made it known to him that he was to die; then they passed cutlasses before his throat, signifying how. But the time had not yet come. They must hold the dance of death, which by tribal custom came at sunset.

As darkness spread across the Sound from the Connecticut hills, the dance of death began. Montes was in the middle of the deck. At a distance and to one side sat Ruiz, watching the horrible performance, helpless to aid the old man. At a distance on the other side were the three girls, not taking part but watching, watching with eyes grown old in misery, lighted by neither hatred nor compassion.

There were no drums on the *Amistad,* so the drummers beat on pans or drummed the deck with their hands, beating a slow hollow rhythm that gradually began to seep into the consciousness of the others. As befitted so solemn an occasion, the Africans had dressed themselves in whatever gaudy material they could find aboard. Some of them were simply wrapped in yards of bright-colored calico. Two had found richly embroidered Spanish shawls. These they tied around for loincloths, leaving the fringe to trail on deck behind them. Others had pantaloons of various colors, pulled from the Spaniards' *bultos de efectos.* Cinqué, master and leader of the orgy, had nothing on below, but above he had on his

89

white coat and planter's white broadbrimmed hat. Like the others, his every movement jingled with the belt and bracelets of Spanish doubloons.

As the rhythm increased, Ka-le, the boy, danced once around, followed by Konoma, his cannibal's face hideous above his finery. Then the others began to circle with shuffling steps around the condemned man. Their voices found the key of a Mendi death song and they began wailing it out as they danced around with sugar cane knives uplifted over the head of their victim. At times they danced near enough to jabber individual threats at the old man, who by now kept crossing himself and muttering his "Hail Marys." At times the circle widened enough for a man to dance like a demon beside him. They slapped his face, swished their knives at his throat, rapped their muskets on the deck beside him.

All the time he sank lower and lower to the deck until he was no more than a heap of yielding flesh—imploring for death or any release from the howling devils around him. On and on they danced until all was dark on Connecticut and Long Island.

Then when the time for death came, Dama raised a question: "If we kill him here, will not his spirit come back to rule us? What have we for fetish against the spirit of a white man?"

Cinqué admitted the question. Had not his own father in Mani been plagued with the spirits of dead men? What would they do?

They would keep him until they were on the broad Atlantic, until they were safe from shoals and treacherous currents. Then they would chop him into small pieces and drop him overboard to the sharks. "Spirits do not return from sharks' bellies," they reassured each other.

The dancers exhausted, Fuleh and Kimbo took Montes below and chained him to a turnbolt.

VI

THE SUN AGAINST US

Morning again, with white mist rising, lifting from the sandy beaches of Culloden Point and the green fields of Long Island, revealing the *Amistad* like a black derelict from some unknown ocean, revealing three houses gray and aged against a blue sky. Cinqué watched the sunrise from his post on deck, pleased with the sight of smoke rising from chimneys, pleased with the land he looked on—a fertile land with cattle grazing on green hills and patches of potatoes and corn ready for harvest. He tied a belt filled with doubloons around his waist. With gold he could fill the holds and casks of the schooner.

He sent Kimbo and Grabo to rouse the other Africans, who were still sleeping away the orgy of the night before. Then he put on a planter's white broadbrimmed hat and a pair of white pantaloons.

Ready for his foraging trip ashore, Cinqué put Ruiz and Montes below, unshackled but with a guard set over them.

Then, taking six of his men and Antonio, who knew the ways of white men, he climbed into the long boat. When they were ready to go, Ka-le begged and cried to go with them. Cinqué refused at first, but relented when Burnah suggested that the boy would be a good messenger if the groups became divided.

No stranger group ever appeared to frighten the residents of Long Island. Four of the men and Ka-le were stark naked.

Con, taken because he was a strong carrier, trained on long treks in Africa, wore a finely embroidered cambric shirt, and nothing else.

Cinqué landed and sent the boat back for another load of men and empty casks, after he had arranged a place of meeting in the protection of some bayberry bushes. They found beach plums ripe, tasted them, threw them away because of their sharp sourness. They pulled ears of corn from stalks beside the path and whitened their faces with milk from the soft kernels as they walked along.

Cinqué sent Kimbo and Con toward a house on the east coast of Long Island, with a warning to flee to the boat if they were attacked by white men. Walking through fields better kept than those in Mani, or any he had seen in Africa, he and the others went to a house on the north shore. Antonio and Burnah were with him, both wrapped in blankets. Grabo was stark naked.

As they approached the house, a dog ran toward them barking. Cinqué, remembering all the times he had wished for a dog in Africa, called to it and stretched a friendly hand toward its white fangs. Burnah, seeing how fat the dog was, said, "We will buy him and eat him."

A white man came from the house and quieted the dog, a tall white man not at all like the Spaniards. He came toward the Africans where they were standing hesitantly on the road.

"Good morning," he said in a friendly voice.

The Africans stared at him without seeming to comprehend his words.

"My name is Fithing. This is my house."

Still they seemed not to understand. Burnah tried some English words on him, but Fithing shook his head.

Cinqué pointed to the dog; then he took a Spanish doubloon from his belt and held it up. Fithing took the doubloon.

"Good," Burnah said, smiling.

Fithing understood him, but kept regarding them suspiciously.

92

"Have you rum?" Burnah asked, enunciating each word slowly, exaggeratedly.

Fithing shook his head that he had none. "Where are you from?" he asked.

"Sierra Leone," Burnah told him. "We go back."

Burnah pointed to the schooner, riding at anchor, with jib and mainsail about half set and her fore topsail set complete.

"Where is your captain?"

Burnah pointed to the *Amistad* again. "Him sick."

"Is he white?"

"Black," Burnah replied. Then he quickly translated into Mendi for Cinqué, who, distrusting white men who asked questions, turned toward the beach.

The dog refusing to following his new master, Fithing brought a rope and tied it around his neck. Cinqué took the rope and, with the others following behind the dog, started toward their meeting place in the bayberry bushes. Their steps were hastened by an approaching wagon with two white men on the springseat, coming from the direction of Sag Harbor.

"Too many white men," Cinqué told his companions. "We will not wait."

When they were at the beach again, they found six of their fellows. They had brought water casks ashore and were filling them at a stream. They had also built a driftwood fire at the foot of the bluff and were boiling potatoes in an iron kettle.

Kimbo and Con returned from the other side of the island. Kimbo was also leading a dog, for which he had given a doubloon. Proudly he pointed to it and said it would make a good feast when they were on their way home. He had a pint of gin, for which he had given another doubloon, and a loaf of bread he had begged for his "sick captain." All of them were full of discovery, talking excitedly of the wonders of this strange country.

"What country is this?" they asked each other.

Before their food was cooked, they saw the white men driving their wagon toward the beach. The two men were still

93

on the springseat. Fithing stood behind them, balancing himself as the wagon shook over the bumpy road. All the men carried muskets. When the Africans saw guns pointed toward them they scattered to hide in beach plum and bayberry thickets.

"Stop," the white men shouted. "We will talk to you."

Leaving their guns on the springseat, the three men got out of the wagon and came to the campfire. Speaking slowly so that Antonio and Burnah could understand them, the two men from the springseat explained that they were Captain Henry Green and Captain Peletiah Fordham, from Sag Harbor, out for a hunt in the sparsely settled reaches of Montauk Point. Some of the Africans stood to face them; the others squatted on the sand at the edge of the bushes.

"What country is this?" Burnah asked.

"America," Captain Green answered.

"Is it slave country?"

"It is free here," Captain Green said, "and safe."

"Is it under the Spaniards?"

"It is not under the Spaniards, and there is no Spanish law here."

When this had all been made known to Cinqué, he gave a low whistle and all the Africans sprang to their feet and shouted. The white men became frightened and ran to get their guns, but Burnah told them the blacks meant no harm. They were only happy to be in a free country. Cinqué, Kimbo, Grabo then ran to the white men, shook their hands, gave them gifts including colored silk kerchiefs. Cinqué took off his white hat and set it on Captain Green's head.

Their jubilation was broken by Grabo, who had sighted a sail low on the horizon, on the Atlantic side and standing east.

"Where come from?" Burnah asked.

"From New York," Fithing told him.

"War brig," Captain Green added. Then, sure that this was the mysterious long low black schooner he had read about in the Sag Harbor *Corrector* and these the blacks who had mur-

94

dered captain and crew, he told them that there were two American men-o'-war searching for them to put them in chains. He named the *Gallatin* and the *Fulton* and tried to tell them about the steamboat. They could not understand what he said about the *Fulton,* but they could understand their danger from warships. Burnah spoke his fears rapidly to Cinqué. Then he pointed to the east.

"Make sail and go," he said.

Cinqué, unreasoningly trusting these first white men who were friendly to them, asked Captain Green to go on board the *Amistad* with them and sail them to Sierra Leone. Excitedly he prompted Burnah and Antonio to convey his words and the promise of great rewards when they reached Africa.

"Money," Burnah said. "Much money on *Amistad.*"

Captain Green heard his words and looked quickly at Captain Fordham. They stepped aside and talked hurriedly in whispers. They would capture the blacks and take all their doubloons. Then they would sail the schooner to Sag Harbor and turn the Africans over to the customs officials. The vessel and cargo would be theirs for salvage—a rich prize for a retired sea captain.

Captain Green made a quick speech, promising to return them safely to Africa. The Africans cheered.

"Bring money here," he said, pointing to the spot where he stood. "Much money."

Cinqué sent Grabo and three others in the boat to fetch the money from Captain Ferrer's cabin. While they waited, Captain Green told them more about the American vessels searching for them. Cinqué, remembering the ships they had seen in the past few days, agreed that what he said might be true.

"I will save you," Captain Green assured them.

Then he tried to persuade them to let him board the *Amistad* and bring her to Sag Harbor. There they could get food and water for their journey. Cinqué held a quick palaver with the Africans. Then he told Captain Green the *Amistad* had to remain where she was that night; next morning he could take her to Sag Harbor. That would give Cinqué time to hide the two Spaniards.

Grabo and the others returned with two trunks in which Captain Ferrer had kept his treasures.

"Four hundred and more," Burnah told Captain Green, holding up four fingers. "Four hundred doubloons . . . much more on ship."

Seeing Captain Green's disbelief, Burnah and Grabo took hold of a trunk and shook it. The white men smiled greedily at the clink of gold against gold. Captain Fordham took hold of one end of the other trunk and motioned Cinqué to take the other. They shook it and heard the same satisfying music of clinking gold.

"We will take the two trunks," Captain Green said. "For them I will sail you to Africa."

While his promise was being translated to Cinqué, Kimbo spied a brig off Gardner's Point and gave an alarm. The Africans became wildly excited and began running back and forth on the beach, shouting to their friends on the *Amistad*. They were in great danger. . . . They must fight together.

As they watched, the brig passed the *Amistad*, tacked, and lowered her boat. Convinced that this was the war brig Captain Green had spoken of, Cinqué implored him to go on board the *Amistad* at once and bring her to Sag Harbor. The time had come when one white man could save them from other white men.

"It's the *Washington*," Green and Fordham agreed. The surveying brig *Washington*. A Navy vessel well known in Long Island Sound.

When he saw the boatload of white men head toward the *Amistad*, Cinqué sprang into their boat and called six of his men to join him. Leaving the other Africans on the beach with the white men, Cinqué shoved the boat from the beach.

Though the *Amistad* was no more than thirty rods from shore, he could soon see that the other boat would reach her first, that strange white men would be climbing aboard, and him powerless to prevent them. He could see the Africans dancing about the deck with muskets and sugar cane knives, ready to fight.

"Kill the white men!" Savagely Cinqué bellowed the command across the narrow strip of intervening water.

He was still bellowing it when the boat from the *Washington* came alongside the *Amistad* and six men armed with pistols sprang aboard, leaving only one behind in their boat.

"Lieutenant Meade of the *Washington*," their leader shouted in English. They stared at him uncomprehendingly. Then in Spanish he called for their captain and demanded their colors.

Still not understanding, urged on by Cinqué's shouting, the Africans rushed toward him with sugar cane knives uplifted. Meade led the attack against them, using his pistol as a club. His men, midshipmen on a summer cruise for training and adventure, clubbed the blacks who tried to resist them. The Africans, led by the fierce-looking Konoma, held their ground for a moment, but they were no match for men armed with pistols. Without Cinqué to lead them, they dropped their knives and fell to the deck, begging mercy from their new captors.

Then Ruiz, who had been below during the boarding, ran on deck. Seeing a white man in uniform, he ran up to him and shouted in English:

"These Negroes are my slaves; they have risen and taken the vessel. . . ." He pointed to Cinqué in the boat still some distance away. "That is the leader. I claim protection from these pirates and murderers."

Meade saw the blacks in the boat and those on shore.

"Porter," he ordered his second in command, "take the boat and arrest them."

Then he ran up the ragged Spanish flag as a signal for Lieutenant Gedney, commander of the *Washington,* to come on board.

Lieutenant Meade went below with Ruiz, and found Montes crouching behind barrels, fearing for his life. When Montes saw the American he rushed to him crying, threw his

97

arms around his neck, and embraced him so hard that Meade thought his intention was to do harm. He thought this wild old man must be on the side of the mutineers. Meade brought his pistol to the crazed man's face and threatened to shoot unless he relaxed his hold. Montes loosened his grip, but he still kept laughing and crying in delight and thankfulness.

"*Ave Maria,*" he prayed over the hands of his rescuer, "you are our preserver."

Then they went on deck to witness the capture of the other Africans.

Seeing the *Washington*'s boat pulling toward them, Cinqué and his men headed for shore. Surely Captain Green and his friends would protect them and help them retake the schooner. They had the trunks of doubloons; there were more on board. . . .

Porter fired his pistol at them, letting his bullets whistle low over their heads. Too frightened to row, the Africans cowered in the boat and let it drift. Porter came alongside and ordered Cinqué into his boat. When Cinqué refused, the white sailors dragged him among them. Then Porter had his men row both boats toward shore.

When Cinqué reached the beach he ran to Captain Green and begged him for protection, falling on his knees before him and clinging to his hands. The other Africans, wailing and crying, fell to their knees around him. Porter shouted above their mumbled pleadings.

"These blacks are prisoners of the United States Navy."

He ordered his men to secure them and the two trunks.

"I claim those trunks for salvage," Captain Green told him. "I rescued them—"

"Make your claims to the United States Navy," Porter answered curtly.

Then he and his men put the trunks in the boats and herded all the Africans in with them. Without ceremony he left Green and Fordham standing on the beach.

On their way to the schooner, Cinqué kept looking back at the white men who had been his friends. The dog he had bought stood beside them. Cinqué looked at them longingly. With them had been freedom. He could expect nothing but slavery from a white man like Porter. He could expect far worse from Ruiz and Montes, who looked down at him from the rail triumphantly. Slavery was a wall around him, chains on hands and feet. Whatever he did to free himself must be done quickly.

As soon as they were on board the *Amistad,* Cinqué eluded the white men and ran below to Captain Ferrer's cabin, which he had occupied since the mutiny. He had given his broadbrimmed hat to Captain Green. Now he took off his pantaloons and stood bare and shining except for the belt of doubloons around his waist. Naked he might escape, he thought. If he failed, he might provoke the white men enough to bring death for himself and his African brothers.

Gathering as much speed as he could, he ran up the ladder, leapt out the main hatch, and at a bound was over the side, in defiance of the shouts of "Halt!" the whites flung at him. He landed in the water and let himself down until he was sure he was hidden from their bullets. Then he began swimming for shore as fast as he could. When he came to the surface some distance from the schooner he heard the whites and blacks shouting, and saw the boat being manned to chase him. He dived again and swam shoreward as long as his breath held—swimming with the strong faith that Captain Green could give him freedom. When he came up again, the boat was cutting him off from shore. He dived again and swam away from the boat until he had to pop his head up for breath, and hear the shouts of white boys on the chase like healthy hunters. Diving for safety, to shut out their voices, he gradually worked his way toward shore. If he could only make the beach. . . .

Forty minutes in the water, forty minutes of bursting lungs and searing head pains—his strength failed and he knew the struggle was hopeless. The white sailors maneuvered their boat too skilfully. Determined that they would not get his Spanish doubloons, he loosened the belt and let it sink to the

99

bottom of the Sound. Then he surfaced again and allowed his white captors to drag him in with a boathook.

When he climbed on board the *Amistad* again Cinqué faced Lieutenant Meade and Lieutenant Gedney, commander of the brig *Washington,* who had come to take charge of the schooner. Behind them were the other captives, with the three little girls standing among them crying bitterly. Near them, lying naked on a hatch, weak from long illness, was Kura, weeping silently. Cinqué smiled at them and made motions with his hands at his throat that he would be hanged.

Using Antonio as an interpreter, Antonio whom the captives hated and who had already ingratiated himself with their new captors, Lieutenant Gedney told Cinqué to get back in the boat. He would be taken to the *Washington* as a prisoner—to solitary confinement from which he could not stir a fresh mutiny. From his speech Cinqué knew Lieutenant Gedney was entirely in sympathy with Ruiz and Montes, knew that he pitied the Spaniards for their suffering at the hands of black men. The whites had grouped together, and there was no sympathy among them for black Africans. He stepped back into the boat and Naval apprentices rowed him to the *Washington* and set up a guard over him.

For the first time since he was captured by Birmaja's men in Mani, Cinqué was completely without hope. Always before there had seemed some way of escape. Now, on a war vessel among strange white men, he was waiting for the noose that would end his life—in payment for the lives of Captain Ferrer and the mulatto Celestino. He still felt no guilt. In *Poro* he had learned no law that would hold him guilty. Beyond *Poro* there must be justification for killing men who took his freedom. He only felt a great sorrow that he would never again see Africa, or his wife and children. In Africa he walked free; in this strange land of America he sat imprisoned on a warship, subject to the whims of his captors.

When Lieutenant Gedney returned to the *Washington* he saw so much uneasiness and anxiety in Cinqué that he decided it was better to return him to the *Amistad* and confine him with the other captives. He was too valuable a piece of property to let die of loneliness and dejection.

When Cinqué went on board the *Amistad* again, the Africans crowded around him, making the most extravagant demonstrations of joy. Some laughed, some screamed, some danced, some wept. Ka-le and Marghru clung to his hands and begged him not to leave them again. Cinqué stood in their midst, but did not even smile. The chance to say farewell to the Africans—to his friends of the Mendi country— had come. Words were taking shape in his mind. When the noise had subsided, he addressed them, speaking slowly as Antonio and Burnah were translating his words for their white captors.

"Friends and Brothers. We would have returned, but the sun was against us. I would not see you serve the white men, so I induced you to help me kill the Captain. I thought I should be killed—I expected it. It would have been better. You had better be killed than live many moons in misery. I shall be hanged, I think, every day. But this does not pain me. I could die happy, if by dying I could save so many of my brothers from the bondage of the white man."

His words stirred the captives to a high pitch. During his absence Kura had died. They pointed to where his body lay on the hatch covering, its rough outlines showing under a black bombazine cloth. "That one is free," they said to Cinqué. Not one among them but would have exchanged places with Kura. They spoke to the dead man as though he were living, begged him to help them escape into death.

"What shall we do?" they asked Cinqué.

He told them to get weapons from the hold and fight again if they could; if they could not, to escape by the rail.

Every way they turned they were stopped by white midshipmen with pistols. Lieutenant Gedney saw that the only way to calm them was to remove Cinqué. This time Cinqué refused to go. Midshipmen took him by force, tearing him from the children. Even this he bore with stoical dignity, though their piercing yells followed him across the water.

101

On board the *Washington* again, the midshipmen put the irons on Cinqué to keep him from leaping overboard. Then they chained him to the deck, where the cries of his African brothers still reached him. A guard sat over him with pistol at ready. Still Cinqué did not give way to the slightest emotion.

Lieutenant Gedney was faced with the question of what to do with the *Amistad* and her mutinous crew. Ruiz and Montes claimed the captives as their slaves and property, and charged them with murder and piracy on the high seas. Gedney sympathized with their claims, but did not feel himself competent to give a final decision on their charges. Nor could he immediately give them possession of the schooner and cargo as they had requested. There was a question of salvage —of the doubloons in the trunks and the cargo and vessel. He and Lieutenant Meade had set their hearts on a share in it. And if the Africans should be declared property. . . . They tried to estimate their reward in terms of what they would bring on the New Orleans market.

These were questions of Admiralty Law, best settled in a United States Court. They had been much in New London, and were acquainted with the courts of the District of Connecticut. Though they were doubtless within the confines of New York and had captured some of the blacks on Long Island, they decided to take their prize to New London, whither they were bound at the end of the day's soundings. They explained their plans to Ruiz and Montes and ordered midshipmen to man the schooner and bring the vessels to harbor before nightfall.

From his place on the *Washington* Cinqué watched white sailors struggle with the *Amistad*'s ragged sails. Then the *Washington* was under way and the two vessels moved toward New London. He was close enough to see white sailors herd the Africans to the slave deck at point of gun. There was nothing he could do now to help his people. He watched the Connecticut shore come close and picked out details of hills and valleys and houses.

It was almost dark when the two vessels were anchored in New London harbor, very near each other and no more than a musket shot from Fort Trumbull.

Cinqué, still manacled, was led to an open space in the hold. There on the bare deck without clothing or blanket he spent the night, chained, brooding, alone.

When morning came Cinqué was still pondering over the misfortune from which no power could save him. He had resigned himself to death. White men would never allow a black to live after he had killed his white master. All he had to do was wait until the noose was put around his neck and pulled tight. The feeling came that he must speak to his countrymen once more. The message he had given must be given again, emphasized, drilled into their minds. They must not accept bondage. They must die first.

How could he get back to them? The answer was gold—that and the white man's greed. He would pretend to have gold.

When Cinqué was brought on deck for food and water, Lieutenant Gedney and the crew of the *Washington* gathered around and stared as if he might have been a dog-faced monkey. Cinqué looked into the staring eyes, the colorless faces.

"Doubloons!" He spoke the word he had heard so often in his long journey.

Lieutenant Gedney heard the word, sent the sailors away lest they hear too much. He asked Cinqué many questions about the doubloons, but Cinqué could not understand his words. Then with signs Cinqué told him that if he could be taken to the *Amistad* he could show him below deck a handkerchief full of doubloons. Gedney had his manacles removed and accompanied him in the *Washington*'s boat.

On the *Amistad* Antonio was the only black on deck. Cinqué hated him for his smiling servility to the white men, for his superiority to *bozales*. Lieutenants Gedney and Meade stepped aside and conferred together. Then they called Ruiz and Montes. After the four had talked, they called Antonio.

103

Cinqué heard but did not understand their instructions to Antonio.

Gedney signalled Cinqué to go below. Antonio followed next to him. Then came the four white men, guarded by sailors with pistols. In his hand Meade carried pencil and paper.

When Cinqué reached the slave deck the Africans broke into demonstrations wilder and more violent than those of the day before. They cried and begged him to take them from the slave deck, to save them from the white men. He patted the children briefly and called Ka-le and Marghru to his side. Then, without making a pretense of searching for doubloons, he addressed the Africans, speaking rapidly, hoping Antonio would not be able to pass on to the whites all he said. "My brothers, I am once more among you, having deceived the enemy of our race by saying that I had doubloons. I came from them to tell you that you have one chance for death and none for liberty. I am sure you prefer death as I do. You can, by killing the white men now on board, and I will help you, make the people here kill you. It is better for you to do this, and then you will not only avert bondage yourselves, but prevent the entailment of unnumbered wrongs on your children. Come— Come with me then—"

All through the speech Antonio interpreted rapidly into Spanish, and Lieutenant Meade took his words down on paper. Ruiz passed the words on to Lieutenant Gedney in English. At this point Antonio made a signal of danger—of mutiny. The Africans were ready for their last desperate uprising. Gedney shouted to the American sailors. They sprang upon Cinqué and dragged him away from his followers.

All through his speech his cheek shone, and his eye often turned to the white sailors. The Africans yelled in savage rage and stared at the whites as fiercely as he did. They leaped about the deck, like creatures under some strange talismanic powers. With their primitive weapons, nail and tooth, they attacked the white men. The sailors beat them back with pistols and dragged Cinqué from the howling demons of the slave deck.

On his way to the *Washington* again, fast bound in chains, he assumed his stoical immobility. He kept his eyes on the *Amistad,* but allowed no emotion to show on his face. The whites, amazed by his courage, touched by his nobility, kept their eyes on him; but there was no established pattern for fathoming his seething feelings. He was unique in their experience—a remarkable blending of savagery and nobility. He might be a cannibal; they were certain he was a prince.

Chained to the deck of the *Washington,* Cinqué sat with his eyes fixed alternately on the *Amistad* and on the Connecticut shore. In the one had been freedom, had he only known how to take it—how to wrest it from the sun and gods against him. In the other lay bondage and death at the hands of white men. His experiences had taught him that America had nothing but the bitterest of fruits for Africans from the Slave Coast.

VII

LAND OF THE FREE. . .

The *Washington* was astir with excitement. Word had come that the United States Judge for the District of Connecticut, with the United States Marshal and newspapermen, waited at the dock to be brought aboard for the trial. The officers and crew of the *Washington* were to be relieved of their black burden. Responsibility for the cannibals would be passed on to someone else. Under Lieutenant Gedney's orders, eager midshipmen lowered the boat and took their place at the oars. Lieutenant Meade went in the boat to escort the party aboard. In their excitement they hardly noticed Cinqué, chained and alone on deck, with a bowl of untouched beans beside him. His eyes followed them into the boat, then returned to contemplating the shore.

Calm and peaceful hills and valleys of Connecticut, houses and farms and factories, coasting vessels between Boston and New York, whalers to the Pacific and return, the unfamiliar sounds of locomotives making themselves familiar as railroads reached toward Boston, New York, Hartford . . . and over all a blue sky and blindingly bright sunlight.

Cinqué thought it a fair land he looked upon, fair almost as Africa itself. He could not see that the blue sky was an illusion—that over America a dark cloud was gathering—that a storm would spread and grow and finally shed its fury on the rooftree of the Nation. He could not know that slavery was an evil sickness in the South, that the mob spirit was endemic in the North.

But Americans read the signs with fear, with dread.

They looked back on the decade that had begun in 1830 and found it bitter with strife. Anti-slavery groups had become firmly, at times violently articulate through public meetings, through the pages of *The Liberator, The Emancipator, The Pennsylvania Freeman*. Abolitionists who before had worked quietly, now fearing the westward expansion, the extension of slave territory, organized the New England Anti-Slavery Society, the American Anti-Slavery Society to pool their resources, to coordinate their fight. Pro-slavery leaders, in power still, applied political pressure nationally, resorted to mob tactics locally.

During the decade four cases had been submitted to mob rule, with decisions that rocked the nation. Four names—Faneuil Hall, Elijah P. Lovejoy, Pennsylvania Hall, Prudence Crandall—became national symbols in the fight in which friends and brothers killed each other over freedom of assembly, of speech, of the press, of education. In none of these was the decision arrived at through due process of law.

Cinqué and the *Amistad* Africans were destined to be a fifth case within the decade—a fifth national symbol. But they became a symbol of human justice achieved through legal procedure. Their case went from the lowest court to the highest—with a final decision that struck a blow for freedom around the world.

All who were touched by the *Amistad* case, prosecution and defense alike, found themselves entangled in the prejudices and hatreds of the times, found every act, every judgment shaded by what had gone before.

Faneuil Hall

A flash lit up Faneuil Hall, Cradle of Liberty, symbol of freedom in Boston, symbol of human liberty bought at the price of blood. . . .

A young man with pale face and fiery eyes looked at the building. Faneuil Hall! What better place in the nation for the Anti-Slavery people to meet? What walls better to echo the oratory of George Thompson calling on American foes of slavery to join their English and Scotch friends in the fight? What platform better for William Lloyd Garrison to thunder aloud the rebukes of the South he wrote in *The Liberator?* Where better could he denounce the mob that broke into the Charleston post office and burnt anti-slavery papers before thousands of cheering citizens. . . .

The young man with pale face and fiery eyes was William Lloyd Garrison. Undaunted by hatred, by threats against him, he presented a plea to Mayor Theodore Lyman, Jr., asking that the hall be opened to an assembly of the New England Anti-Slavery Society.

Mayor Lyman denied the request. "Incendiary," he said of the proposed meeting. "Put down Garrison and his friends," shouted slavery sympathizers in Boston. The editor of the *Gazette* proposed throwing the mischievous Garrison and his followers overboard like the tea spilt in Boston Harbor during the Revolution. "A cold bath would do them good."

"The cause of bleeding slaves shall yet be pleaded in Faneuil Hall," Garrison prophesied. But the Hall was denied him, and then church after church closed its doors against the Abolitionists.

Garrison was stunned by a petition in the *Daily Advertiser* signed by fifteen hundred names, a list filling one and a half solid columns of fine print, calling for an anti-Abolitionist mass meeting at Faneuil Hall in the afternoon of August 21, 1835. Among the names were those of the highest social, political, religious, intellectual position in Boston—all moved with the same desire to show Southron slaveholders their eagerness to put down the rabble Abolitionists among them. Present also were many Southrons, who had journeyed to Boston by stage or boat to help their Yankee friends in their fight against insurrection. Among these, not a few kept their eyes open for slaves who had escaped from their plantations and made their way North by the Underground Railroad. . . .

This was a great meeting for the slavery forces, a meeting

called to put law on the side of slavery, to write new laws which would put Abolitionists forever in the wrong. It was not by chance they had chosen Faneuil Hall as a place of assembly—not by chance that Mayor Lyman of Boston presided at the meeting and gave the keys of the city to pro-Slavery speakers who accused the Abolitionists of attempting to scatter among our Southron brethren firebrands, arrows, and death. . . .

Oratory, oratory, oratory, words piled on words—all directed at keeping the Abolitionists silent under law, at keeping slaves in chains, at keeping the clock of human freedom turned backward. Tempers raged, brickbats flew, the violent rabble kept kettles of tar and bags of feathers ready in case an Abolitionist should raise his voice.

"Thompson!" "Garrison!" "Get us Thompson and Garrison!" the rabble cried on street and Common.

The meeting broke up, but the crowds did not disperse. They waited for an Abolitionist meeting that had been announced. Mayor Lyman urged the Abolitionists not to hold their meeting while the public mind was so heated, refused to promise police protection in case of an outbreak. Still the mobs cried for Thompson and Garrison. But their victims were beyond their cries: Thompson, the alien Scotchman, was traveling the length and breadth of New England speaking his doctrine in churches and at crossroads, suffering indignities from a mob at Concord. Garrison was in Brooklyn, speaking and writing against mob violence in Boston. . . .

A meeting of the Boston Female Anti-Slavery Society had been announced for three in the afternoon on October 21 at the Anti-Slavery Society Building, No. 46 Washington Street. Garrison arrived at the *Liberator* office at No. 48 Washington Street shortly after noon and was met by Charles Burleigh.

"Have you seen this?" Burleigh asked.

He handed Garrison a placard.

THOMPSON
THE ABOLITIONIST ! ! !

That infamous foreign scoundrel Thompson, will hold forth this afternoon, at the *Liberator* Office, No. 48 Washington Street. The present is a fair opportunity for the friends of the Union to snake Thompson out! It will be a contest between the Abolitionists and the friends of the Union. A purse of $100 has been raised by a number of patriotic citizens to reward the individual who shall first lay violent hands on Thompson, so that he may be brought to the tar-kettle before dark. Friends of the Union, be vigilant.

"Cowards," Garrison said. Then he turned to his desk to write an editorial.

Burleigh hovered over the desk. "They say they have indelible ink and are going to make Thompson's face forever black."

Garrison continued writing.

"Are you going to the meeting?" Burleigh asked.

"God willing."

At twenty to three Garrison laid aside his quill and with Burleigh clutching his elbow went down the steps from the *Liberator* office and toward the entrance under the ANTI-SLAVERY ROOMS sign. There were already more than a hundred men crowded around the entrance and more arriving at a run. He worked his way up two flights of stairs through crowds of young ruffians. Others had already pushed their way into the assembly hall. There Garrison found about twenty women in prayer. Most of them were white and from respected Boston families; a few were colored or mulattoes. Among them Garrison recognized Mrs. Maria Chapman and Miss Elizabeth Whittier, sister of his friend the poet.

"That's Garrison," the ruffians shouted to each other as he took his seat.

Garrison went to them and tried to persuade them to leave. He tried common courtesy, he tried ridicule. They did not budge. More pushed their way inside the room. Their taunts became brazen, obscene.

Outside, the mob, disappointed at not getting Thompson, took up the cry of "Garrison! We'll tar and feather Garrison!"

The President of the Society led the group in prayer, but the mob drowned out her words. Garrison rose and went to her.

"I do not want to endanger you ladies by making a speech today," he said. "With your permission I will go—"

The President grasped his hand.

"God go with you," she said fervently.

Burleigh led the way through a door in the board partition to the *Liberator* office. There Garrison sat down and began to write an account of the mob.

But he was not to be left in peace. News of his escape had filtered down to the mob in the street. Men now gathered at the door and began beating and kicking at the flimsy panels. The lower panels gave way and the leaders stooped down to peer inside the office.

"There he is! That's Garrison! Out with the scoundrel!" they cried.

With a calmness born of conviction, Garrison turned to Burleigh and said, "You may as well open the door, and let them come in and do their worst."

But Burleigh, calmed by danger, went out, locked the door, put the key in his pocket, and faced the mob. Men who a moment before had demanded the body of Garrison stood irresolutely facing this cool, self-contained man.

Their attention was distracted by the arrival of Mayor Lyman, who went immediately to the hall where the women were still in meeting. He persuaded them for their own sake and the safety of others to adjourn their meeting. While the mob stood sullenly aside the women in a close column of twos came down the stairs. Before they could get outside a wave of brutal comments, of groans, hissing, laughter, swept the mob.

With the women out of sight, the men turned to the ANTI-SLAVERY ROOMS sign above the door. Mayor Lyman stood aside and let them pull it down and destroy it. While they were breaking the sign to splinters and grabbing fragments for souvenirs, Mayor Lyman and his deputies went to the *Liberator* office to help Garrison escape.

"We cannot protect you," Mayor Lyman assured him. Then they persuaded him to climb out a back window on Wilson's Lane.

"Garrison is gone," a deputy told the mob. "Return to your work. Return to your homes. . . ."

But watchers for the mob caught sight of Garrison and Burleigh crawling along roof tops. They started clamoring after him. Garrison hid in a carpenter's shop and Burleigh stood planks up around him to conceal him. There was no concealment from the angry mob. They caught him and dragged him out of the shavings. They dragged him to a window with the intention of throwing him to the mob below.

"Don't kill him outright!" one of the leaders shouted.

They coiled a rope around his body to drag him through the streets of Boston. Abolitionists should see, Southrons should see. . . . Then they made him climb down a ladder set against the window for him.

As he clutched at the rungs he looked on the mob, now grown to thousands, and not one among them to save him from death, the tar-kettle, indelible ink. When he reached the ground he fell to his knees and muttered an incoherent prayer. His face was ghastly pale, his body trembling. All will to fight back had gone out of him.

Three strong men from the mob grabbed him and half pushed, half dragged him through State Street.

"They're going to hang him. For God's sake save him," a voice wailed from the crowd.

"He shan't be hurt. . . . He shan't be hurt," his three captors cried.

The mob reiterated, "He shan't be hurt. . . . He is an American." They were not yet ready to murder their own for the cause of slavery.

The mob flowed to the south door of the Old State House —among them a young Massachusetts legislator, John Greenleaf Whittier, whose passion for Abolition had been aroused by this man, whose Quaker heart melted at the sight of Garrison in the hands of the mob.

The three men set Garrison on the steps of the Old State House and disappeared into the crowd—three draymen, enemies of black men, who had saved a man's life to preserve constitutionality.

Again Mayor Lyman intervened.

"Night is drawing on," he told the mob. "I propose to lock this man up for the night on a charge of disorderly conduct."

The mob, not quite committed to violence, stood back until Garrison, surrounded by deputies, was placed in a carriage. Then they surged around the carriage and fought the deputies all the way through Boston to the jail.

In the darkness of a cell, his clothing torn, his spirit lacerated, Garrison waited through the night. He knew the lightning flash had kindled a flame. . . .

Elijah P. Lovejoy

Francis McIntosh leaped to the steamboat landing as soon as the *Flora* touched. He was free from his work in the galley, free after the long journey down river from Pittsburgh, and all St. Louis lay before him.

"Gonna have myself a time," he said to crewmen of the *Flora*.

Before he could leave the dock, he saw two boatmen swinging their fists at each other. Then two policemen came at them with clubs. In Pittsburgh a free mulatto could help white men. McIntosh set upon the policemen with his fists. They turned on him with their clubs and curses. While the two strange white men fled down an alley, the policemen arrested McIntosh for interfering with an officer of the law.

They took him before a Justice of the Peace, who quickly found him guilty, sentenced him to jail, and commanded the two policemen, George Hammond and William Mull, to deliver him to the jailor. On foot the three men started along a street leading from the River.

"What's my fine gonna be?" McIntosh asked.

Five years in the penitentiary . . . five years in a black man's hell. Gonna have myself a time. . . .

He jerked loose from the officers and pulled a long knife from under his shirt. He slashed at Mull and missed. He slashed again and caught Mull in the side. Hammond grabbed him by the shoulder and turned him away from Mull. McIntosh stabbed at Hammond and caught him in the neck, cutting the jugular vein. Hammond took a few steps and fell dead.

McIntosh ran for the River, but Mull was after him and soon had a mob raised with his cries. They caught McIntosh in sight of the *Flora* and took him to jail.

A mob gathered around the body of Hammond, still lying on the bloodsoaked ground. Without speeches, without urging, stirred to violence by the sight of the dead man, the men moved on the jail. All was still; men spoke to each other in a whisper, but it was a whisper which made the blood curdle to hear it, and disclosed the awful purpose with which they approached the sacrifice of their victim. Armed guards, selected from the mob, protected the men who volunteered to break down the doors.

Between eight and nine at night they reached his cell. A shout of triumph rose from the waiting mob. They dragged him to a large locust tree in the rear of the town, not far from the jail. They chained him to the tree with his back against the tree and his face turned south. They piled planks, rails, and twigs around him up to his knees. Then the leader brought shavings and a lighted torch and set the fire.

McIntosh had watched their preparations without a sound. When the fire touched his feet he lifted his head to the crowd and begged, "Shoot me! Shoot me!"

No one in the crowd stirred. He watched the flames light up hard cold faces. No help there.

He began singing

"Oh, my loving brother, when the world's on fire,

Don't you want God's bosom to be your pillow. . . ."

Unable to finish, he stopped and began a prayer. The flames climbed higher and he dropped his head and was silent.

"He must be out of his misery," a man near the fire said.

Again he lifted a head that had lost all semblance of humanity. Though he was covered with flames to the top of his head, he spoke distinctly.

"No, no," he shrieked. "I feel as much as any of you feel. I hear you all. Shoot me! Shoot me!"

No one answered him, and within twenty minutes he was dead. Satisfied with their vengeance, a little shamed by the suffering they had seen, the men began to drift away into the edge of darkness. Their places were taken by a rabble of boys with stones in their hands. Moving close to the circle of fire, they cast their stones at the charred body still chained to the tree.

"I'll be the first to bust his skull," they boasted to each other. . . .

McIntosh dead, and only one person to speak out against mob violence.

Elijah P. Lovejoy, editor of the Abolitionist St. Louis *Observer*, spoke out with a passion that aroused fresh fury. He spoke not in favor of the hardened wretch McIntosh but against the denial of the courts of justice. His editorials forced the case to the grand jury, but the presiding judge dismissed the case as one of practical justice, beyond human law.

Lovejoy received threats of death—death to him and destruction of his *Observer*. St. Louis would no longer tolerate his Abolitionist views. Seeing the strength of anger against him, he decided to move his press to Alton, Illinois.

Before he could act, a mob entered the *Observer* office and tossed the furniture and part of the press into the Mississippi

River. Lovejoy gathered what was left of the press and shipped it to Alton. The crates were discharged on the River bank at Alton before daylight on Sunday morning. A mob gathered and rolled the crates into the Mississippi. In Alton they also knew of the editorials on the burning of McIntosh.

Abolitionist friends bought another press and set it up in Alton. Lovejoy began a new series of editorials on the evils of slavery and mob rule.

Lovejoy's wife became desperately ill. Still he wrote his editorials. One night at eleven o'clock he started on foot for the drugstore in Alton for medicine she needed. The distance was half a mile through dark roads. As he reached the main thoroughfare a group of disguised men sprang from the bushes. They struck Lovejoy with clods and then one armed with a club caught hold of him.

"It's the damned Abolitionist," he yelled. "Give him hell."

The others linked arms and surrounded him. "Rail him! Rail him! Tar and feather him! Set him adrift in a boat in the Mississippi in tar and feathers. He'll find niggers his color down South. . . ."

Lovejoy knew fighting was futile. He could never escape ten men. With calmness and composure he said:

"Gentlemen, I have but a single request to make of you. My wife is dangerously ill, and it is necessary she should have this prescription immediately. I was on my way to town for it. Will one of you take it and see that it is delivered at the house, but without intimating what is about to befall me. I am in the hands of God and ready to go with you."

For a moment the men were silent. Then a doctor in the group, a Southerner, spoke up:

"Boys, I can't lay my hand upon as brave a man as this."

He turned away and the others followed. But they spent their wrath that night destroying the *Observer* press.

Lovejoy bought a fourth press in Cincinnati and had it shipped to Alton, where it was received by the Mayor and stored in a building belonging to one of the most respected firms in the city.

A few of Lovejoy's friends met him at the building to guard the press. His wife, somewhat recovered, had been secretly moved to the home of a friend. Lovejoy himself was obviously nervous, apprehensive.

A scattered mob moved around in the darkness outside. Enoch Long, leader of the defenders, placed his men at strategic points. "Shoot if they attack," he told them.

The mob moved against the building with logs for battering rams.

"Shoot," Long commanded.

A shot rang out and a man fell dead. The mob drew back, hesitated, and then went away to fortify themselves with drinking. All was quiet. The moon rose, shedding a clear light over building and grounds.

Toward midnight the mob returned. Drunkenly they fired at the black window squares. Then a dozen men rushed the building with flaming torches.

"They're firing the building," Long shouted. "Who will volunteer to fight fire?"

Lovejoy stepped forward.

"I will go," he said. "They don't dare harm me."

Two others followed him.

Lovejoy opened the door and stepped into the calm clear moonlight.

"Lovejoy!" the mob snarled.

Then five shots rang out.

Lovejoy ran back inside the building and up the stairs shouting, "I'm shot! I'm shot! I'm dead—"

He fell dead in the arms of a friend.

The roof was on fire and the men inside in danger of being burned alive. Long went to the window.

"Lovejoy is dead," he shouted.

A roar came from the mob below.

"We will surrender."

The mob agreed to let them escape and to save the building. When the friends of Lovejoy came down, leaving his dead body behind, the mob fired hundreds of bullets above their heads to hasten their flight.

Then they stormed into the building to destroy the thing they hated—the PRESS. . . .

Pennsylvania Hall

In the whole of Philadelphia there was not a hall where members of all sects and those of no sect—of all parties and of no party—could speak publicly. Then on May 14, 1838, Pennsylvania Hall was opened and dedicated to the free discussion of liberty, of the equality of civil rights, of the evils of slavery. Built with contributions from laborers, farmers, housewives, presided over by a committee whose sole interest was in human justice, the hall was a temple of hope to the slave, to the persecuted.

During the long months it was abuilding, pro-slavery men whispered that it was to be a meeting place of nigger lovers, male and female . . . of people who in truth practiced miscegenation to color the pure stream of the white race.

For the opening exercises John Greenleaf Whittier, the young sensitive Yankee poet, wrote a dedication ode, into which he poured all the emotion he had stored up as Abolitionist organizer, speaker, editor of the *Pennsylvania Freeman*—wrote it in his new editorial offices in Pennsylvania Hall.

The whisperers had done their work well. Philadelphia was seething with unrest before the doors opened. Abolitionists from New England, from the Middle West, from Philadelphia itself, were hissed and ridiculed in the street. Crowds followed them to Pennsylvania Hall, milled outside, stamped, yelled, threw brickbats. Spies for the mob listened at windows, doors, heard Abolitionists speaking, discussing the Fugitive Slave Law and all the damnable trappings of slavery, reported seeing white women walking arm in arm with Negro men.

"We've got to break it up," they told the mob. But the mob had not yet worked up to a fury.

Two nights later the mob outside the hall was larger, more threatening. "Garrison's speaking tonight," the word went round. When Garrison rose to speak, they hurled rocks through the windows, breaking glass and pelting his hearers. But the meeting went on.

The next morning the mob was larger still, and tense to the breaking point. Something had to be done or Philadelphia streets would run with blood. The Abolitionists demanded protection from Mayor John Swift.

The Mayor replied, "It is public opinion that makes mobs, and ninety-nine out of a hundred of those with whom I converse are against you."

By that afternoon the crowd, swollen to at least fifteen thousand, lashed into fury by inflammatory placards in all the streets, jeered at the Abolitionists in a maddening rush of voices. Word got around that the police had been ordered not to make arrests in connection with the agitation. There would be no punishment for a few lessons to the nigger lovers.

At sunset Mayor Swift came to Pennsylvania Hall and promised to restore order if the meetings were cancelled and the keys handed over to him. With the keys in his hand, he made the speech which set the mob free:

"There will be no meeting here this evening. This house has been given up to me. The managers had a right to hold their meeting; but as good citizens they have, at my request, suspended their meeting for this evening.

"We never call out the military here! . . . I would, fellow citizens, look upon you as my police, and I trust you will keep order.

"I now bid you farewell for the night!"

The crowds cheered, the Abolitionists trembled. Whittier, experienced in taking the temper of crowds, slipped away from his friends and lost himself in the mass. The Mayor made his word good and disappeared for the night. Then the mob, led by a group of Southern medical students, set to their business of destruction.

They battered down doors with battering rams. They ransacked the desk and files of the *Pennsylvania Freeman*. They piled papers and wood high on the speaker's desk, turned on the jets, lit the gas, and let the building burn. When the fire companies arrived, the mob let them save surrounding buildings but not Pennsylvania Hall.

Among the mob ransacking the building was a tall frail young man wearing a gray wig and a long white overcoat— Whittier in disguise stuffing his own valuable manuscripts into his pockets while the mob destroyed Abolitionist books and papers.

When the building was no longer safe, he went out and mingled with the mob, letting their jubilation, their vile words sear into his mind. Then at dawn he sat down to write another flaming editorial:

"Pennsylvania Hall is in ashes! The beautiful temple consecrated to Liberty has been offered a smoking sacrifice to the Demon of Slavery. In the heart of this city a flame has gone up to Heaven. It will be seen from Maine to Georgia. In its red and lurid light, men will see more clearly than ever the black abomination of the fiend at whose instigation it was kindled . . .

"Let the abhorred deed speak for itself. Let all men see by what frail tenure they hold property and life in a land overshadowed by the curse of slavery. . . ."

Prudence Crandall

Canterbury, Connecticut, was a proper New England village, with fifteen hundred citizens, most of them of original Puritan stock, with regular stagecoach service to Hartford and Providence, with a first class Ladies' Academy.

Prudence Crandall, the proprietess of this Academy, had often given Canterburians samples of her good faith and strong conscience. A vigorous woman with rather masculine

120

features and tastes in grooming, she was of good Quaker family. She was an accomplished woman and a well-trained teacher. Her school was in good standing in the community and the particular pride of her nearest neighbors, Dr. Andrew Harris and Attorney Andrew T. Judson.

Then Sarah Harris, a Negro girl from a neighboring community, applied for admission to take teacher training so she could become a teacher of colored children. Prudence Crandall admitted her to full membership in the Academy.

The village was immediately in an uproar. Sarah Harris would have to go. They favored education for ladies of color, if it could be given elsewhere.

Judson and Harris were the first to call on Miss Crandall about the matter. They pointed out what keeping Sarah would mean to the reputation of the school, the community. Decent people would leave Canterbury. Real estate values would go down. Their own pleasant homes would be distasteful to their wives if nigger girls lived at the Academy.

Without flinching Miss Crandall replied, "The school may sink, but I will not give up Sarah Harris."

Then the wife of the Episcopal minister called. "I will not have it said that my daughter went to school with a nigger girl," she threatened.

"Sarah Harris stays," Miss Crandall replied.

The white girls withdrew, leaving Prudence Crandall with her one pupil, and only her sister Almira to help her. She appealed to William Lloyd Garrison for Negro pupils and advertised in the *Liberator* that henceforth her school was for young ladies and little misses of color.

Canterbury neighbors rebelled at the idea of having a nigger school in the middle of their beautiful New England village.

"Do you want the town filled with niggers?" people asked each other.

"No! God forbid!"

A committee of Canterbury citizens—attorney, squire, farmer, temperance reformer, minister—waited on Prudence

Crandall and protested officially. They were led by Andrew T. Judson.

"Africans are naturally as well as actually inferior to whites," he said. "Letting them stay here will lead to inter-marriage and a general leveling of society."

"Moses had a black wife," Prudence Crandall answered. And they found the remainder of the interview as unsatisfactory.

Judson then brought the problem to town meeting. People from Canterbury, Brooklyn, Plainfield, as far away as Providence, crowded into the meeting. Miss Crandall stayed away, but sent two of her Abolitionist friends to speak for her. Her neighbors applauded when Judson, in violent and abusive language, told of the degradation threatened by this Quaker wolf and her misses of color. Under the spell of his oratory, they passed a resolution prohibiting the school. When her friends tried to speak for her, they turned the meeting into an angry, shouting mob.

Prudence Crandall listened to a report of the meeting, and then went to New York, Philadelphia, Boston, Providence seeking pupils. One day Canterburians watched her lead twenty little misses of color through the village. They crowded outside the school to watch as the little girls set about learning white folks' arithmetic, grammar, moral philosophy.

The men of Canterbury, assisted by their wives, aunts, and children and by the power of church, meat market, and grocery, began a siege against the Quaker lady and her misses of color. Traders refused to sell them provisions; freemen assailed them and abused them on the streets; their doors and doorsteps were smeared with filth—all in the interest of purity. Neighborhood boys filled her well with manure from a horse stable; neighborhood women refused her a pail of drinking water when she begged for it. The trustees of the church found them to be rabble unfit for sanctuary. The doctor feared to treat the sick, had he wanted to. Still Prudence Crandall hung on.

The village turned to Judson, the man of the law. With their petitions and letters, he went to Hartford. Soon thereafter a law was enacted forbiding any person, under severe penalty, from establishing in any town in Connecticut, without written permission from its selectmen, a school for the education of colored people not inhabitants of Connecticut, and from teaching, boarding, or harboring Negroes born outside of Connecticut.

Canterburians went wild with the news. They rang bells, fired cannon. Law was at last on their side. They waited for Prudence Crandall to march her pupils out of Canterbury.

When she did not, they committed her to jail in the neighboring village of Brooklyn, assigning her to a cell just vacated by a condemned murderer.

From her vigil in that cell Prudence Crandall went to her trial before the Windham County Court. Andrew T. Judson was prosecuting attorney, and the court room was packed with friends of slavery waiting for him to state their case. Judson had never before been given such an opportunity to speak the mind of the white North. He twanged every chord that could stir the coarser passions. He appealed to popular prejudice on the question of amalgamation. He appealed to constitutionality, showing that since Negroes were not enfranchised they could not be regarded as citizens, or as having the rights of citizens. With the audience applauding, he ended his plea, "I am not opposed to their improvement, except so far as it violates the Constitution and endangers the Union. . . ."

He finished his plea, and seemed to have won, but when the count of the jury was taken, some voted in favor of the Quaker woman and her school for nigger girls. In spite of the haranguing of pro-slavery jurymen, they remained firm and returned no verdict. The case was taken before the Supreme Court of Connecticut and the Court of Errors. Still no jury would convict her.

While Prudence was spending her days and nights fighting for her freedom, Almira kept the school going. Then one day Prudence Crandall returned to Canterbury a free woman. The law was on the books, but in all Connecticut no jury could be found to convict her.

Canterburians, feeling cheated by the due process of law ideal, took the case into their own hands. To them that meant justice through violence. First they set her house on fire. Prudence and her colored girls put the fire out. Then at midnight a mob armed with clubs and iron bars attacked the house. They broke in windows and doors, and smashed rooms and furniture until they made the building unfit for animals. Then they went away.

Prudence Crandall at last had to give up. She took her colored misses away, returned them to their homes, and the town could again feel itself free of the black menace. Andrew T. Judson could again enjoy his big house without being offended by the sight of little black girls at school next door. . . .

Cinqué watched the *Washington*'s boat touch dock at New London. Lieutenant Meade leaped out and walked toward the group of waiting men. They shook hands in the manner of white men, and then Lieutenant Meade led them to the waiting boat. Having seen them comfortably seated, he took his place standing in the prow and barked an order to the oarsmen.

The boat came near enough the *Washington* for Cinqué to see the faces of the men. As he studied them his hands went to his throat unconsciously. There was not one among them to save him and his comrades from hanging.

Cinqué watched the boat pull alongside the *Washington*. He watched Lieutenant Meade deferentially help a white man from the boat to the deck. He watched Lieutenant Gedney hurry forward and greet him. He could not know that the man was Andrew T. Judson, United States Judge for the District of Connecticut, come to try the *Amistad* Africans on charges of mutiny and murder.

124

VIII

TRIAL BY ERROR

Judge Judson, his black breeches tight against his legs, his long coat whipping in the sea breeze, strode across the deck to where Cinqué sat, naked except for chains on his ankles, manacles on his wrists. With the authority of years and position, Judge Judson leaned over the Negro and stared at him.

"Get up, boy," he said, and motioned for Cinqué to rise.

With a rattle of chains Cinqué rose to full height, and found his face level with the Judge's eyes, his eyes looking straight into the unfriendly eyes of the white man. He shifted his gaze to the men standing behind the Judge, but there was no sympathy among them, either in the court officials or the ruddy-faced mid-shipmen crowding behind them.

"What's he worth, John?" the Judge asked one of his companions.

John J. Hyde, editor of the New London *Gazette,* stepped up to Cinqué with the air of a professional slave appraiser. He felt the muscles in Cinqué's arms and thighs, buried his fingers in the black fleece to test the soundness of his skull, parted his lips with thumb and forefinger and studied his teeth.

"In New Orleans that nigger'd bring at least fifteen hundred dollars under the hammer," he said.

Lieutenant Gedney and Lieutenant Meade exchanged looks, read each other's mind. Fifteen hundred dollars for

Cinqué. At least a thousand each for the other men. Perhaps five hundred each for the children. In prize money each could claim more than ten thousand dollars. Even at the usual salvage rate of one third, their reward would be large. Without saying a word the two men pledged a fight to the finish to establish their claim.

Then Lieutenant Meade introduced Norris Wilcox, United States Marshal, and Charles A. Ingersoll to Lieutenant Gedney.

"I am appearing for W. S. Holabird, United States Attorney for the District of Connecticut," Ingersoll announced. "Mr. Holabird remained at his home in Winsted, not wishing to undertake the journey in his present state of health."

Cinqué turned from the white men and looked at the water to where Montauk Point made a dark blue line in the blue haze.

"I brought James Sheffield along with me," John Hyde was saying. "He is an artist and lives in New London. I thought he could take a likeness of Cinqué for my paper."

"You want to wait till the hearing is over?" Lieutenant Gedney asked.

"If you have no objection, sir, I will begin at once and be ready to return with Mr. Hyde to New London."

Lieutenant Gedney offering no objection, Sheffield put a fresh sheet of paper on his easel and began sketching the outline of Cinqué's head and shoulders.

"Where are the two Spaniards?" Judge Judson asked Lieutenant Gedney.

"Below . . . resting. They need it too, by God. No one knows what they've suffered at the hands of those black cannibals."

"They'll have to be present for the hearing."

"I'll call them. First, I want to tell you some of the circumstances. . . ."

Briefly he summarized the story as he had heard it from Ruiz and Montes. Then he told of the Spaniards' wish to take schooner and captives to Havana. Almost as if an after-

126

thought, he added that he and Lieutenant Meade felt themselves entitled to prize money or salvage on schooner and cargo.

He sent an orderly below to summon Ruiz and Montes.

"The old man is still nearly crazy from fear and worry," Lieutenant Gedney told Judge Judson.

Sure he had made his own position clear, Lieutenant Gedney turned to welcome Ruiz and Montes on deck and introduced them to the Americans.

"These gentlemen own the slaves," he said.

"Where did you get them?" Mr. Hyde asked.

"I bought them in Havana—at the barracoon for native Africans," Ruiz replied.

"Do they speak Spanish?"

"Oh, no. They are too recently from Africa."

"Lieutenant Meade tells me one of them speaks English. How is that?"

"He no doubt learned it on the coast of Africa. English is much spoken on the Slave Coast."

Mr. Hyde turned to Cinqué.

"Do you speak English?"

The circle opened to include Cinqué.

"No . . . no English," Cinqué managed.

The circle closed again, leaving Cinqué no chance to speak for himself.

Lieutenant Gedney suggested the cabin of the *Washington* as the best place for the hearing. "You can examine the *Amistad* later," he added. "You will not be able to stand the sickening smell long."

Leaving Cinqué chained on deck, with Sheffield at work on his likeness, they followed Lieutenant Gedney below.

Judge Judson seated himself behind a desk at one end of the cabin. When the others had seated themselves in chairs facing the Judge, or had found places to lean against painted bulkheads, Wilcox opened the court.

"We will hear the Spaniards together," Judge Judson announced.

Don Pedro Montes and Don José Ruiz came before the court, accompanied by Lieutenant Meade as interpreter. Ruiz, his face dark and handsome above fresh linen, faced the court with confidence, sure he had the sympathy of these white men, sure the vessel and cargo would be restored to his possession, sure Cinqué and his fellow cannibals would find justice in Havana. Montes was still pale and haggard from his experience, still casting his eyes aloft as if every breath was a prayer of thanksgiving for finding himself so providentially surrounded by white men.

Wilcox read the oath and Lieutenant Meade, in Spanish learned in his youth in Madrid and Cadiz, interpreted, selecting his words from courtly usage, bowing in deference to the Spanish gentlemen.

Ruiz and Montes, duly sworn and with Ruiz as spokesman, lodged a complaint against Cinqué and the thirty-eight other Africans still alive, the four children being specifically exempted. On the complaint, the Judge, the Marshal, the Acting District Attorney, framed an indictment, charging the Africans with murder and piracy on board the Spanish schooner *Amistad*. Wilcox read the document aloud, Lieutenant Meade interpreted it, and the Spaniards spoke their "Sí, Señor," their "Gracias, Señor."

At a nod from Lieutenant Gedney, two sailors from the *Washington* brought Cinqué, still manacled, to the cabin and stood him before the court. The change in his appearance caused a rustle through the cabin. He had been allowed to wash, and his skin shone like smooth velvet. He wore a red flannel shirt, buttoned low to expose the *grisgris* marks on his chest, and white pantaloons, clothing the sailors had salvaged for him from the *Amistad*. He had a cord about his neck from which hung a silver snuffbox, a gift from one of the sailors.

Not knowing what they were saying to him, but aware that this must be a white man's palaver, Cinqué stood before them with the calm dignity of an African chief. His mind went back to palavers he had attended in Mani, with his

128

father at the head of the council. His father and Judge Judson were near the same age, they both held office with dignity. But the differences between them were greater than in color of skin. Cinqué thought of his father, the sense of justice his father inspired. He looked at Judge Judson's face, its character lines hidden by the beard. But the eyes that looked at him, the prisoner at the bar, were cold, contemptuous.

Near Cinqué sat Sheffield with his easel on his knee, with his pencil flying as he sketched the portrait for Hyde to lithograph in his *Gazette*. Those near him could see he had the set of head and shoulders right. Now he was working on details. He drew in the thick lips, slightly upturned, revealing strong, regular teeth. He paused at the nostrils, finding them the most difficult feature to capture. They seemed always in motion, dilating, contracting, responding to the African's every emotion.

Wilcox repeated the charges, addressed them directly to Cinqué, who listened with dignity and then signified that he did not understand. He was calm and collected, resigned to his fate at the hands of white men. When Wilcox had finished with the charges and his voice died away in the cabin, Cinqué smiled with a melancholy but determined expression. When the two sailors led him to a position at one side of the cabin, he gazed intently at Ruiz and Montes and then motioned with his hands that he expected to be hanged.

He knew enough of hate to know the hatred in these men's eyes—to know they would not relent until he had repaid Captain Ferrer's life with his own.

He could not know that, under agreements between England and Spain, slavery was piracy—that in parts of the white world the slave who murdered for freedom was no murderer at all—that if he had fallen in with a British vessel after the mutiny, he and his companions would have been considered injured freemen, not pirates and murderers. But they had been taken by a vessel of the United States, a country whose conflict over slave and free tipped the balance away from justice, whose Judge had brought him to trial and had not

129

offered him the counsel to which by law freemen were entitled.

Perhaps if he spoke . . . A few words of Mendi tumbled from Cinqué's lips. Judge Judson stopped him impatiently and asked for the hearing to proceed without delay. Lieutenant Meade was sworn and testified that he boarded the *Amistad* off Montauk and asked for her papers.

"Where are the papers?" Judge Judson demanded.

Lieutenant Gedney took a leather folder from his desk and extracted several packages. "Here, Your Honor." He handed them to Judge Judson. Judge Judson saw they were in Spanish and passed them on to Lieutenant Meade for translating. He read those with broken seals to the court. They were chiefly commercial letters, lists of purchases, commissions to transact business. He also read the two *traspasos* from the Governor General of Cuba permitting Ruiz and Montes to transport their slaves to Puerto Príncipe.

"These are official?" Judge Judson asked.

Ruiz examined them and then said, "Si, Señor."

"Enter them for evidence," Judge Judson directed.

Cinqué, seeing the interest taken in the letters, wished he had weighted them and sent them to the bottom of the ocean.

Then Lieutenant Meade told how he captured Cinqué and the remaining Africans on shore at Montauk, and how he took the two trunks from Captain Green.

"We must examine the trunks," Ingersoll said.

Lieutenant Gedney had his sailors bring in the two sea chests. In the presence of the court Ingersoll opened them. He lifted out clothing and gear that had belonged to Captain Ferrer, including a finely wrought leather holster. Cinqué leaned forward with the others to look. There was not a doubloon in the trunks, not a clink of the gold he had heard last on Long Island.

"Was there gold on board?" Judge Judson asked.

"We found none," Lieutenant Gedney assured him. Then

130

he told the court of the belt of doubloons Cinqué had dropped to the bottom of the Sound.

"Do you believe that was all the money on board?" Judge Judson asked.

"I do indeed."

Judge Judson excused Lieutenant Gedney and called Señor Ruiz.

"Will you give a full account of all that happened since the day you bought the slaves at *Misericordia?*" he asked.

With the skill of a dramatist Señor Ruiz began the story of the voyage in a low tone, gradually increased the volume, made strident his tones as he described in all its fury the mutiny on the *Amistad*. He made vivid the murders he had not witnessed. He made his hearers wince at the threats against the survivors. Again and again he thrust an accusing hand at Cinqué.

Cinqué could not understand the words, but the accusing hand he knew well, and he felt the hatred Ruiz was building up in the hearts of these Americans.

Calm again, Ruiz stepped back and Señor Montes addressed the Judge. In halting Spanish, which Lieutenant Meade translated with difficulty, he told of his own night of horror during the mutiny. As his tale progressed he became more agitated until his voice broke and tears stood on his cheeks.

"Had I been chained ten years in a dungeon, it would not have broken me down as much as this has," he moaned. "I shall never recover from the effects of this trouble."

When his story was finished, Lieutenant Meade took him gently by the arm and led him to a seat.

"I had no wish to kill any of them," he repeated from his chair. "I only wanted to protect them from themselves."

From the beginning it had been obvious the Americans wanted to believe the black men guilty. Now there were those among them who would have swung Cinqué from a yardarm, and every last African beside him.

The testimony being taken, Judge Judson adjourned the

131

court to make an investigation of the *Amistad* and to take the testimony of Antonio. The sailors took Cinqué to the deck again, where Sheffield posed him looking out to sea.

When Judge Judson stepped on board the *Amistad,* he saw a group of Africans under guard on deck, some in emaciated nudity, some in fantastic finery taken from the cargo. The four children, free to roam, ran at the sight of strange white faces, huddled around the windlass. Judge Judson and Hyde walked warily through a jumble of crockery, saddles, bridles, looking glasses, olives, raisins, and books, all mixed up in a strange medley.

On the forward hatch Hyde unconsciously rested his hand for a moment, then drew it quickly away from a cold clammy touch. It was the body of Kura, still lying naked under the black bombazine. Hyde pulled a fold away and he and Judge Judson stared at the rigid countenance and glazed eyes of the dead Negro. The mouth was open and still wore the ghastly marks of his last struggle.

"He died hard," Judge Judson observed coldly.

Near him, like some watchful fiend, sat Konoma, who with his filed tusks and demon's eyes aroused the white men to fear and loathing. He was confirmation of all they had heard from Ruiz and Montes, confirmation that these savage cannibals from Africa were worse than beasts from the jungles. Hyde stepped back a safe distance and scribbled notes on a pad. Judge Judson demanded that Lieutenant Gedney bring Antonio at once. He had seen enough of the nightmare the Spaniards had endured.

Lieutenant Meade brought Antonio on deck. Like comrades they crossed the deck together and stood before Judge Judson.

"This is Captain Ferrer's cabin boy," Lieutenant Meade said.

Antonio bowed and smiled ingratiatingly. Slowly, in Spanish, Lieutenant Meade explained to Antonio the nature of an oath. Antonio understood readily.

"I am a Christian," he said.

Then he was sworn. In his testimony he could at last speak his hatred of Cinqué, avenge himself for the harsh words, the blows he had suffered during the long voyage. With the confidence of an eyewitness he named Cinqué as the murderer of Captain Ferrer.

"I swear I saw the knife fall," he insisted.

Then he pointed to Grabo and Konoma as accomplices.

"They tried to kill me," he said to Judge Judson. "Will you protect me?"

Judge Judson turned to Lieutenant Gedney.

"Can you provide temporary quarters for this boy on the *Washington?*"

"Yes, Your Honor."

Judge Judson had come to the end of his investigation as bewildered as he had started. It was not a clear case like the affair at Canterbury. The blacks were guilty, of that he was convinced. But how should they be punished? And by whom? His own ignorance of Admiralty and International Law left him feeling unsure, incompetent. He was glad enough to leave the evil-smelling slave ship. He would have been gladder to be quit of the case entirely.

When they arrived on board the *Washington*, Sheffield was making kinky loops to indicate Cinqué's fleece. The likeness was good, but too romantic for Judge Judson.

"You have made this black savage too heroic," he complained.

Hyde studied the portrait intently, and then the original, its every detail now clear in the mid-morning sun. His face was puzzled and then relieved. The artist had helped him for the first time to look on Cinqué as a man.

"I don't agree," he said. "I think it is deficient in the heroic-like expression of the eye and brow."

"I agree with you, sir," Sheffield said to Hyde. "It is the noblest face I have ever looked on. It is my fault the portrait does not convey the heroic qualities I see in him."

Judge Judson set Ingersoll and Wilcox to preparing copies of the evidence. Then he drew Lieutenant Gedney and

133

Meade aside. Doubt, not conviction, had driven him to seek an escape for himself.

"This case could be easily settled," he said. "The indictment could be destroyed . . . the schooner and slaves turned over to the Spaniards—"

"What about our claim for salvage?" the officers interrupted. "What about punishment for their crimes?"

"I would trust the Spaniards to punish them, once they got them to Havana. You can bargain with them for prize money. A settlement with them would probably be more profitable to you than court proceedings, with all the expenses."

"We have spoken to Señor Ruiz," Lieutenant Gedney said, "on the subject of prize money. They are not willing to pay a cent, believing that we as officers of the United States Navy did no more than our duty."

Judge Judson tried to persuade them to withdraw their claim for salvage in favor of an immediate settlement of the case.

"In our own interest we will pursue the process," Lieutenant Gedney said. "We demand an American court to protect the rights of American citizens."

Acceding to their demands, not considering the competence of his court or the question of justice for all, Judge Judson accepted the documents prepared by Ingersoll and Wilcox. They committed Cinqué and thirty-eight others to stand trial before the next Circuit Court, to be held in Hartford on the seventeenth of the following September. They were to be held in the county jail at New Haven under two processes: the charge of murder and piracy, and the libels on them as property filed by the Spaniards and the American officers.

Señor Ruiz objected volubly to the claim for salvage filed by Gedney and Meade.

"These gentlemen are officers of a public vessel of the United States," he argued. "They are not entitled to additional reward for performing their duty. They bore no hardship, no danger. The case is covered by treaties—"

"It is a question to be settled by the Circuit Court," Judge Judson told him impatiently. "You will have ample opportunity to present your arguments in the case. You may have whatever counsel you will."

The three little girls, Ka-le, and Antonio, not indicted but included in process as property, were ordered to give bonds in the sum of one hundred dollars each to appear before the Circuit Court as witnesses in the case. For want of bonds, they also were committed to the New Haven jail.

Lieutenant Meade, Señor Montes, and Señor Ruiz were ordered to recognize in the sum of one hundred dollars each to appear at the trial.

"Where will you be stopping?" Judge Judson asked the Spaniards.

"Where is the nearest Spanish consul?"

"Señor Antonio G. Vega in Boston."

"Then you may reach us through him. We will ask him to present our cause to Her Majesty's Government."

Wilcox laboriously copied the names of his new charges from the Spanish *traspaso*. He dated the document New London, August 29, 1839. Judge Judson made sure that Ingersoll had copies of all documents for District Attorney Holabird. Then Lieutenant Meade escorted the party to the *Washington*'s boat.

As they were about to leave, Señor Ruiz handed a card to Mr. Hyde.

"Will you do me the favor of publishing this in your paper?" he asked.

On their way to New London, Mr. Hyde read the card aloud:

The subscribers, Don José Ruiz and Don Pedro Montes, in gratitude for their most unhoped for and providential rescue from the hands of a ruthless gang of African buccaneers, and an awful death, would take this means of

135

expressing, in some slight degree, their thankfulness and obligation to Lieut. Com. T. R. Gedney, and the officers and crew of the United States surveying brig "Washington," for their decision in seizing the "Amistad," and their unremitting kindness and hospitality in providing for their comfort on board their vessel, as well as the means they have taken for the protection of their property.

We also must express our indebtedness to that nation whose flag they so worthily bear, with an assurance that this act will be duly appreciated by our most gracious sovereign, Her Majesty the Queen of Spain.

"They have put their case well," Judge Judson said.

"They have indeed," Mr. Hyde answered. Then he added, "With your approval, sir, I will print this in the *Gazette* and send a copy on to the New York *Sun*, along with my story."

As the Spaniards had anticipated, it was published and read the length and breadth of America. It did what they expected—curried favor for themselves and set hatred against the savage Africans.

While Cinqué, chained in the hold of the *Washington*, awaiting transfer to the New Haven jail, had neither language nor spokesman to tell his plight to the American people. He had only the steadfastness that had so far held firm in his fight for freedom. That, and a small sketch made by James Sheffield.

IX

THE VILLAGE GREEN

From the deck of a government cutter Cinqué watched the harbor at New Haven open up and the village spread itself before him. He was manacled, but the Reverend Cutter Wolcott and Captain Mather Herald, detailed by Marshal Wilcox to convey him to jail, allowed him the run of the deck. Leaving New London at Saturday noon, they had sailed leisurely along the Sound. At times Cinqué had leaned on the rail, staring moodily at Long Island, a thin blue-white line edging blue water; more often he had searched the green hill-studded shore of Connecticut, seeking the answers to his questions: Where were they taking him? When would they put the noose on him?

Now as they approached New Haven Harbor, the white men stood on either side of him at the rail, pointing out landmarks as they took shape in the sunlight: the Light House, Fort Hale, East Rock, West Rock, where long before him the Regicides had sought refuge in the "Judges' Cave," having, like him, killed for freedom. For each he smiled and grunted, but their talk was like waves slapping the hull of the cutter.

The cutter put in at Long Wharf and the three men began their walk through the village to the jail. Though it was Saturday afternoon and many people were on the streets, they caused little excitement. Strange faces and strange garbs, crews from sailing vessels from around the world, often walked the water front or sang their way from taverns near the Green. Cinqué, in his red shirt and white pantaloons, with his wrists manacled behind him, might have been any fugitive slave being dragged to jail for his master. Walking on solid ground, separated from the *Amistad* and his companions, he seemed less heroic than Sheffield had pictured him, or than Hyde had described him for the New York *Sun*, both sketches familiar now to the people of New Haven.

Mani, Havana, New Haven—grass hut, red-roofed palace, white clapboard house—African jungle, Cuban luxuriance, well-trimmed groves and hedges of New England—Cinqué's mind was alive with impressions thrust upon him by his journey. Nothing he had seen was like this village of New Haven with its white clapboard and red brick buildings surrounding an open square. Up Chapel Street they walked, and the Village Green lay before them, with its three church spires and the State House in the background, with its elms stripped bare as winter by canker worms, its grass browned by end-of-summer dryness. These impressions of clean orderliness flooded Cinqué's mind as they led him past the Tontine Hotel and to the rear of the County House.

The County House, kept by Colonel Pendleton and his lady, was both jail and tavern—with the only entrance to the jail through the tavern. The prisoner had to be led past men enjoying their talk and spirits before reaching at last one of the six cells in the three-story building.

Captain Herald held the door to the tavern open and the Reverend Wolcott led Cinqué inside. The men at their drinks barely glanced up at first. Then someone said, "Where'd you get that nigger?"

"From the *Amistad*," the Reverend Wolcott answered.

"The *Amistad!*"

"The nigger's from the *Amistad*."

"That's one of the cannibals."

"What will they do with him?"

The men crowded around Cinqué. A kitchen boy shouted for Mrs. Pendleton.

"Where are the Spaniards?" one of the men asked Captain Herald.

"They have gone to the Spanish Consul at Boston."

Mrs. Pendleton, in drab gray dress and cap, came from her work in the kitchen. Cinqué stared at her heavy white face and white hands showing from the folds of dress and cap.

"Bring him this way," Mrs. Pendleton said to Captain Herald.

She took keys from her pocket and opened a door leading into a narrow passageway between the two first-floor cells. The only light was from the sunset, and Cinqué, following her, nudged along by Captain Herald, had difficulty adjusting his eyes to the dimness.

"We'll put him in with the local prisoners until Colonel Pendleton brings the other Africans," Mrs. Pendleton said.

She peered through the wicket into a cell and then unlocked the heavy plank door.

"Should I take off the irons?" Captain Herald asked.

"Yes."

He unlocked the manacles and pushed Cinqué into the cell. Then Mrs. Pendleton closed the door behind him. Cinqué heard the rattling of keys as Mrs. Pendleton locked the two doors between him and freedom. Then he turned to see if there was some way to escape.

Cinqué found himself facing six prisoners—four colored like himself, two white—all withdrawn to the windows, from which they had been watching passers-by on Church Street and the Village Green. Cinqué stood erect, his back to the oaken door, his hands drawn to his sides. If they meant to do him harm—

"What'd they get you for?" one of the colored men asked, his voice thick from rum.

Cinqué shook his head.

"Won't talk, eh?"

The man raised his hand threateningly.

"My brothers," Cinqué began rapidly in Mendi. They stared at him uncomprehendingly, their attitudes belligerent.

"English . . . no . . . no," Cinqué pleaded.

The colored men came closer to him.

"Fresh from Africa, eh?"

They surrounded him and ran their hands through the pockets of his shirt and pantaloons. Finding nothing, they stepped back. With signs they tried to ask how long he had been in America. Cinqué, unable to understand what they asked, asked questions meaningless to them.

With a shrug they returned to the windows, leaving Cinqué to lie down on a blanket near the door, his fear of the strangers somewhat abated. A group of white men gathered in front of the County House, drawn there by rumor, and peered into the darkening cell.

"Where is the cannibal?" they asked. "Let us see the cannibal from the *Amistad*."

The prisoners pressed together at this word *cannibal*. They begged the men outside to tell them more about Cinqué, became frantic at the garbled stories of the mysterious black schooner. They shouted for Mrs. Pendleton to rescue them. What right had she to put a cannibal in with them?

By now it was too dark to see him, but they could feel him near the door.

"We must keep watch all night," they whispered.

When the men outside had drifted away, the six prisoners spread their blankets near the windows and stationed two guards to keep watch. On the other side of the room Cinqué huddled in his blanket, fearful of the harm these men might do to him.

Long after footsteps had ceased echoing along Church Street, when darkness and silence had separated Cinqué from the other prisoners, he heard Mrs. Pendleton's key in the lock. She opened the door and, holding her candle before her, pushed another prisoner into the cell. He was an old man, colored, and staggering from a night of rum.

"Give us a light. Give us your candle," the prisoners begged. "We want to see the cannibal."

Mrs. Pendleton followed their eyes to the inch of candle

140

in her hand. She set the holder on the floor and closed the door behind her. Then she put her face through the wicket.

"You can let that burn down," she said.

The men jerked the old man to their side of the cell and rifled his pockets. They divided the coins they found among themselves and passed around his snuffbox. Then they left him lying on the floor, too drunk to share their fears of inevitable darkness and a man-eating savage.

Like a caged eagle, Cinqué stood with his back to the door, the light of the candle making him larger, fiercer in the outlines of his shadow. Two men sat facing him on guard while the others wrapped their blankets around themselves and slept. The candle burned low and went out, leaving Cinqué and the guards to adjust their eyes to darkness, to feed their fears to monstrous growth.

When daylight came Cinqué still had not slept. Facing him were the two white prisoners, at their turn on guard, their faces sickly pale in the morning light. A clanging of church bells roused Cinqué to new fear, wonder, made the sleeping prisoners sit up and stare at Cinqué. Their anxiety allayed, they resumed their watch at the windows. Mrs. Pendleton came and took four of the colored men to work in the kitchen.

Soon after sunup people began passing along Church Street toward the harbor.

"Where are you going?" the prisoners asked from their County House windows.

"To Long Wharf to see the cannibals. They have come by sloop from New London."

Before church time the streets and Green were full of people who had for the moment put away their Sabbath seriousness, as they waited for the *Amistad* Africans to come like a procession to the County House. With the men in their long coats and tall hats, the women in billowing dresses, it was like a political rally or an auction. Indeed, some of the Whigs, confident of party strength, repeated the cry against

141

the President: "Van, Van, the used-up man." And a few Southerners among them, summer guests at The Pavilion on the water front, marveled at the excitement a "passel o' niggers" could stir up.

There were present many who could remember the last slave auction on New Haven Green, fourteen years before, at the spot still marked by the whipping post. Present also was a colored woman, one of the last two slaves sold, manumitted after the sale, living free and content in the village of New Haven, taking her place among its fourteen thousand. . . .

"Here they come," the crowds shouted.

Cinqué, made curious by their excitement, crept close to the window and looked down Church Street. He joined the shouting when he saw his friends from the *Amistad* coming toward him.

Konoma, his tattoo marks and filed tusks enough to cause shivers among the whites, led the group.

"Look at the man-eater," people whispered to each other. Women jerked their children back at sight of him.

Behind Konoma came the men able to walk, following in columns headed by Grabo and Kin-na. The three little girls and Ka-le ran in and out among the Africans, or darted to one side of the street or the other to accept gifts of fruit and coins from outstretched white hands. Two wagons, loaded with men too weak to walk, ended the procession. On either side marched guards from the *Washington*, scrubbed young men in uniform.

Thinly clad, emaciated, gaping, the Africans marched along Church Street. "Colonel Pendleton's got his hands full with that crew," the people said to each other. "They won't be as easy as Saturday night drunks."

Colonel Pendleton guided his prisoners to the rear of the County House, through the tavern, and into the cells. Those able to walk were marched to the cells on the second floor. The sick were carried to a cell on the third floor, which Mrs. Pendleton had prepared as a hospital ward. Colonel Pendleton sent a messenger to Dr. Charles Hooker, Professor of Medicine at Yale College, to see if he could control the flux among the captives. Mrs. Pendleton took the three little girls and Ka-le to a room in her own quarters, where they were to sleep four in a bed.

With the prisoners settled, the guards from the *Washington* dismissed, Colonel Pendleton and Marshal Wilcox decided to check the commitment order against the captives. From cell to cell they went calling "Manuel, Evaristo, Escolástico. . . ." The Africans looked at them dumbly. When it was obvious they could not apply these Spanish names given by Ruiz, they went through the cells and with Burnah and Antonio to help them, laboriously spelled out the names the Africans gave them.

Noontime came, and the four colored prisoners, supervised by Mrs. Pendleton, brought them stew in pewter plates. The Africans pushed their forks and spoons aside and ate with their fingers. Then when they had finished they tossed their plates away as lightly as they had tossed away banana-leaf dishes in Africa.

Sunday sermons, Sunday dinners over, the people of New Haven gathered around the County House, drawn there by curiosity to learn more about the survivors of the mysterious long low black schooner. All morning long Colonel Pendleton had escorted his special friends to the cells and let them look through wickets at the captives. Now, when the afternoon had brought a pressure of crowds, he set a fee of a shilling each and allowed the people to file through the upper passageways and peer through wickets at the Africans lying on their blankets.

"The money will be used for the Africans," he announced, "after expenses have been defrayed."

Some found them objects of pity or terror. Some saw them for what they were: a bedraggled group of forlorn Negroes alone and friendless in a strange land—desperately in need of help.

Among those who came were the phrenologists, the sketchers, the painters. Those who paid their shillings filed upstairs with the crowd. Only a select few, friends of Colonel Pendleton, were let in to see Cinqué.

A phrenologist studied Cinqué, felt his head, measured his skull. Then he drew an audience around him on the Green.

"Did you see that Cinqué? What a powerful frame!"

"What do you make of him?" his audience asked.

"I judge him of bilious and sanguine temperament, with bilious predominating. What a head! Well formed and such as a phrenologist admires. Such an African head is seldom seen . . . and doubtless in other circumstances would have been an honor to his race. . . ."

The drops of Berber blood!

The painters saw in him the noble savage, the perfect model for a canvas romanticizing the primitive. And they sketched and painted him, with a little less accent on lips and nostrils, with a careful remodeling of head and ears to Caucasian ideas of manly beauty.

The professors from Yale College came, among them Josiah Willard Gibbs with Mungo Park's *Travels* and Mollison's *Travels in Africa* under his arm. Learned in Greek, Latin, and Hebrew, famous in New Haven and outside for his skill with languages, he had come to work out a method of communication with the Africans. Colonel Pendleton, helpless without an interpreter, took him to the second story and brought the Africans together in one cell.

When they saw this stranger, the Africans drew back in alarm. Tall, thin—thin almost as any of them—stern in face and manner, he was not a man to inspire easy confidence. But when he spoke his voice was gentle, and gentleness shone from his deep-set eyes.

Professor Gibbs turned to the African dialects in Mungo Park and read a few words at random. The Africans laughed foolishly, uncomprehendingly. Then he tried to build a vocabulary from their own words.

He held up a finger and said, "One."

They watched intently but silently, caught by the white man's seriousness.

He held up a coin and said, "One."

Some of the men seemed to understand.

He held up one finger again.

"*Eta*," Grabo shouted. The others shouted *eta* after him and laughed like children.

Professor Gibbs held up one finger again and said, *"Eta,"* imitating the Africans carefully, smiling at the good-natured laughter his failure provoked.

With them in a circle around him he tried with two, three, up to ten fingers: *fili, kiauwa, naeni, loelu, weta, wafura, wayapa, ta-u, pu* the numerals developed. While the crowds filed by, Professor Gibbs worked as patiently as if he had a beginning class in counting.

As the vocabulary grew, he noticed that some of the Africans did not respond to the words. One by one he worked out the numerals with them until he had determined that there were at least three languages among them. But most of them were from the same people.

"Mendi," they said to him repeatedly. Not knowing an African people of that name, unable to find it in his books, he decided they must be the Mandingoes described by Mungo Park.

By late afternoon he had said the numerals over and over until the Africans no longer laughed at him. Then he left the jail to find some colored person who could talk with them. He felt sure there must be some sailor along the New Haven water front who would understand the words. Afire with his mission, he trod the water front and Long Wharf, stopping every colored person he saw, counting out the numerals over and over, asking again and again for help for these poor primitive Africans. . . .

The next morning after breakfast Norris Wilcox arrived at the jail with clothing for the Africans—pants and shirts made of striped cotton cloth, the kind called "hardtimes," for the men, and calico dresses and woolen shawls for the little girls. The men struggled into their pants with a great deal of laughter. But when they put on their shirts, their *grisgris* marks were entirely hidden. They jerked the shirts off and threw them aside, proudly showing again their crosses, diamonds, cicatrices.

The little girls put on their dresses and wound their shawls around their heads like turbans, African fashion. Then they pulled on the long woolen stockings Wilcox had brought them.

"Cinqué?" they asked of Wilcox and Pendleton. Close knit as they were by suffering, they still needed their leader.

But Cinqué was not brought among them. They thought he surely must have been hanged.

When Mrs. Pendleton showed them a copy of the lithograph made from Sheffield's sketch, they cried "Cinqué" over and over. Still he was kept from them, and they were not told he was in the cell below them.

Cinqué, in the cell with the other prisoners, begged to be taken to his people. He shouted to them, but was not sure his voice had carried. When there was no reply he shrank to a corner and brooded. How long must he bear the torture of being so separated from them?

View of NEW HAVEN and FORT HALE.

a. West Rock. b. Long Wharf. c. New Haven Gymnasium. d. Steam Boat Office. e. East Rock. g. Tomlinson's bridge. h. Fort Hale.

Drawn & Engraved by J.W.Barber

Fig. 6 (Courtesy of Yale University Library.)

Drawn & Engraved by J.W.Barker

E.VIEW OF THE PUBLIC SQUARE OR GREEN, IN NEW HAVEN CON.

Fig. 7 (Courtesy of Yale University Library.)

X

FRIENDS STORM SENT

While Cinqué lay on his blanket in New Haven jail, surrounded by drunkards, panderers, criminals, waiting for the
noose around his neck, newspapers spread his story around
the world, Sheffield's lithograph passed from hand to hand.
In hamlet and town, small groups gathered to hear the story,
to study the black man's face, trying to find in it the answer
to a national enigma. No answer came—only louder rum-
blings of thunder. "Southrons," by birth or by sympathy,
jeered at the picture. "He will be precious poor property for
the Abolitionists," they said. "He is hardly above the apes
and monkeys of his own native Africa, the language he jab-
bers incomprehensible to civilized men." The Abolitionists,
taking his cause as their own, thanked God for a heroic symbol that would bring them closer together. Officers of the
law, from Chief Executive to local constable, already fore-
warned of the gathering storm, shivered at what might come
if both sides stirred themselves to action over Cinqué. In New
York, Philadelphia, Havana, men who had suffered long for
black men's rights turned their eyes to New Haven and prepared to fight—legally if they could, by trickery if they
must. . . .

Lewis Tappan sat at a small desk in the middle of his Hanover Square warehouse in New York City, surrounded by
the trappings of a merchant's trade: bales of goods from Eng-

147

land and France, cases of cutlery, boxes of guns, kegs of powder. Middle-aged, slight of build, careful of his black cloth and white linen, he ruled this part of the commercial empire he had built up with his brother Arthur.

But on this morning his mind was not on the men at the counting desks, or on those who prepared shipments of merchandise for their diminishing trade to the South, their growing trade to the West. He had a copy of the New York *Sun* spread on the desk before him, and had just finished reading the story of the *Amistad* Africans. Their heroic fight for freedom, their fate in New Haven jail, rekindled the Abolitionists' fire that had long burned in him.

He stared at the windows, iron-shuttered against pro-slavery mobs who had tried to destroy him and his brother. He asked himself, "What can become of those unfortunate Africans?"

The answer was suggested by the newspaper. They would be returned to Havana, to find justice in Spanish courts for murdering the Captain and the cook.

In that moment Lewis Tappan decided to use his strength, his wealth to fight for the Africans. He took the newspaper to his brother, who was busy at the counting desks, and waited while he read the story.

"I am going to New Haven," Lewis Tappan said.

No explanation was needed. In the same way Arthur Tappan had spoken and gone off to Canterbury to lend his advice and money to the defense of Prudence Crandall. In the same way both had supported the American Anti-Slavery Society, or supplied the needs of fugitive slaves.

"What help will you need?"

"Money, but I don't yet know how much. Enough to employ legal counsel at least. Before I go I will talk with Joshua Leavitt and Simeon Jocelyn. I will try among my colored friends to find some African who can speak their language."

Lewis Tappan walked out of the dim warehouse into the bright September sunlight. Shunning hacks, he walked first

148

along Pearl Street toward the Battery until he found a colored friend, a member of the colored Baptist Church the Tappans supported. Tappan told him to gather what colored men he could who could speak African dialects and bring them to Simeon Jocelyn's office. Then he went up Broad to Nassau, to the office where Joshua Leavitt edited *The Emancipator* for the American Anti-Slavery Society.

He was conscious that people stared at him as he passed. "Lewis Tappan," their voices came to him. "Lewis Tappan . . . Abolition personified." It was an old face he turned toward them, lighted by old eyes grown weary from much suffering. He could look back over fifteen years of struggle for Abolition in Boston, New Haven, New York. Long before his hair became mixed with gray and fell away from his skull, he had been jeered at by enemies who laughed at his physical appearance. They could not laugh at his sincerity in the fight for human rights.

The jeering led to worse. "Southron" customers shunned his warehouse. "Southron" politicians had offered ten thousand dollars for his head if he ever came South. His house at No. 40 Rose Street, from which many a fugitive slave had headed north on the Underground Railroad, had been ransacked by a mob, the furnishings dragged into the street, the house burned to the ground, while the owner and his family were fortunately visiting in Harlem. Mobs had moved on his warehouse and broken windows, destroyed goods. It was no longer safe for members of his family to be caught abroad. Still he fought on.

Lewis Tappan came to the offices of the American Anti-Slavery Society, where he found Joshua Leavitt copying for *The Emancipator* stories about the *Amistad* Africans from the New London *Gazette* and the New York *Sun*. It was a shabby office, but the heart of the anti-slavery movement. The Administration at Washington, the "Southron" politicians would have been surprised at how strong the heartbeat had grown in ten years of agitation.

"What is your opinion of the case?" Tappan asked Leavitt.

149

"The opinion of any right-thinking man. Cinqué killed for freedom, and should be free. That is his right . . . in a free country. In a slave country, slaveholders have prisons and gallows for slaves who rise against their masters. Something has to be done soon or they will be turned over to the Spaniards."

"Is it a case for the Executive?"

"The Executive will make it so if it suits his purpose."

"I agree . . . but what can we do? I am going to New Haven tomorrow to see them. I want to offer them all the help I can."

"We can provide counsel for the trial at Hartford."

"I had thought of that. We will need to raise considerable money. I would pay all, but our business has not fully recovered from the shock of panic and fire. I suggest that we form a Committee of Friends of the *Amistad* Africans and ask for donations."

"You can count on me."

They shook hands gravely.

"I would like to include Brother Jocelyn," Tappan added. "Will you call on him with me?"

Tappan and Leavitt crossed over to Broadway, passed Trinity Church, and turned into Wall Street. As they walked, they talked of President Van Buren and the possibility of his surrendering the Africans to the Spaniards without waiting for court proceedings.

"I would not trust him," Tappan said. "He has courted favor with Southrons and Northern friends of slavery too often. If he thinks this case might endanger him in the coming election, I feel he will settle quickly against the Africans."

"He is the most cunning political trickster in our history. I agree with what Davy Crockett said of him: 'He could take a piece of meat on one side of his mouth, a piece of bread on the other, and cabbage in the middle, and chew and swallow each in its severalty, never mixing them together.' "

Not smiles but bitterness came to Tappan's face at the words.

Their walk brought them to the office in Wall Street from which Jocelyn carried on his work with colored people. Jocelyn, too, had felt the touch of lightning. He had been pastor of the colored church in New Haven, where he tried to apply the teachings of Christ to black and white alike. But New Haven was not ready to go that far in Christianity. Mobs threatened him on the street, attacked his church with rotten eggs, assaulted his house, finally drove him from New Haven. Now he had come to New York, where he could devote all his energy to helping colored people.

Tappan and Leavitt passed a group of colored men and women waiting outside the door for help and stepped inside the office. They waited while Jocelyn dismissed an old man whose bowing and scraping revealed how recently he had been manumitted.

"Have you read of the *Amistad* case?" Tappan asked.

"Yes."

"What do you think of it?"

"If the United States judges murder that man, the mark of Cain should be burnt upon their foreheads."

"The judges won't murder him alone," Leavitt said. "The Southrons will make much of this case. We must be prepared to fight them at every turn."

"It's not the Southrons I fear so much," Tappan added, "no matter how much their papers may shout. I fear proslavery Northerners more—people who are making money out of slavery without being contaminated by it. Their voice is loud in Washington. Their influence will be harder to fight."

Their discussion turned to lawyers with Abolitionist leanings who might defend the Africans. Rufus Choate of Boston was their first choice, but he was old and in ill health. He would not have the strength to carry the fight to the end. David Brown of Philadelphia had already offered his services to Leavitt. But they were unwilling to consider him seriously. There were left only Roger Sherman Baldwin of New

151

Haven and Seth P. Staples, Jr. and Theodore Sedgwick of New York City.

"Would you agree for me to speak to Baldwin when I go to New Haven tomorrow?" Tappan asked.

They agreed, and assured him that Baldwin should be asked to assume the position of chief counsel. Staples and Sedgwick were eager and talented, but too young to bear the burden of a case on which so many lives depended.

"I have some work with Sedgwick concerning his pamphlet, 'Is Slavery a Good or an Evil in These States?' " Leavitt said. "I will speak to him and to Staples, if you gentlemen are willing."

The question of counsel settled, the men turned to the question of providing funds. They drew up a statement of their purposes and a request for public donations, both to be printed in *The Emancipator*.

By nightfall four Africans who spoke native dialects had come to Jocelyn's office to meet Lewis Tappan. Three of these were Congoes, old men who had been away from Africa since childhood. The fourth was John Ferry, a native of Kissi, a man about thirty years old.

His story was one to arouse compassion among friends of black men. He had been kidnapped when he was twelve and sold as a slave. He had been brought by Baltimore clipper to St. Thomas and then to Colombia, where he was a slave five years. When Simon Bolivar began his revolution with the manumission of slaves, John Ferry was freed. Since then he had drifted from one English-speaking country to another, and had finally settled in New York in 1830.

The following morning Lewis Tappan set out by boat for New Haven, accompanied by the three Congoes and John Ferry. . . .

In the office of the New York *Evening Post*, William Cullen Bryant, the mild-mannered poet-editor, faced Theodore Sedgwick across his desk. Sedgwick, a big man with long face, beak nose, black shaggy beard, leaned forward as he spoke.

"I have already taken some interest in the *Amistad* case."

"Good. I fear the case may be regarded from an emotional rather than a legal viewpoint. My plan is to run a series of discussions which will present to the public the real merits of the cause. Will you study the case and prepare some articles on it?"

"Previous commitments may prevent me. Joshua Leavitt called on me today as a member of the Committee of Friends of the *Amistad* Africans and asked me to serve as counsel in the trial at Hartford."

"Did you accept?"

"Yes, sir."

"That offers no difficulty as far as the *Evening Post* is concerned. You could continue to sign your articles *Veto*. No one need know your identity."

"I am willing."

"Then I will count on you for an article within the week."

The two men shook hands and Sedgwick went out. Then the poet resumed work on his editorial in defense of the *Amistad* Africans. . . .

In Philadelphia another poet, John Greenleaf Whittier, frail in health, saddened by failures in his fight for Abolition, agonized over the fate of the unfortunate Africans, in an editorial for the *Pennsylvania Freeman* poured out his heart for Cinqué, the hero of the African buccanneers:

What a master spirit is his . . . what a soul for the tyrant to crush down in bondage. . . .

His words added to the crescendo of voices crying for justice for the Africans. . . .

In Quincy a lawyer, John Quincy Adams, who had been President and who was now a Congressman from Massachusetts, read the story of the Africans and set his mind to analyzing legal questions involved. . . . to puzzling over what the Administration would do when the human problems of the Africans came to be considered . . . to framing a speech in their defense to be delivered from the floor in Congress. . . .

. . . In New Haven Lewis Tappan went first to the office of Roger Sherman Baldwin, who immediately accepted the place as chief counsel for the Africans.

"I saw them arrive from New London," he told Tappan. "Their condition is enough to inspire the deepest sympathy."

Then, with Professor Gibbs and the four Africans from New York, they went to the jail. On the way, Professor Gibbs tried *eta, fili, kiauwa* on the Africans. The three Congoes were silent, but John Ferry repeated the words and counted through ten quickly.

"That is the language of the Mendis," he said. "Their country is near mine in Africa."

Colonel Pendleton met them in the tavern and told them that Bootah had been buried that morning and that Tuar would be buried in the afternoon.

"We want to see Cinqué," Tappan said.

But Colonel Pendleton took them first to the second-story cells, where the captives lay on cots. At the suggestion of Professor Gibbs, the three Congoes, one at a time, put their heads through the wickets and spoke to the Africans in native dialects. They were met with blank stares. Then John Ferry looked in and shouted a greeting in Kissi. This brought the Africans running. When he spoke to them again, this time in Mendi, they began to laugh and cry with happiness.

Colonel Pendleton brought the captives to one cell to let the white men talk to them through John Ferry. But his knowledge of Mendi was slight, and theirs of Kissi so imperfect that no satisfactory account of their experiences could be taken. Professor Gibbs knew his search for an interpreter must go on.

Then Colonel Pendleton took Tappan and the others to see Cinqué, in the cell with local prisoners. They found him stretched on his blanket on the floor, wholly naked, with a part of the blanket wrapped around him.

"Cinqué," Colonel Pendleton called.

He arose rather reluctantly and came towards them with great native dignity. He had grown used to being called for curious white men to stare at. But when he looked into the face of Lewis Tappan he knew he had found a friend, a white man he could trust. Tappan held out his hand. "Massa," Cinqué said simply, and took his hand.

With Ferry as interpreter, Cinqué told his story, but imperfectly. There were many gaps left to puzzle the white men —too many for Baldwin to prepare an adequate defense. When he mentioned Ruiz and Montes, it was with bitterness.

"They made fools of us and did not go to Sierra Leone," he said.

Then he asked about the other captives, his people.

"Why have you kept them separated?" Baldwin asked Colonel Pendleton.

"I was afraid he might cause them to mutiny again."

When Tappan and Baldwin insisted, Colonel Pendleton agreed that Cinqué could visit the other captives and attend Tuar's funeral.

Tappan took Cinqué's arm and led him gently from his cell. When they entered the second-story passageway the Africans from both cells crowded around Cinqué, chattering, calling him "Massa," offering him snuff and the coins they had been given by white visitors. He accepted the coins and put them in his pocket.

After he had spoken to each of the Africans individually, Colonel Pendleton took his arm to return him to his cell. Cinqué suddenly took the coins from his pocket and gave them to Bato.

"White men take," he said, remembering how the other prisoners robbed each other.

In the afternoon, when it was time for the funeral, Colonel Pendleton and Lewis Tappan went to Cinqué's cell. They took him to the largest room in the jail, where Tuar lay in his coffin, the other Africans squatting around it, native fashion.

The Reverend Leonard Bacon, a New Haven minister who had long interested himself in the cause of Abolition, stood at the head of the coffin. Antonio and John Ferry stood at the foot to serve as interpreters. Enough white visitors had been gathered to sing a hymn.

Carefully Mr. Bacon told them about the coffin, the manner of dress for the dead, preparation of the body for burial in the Christian ritual. Antonio and John Ferry stumbled after him, trying to put the words in Mendi, but leaving the Africans with blank faces.

After another hymn, Mr. Bacon read a long prayer, through which the whites stood with bowed heads. Observing them, Cinqué motioned for the Africans to imitate them.

Then Cinqué approached the coffin and again looked on the face of a friend he had first met on the *Amistad*, a friend who had not shirked in the fight for freedom, a friend who had stayed close at his side until they were separated in this strange, well-ordered land.

Gazing steadily at the corpse, he spoke half to Tuar, as if he were still alive, half to the other Africans, recalling their fight for freedom and their hardships together, consigning his soul to Ngil-li, the maker of all good and evil, in the manner of his father in the village of Mani. As he spoke, the others answered him in short affirmations like the amens in a responsive prayer. After four or five minutes of speaking, Cinqué stepped back from the coffin and squatted with the others.

Mr. Bacon selected one African from each cell to act as pall bearer and to report to the others the place and manner of burial.

They lifted the coffin into a wagon and whites and blacks alike followed on foot. The little cortege moved slowly along Church Street, past the Village Green, past Yale College, to the cemetery on Grove Street. There they found a mound of newly-dug earth beside an open grave that had received Bootah that morning, and the old sexton waiting.

It was in ground consecrated by Jehudi Ashmun, the first American representative to Liberia, and he rested there in his red stone tomb patterned after Scipio's. He had given his life in the service of black men, and had willed that, having no family, he would share his plot with black men.

There were more hymns and prayers, and then Mr. Bacon signalled for the coffin to be lowered into the grave. Intently the Africans watched as he spread a little dirt on the coffin and said, "Ashes to ashes, dust to dust. . . ." Then there was silence except for the sound of spades on earth.

When the white men seemed ready to turn away, the Africans stepped to the grave and began circling it, casting on stones they had picked up along the way, speaking to Tuar. Cinqué led the circle, Burnah closed it.

"Walky good, hear," Burnah said, and cast a stone.

Again they circled.

"Good-bye, hear," Burnah chanted.

A third time they circled.

"I am coming, hear."

The Africans broke their circle and became a part of the procession returning to the jail. The old sexton took out his record book. For years he had entered "niger." For Tuar he scrawled "African" across the page. . . .

In Havana, Dr. Madden once again stopped by Consul Trist's office to ask if there had been news of the *Amistad*.

Weeks had passed since Jacinto and Vicente had brought the *Amistad*'s boat ashore and told their terrified story of mutiny—weeks in which Dr. Madden had hoped the mutineers would make their way back to Africa. That was a vindication to hope for, a heartening thing among his frustrations at being shuffled from one Spanish official to another.

Consul Trist was out, but a clerk brought Dr. Madden the New York papers. He pointed to a story in the New York *Sun*.

"This will interest you, sir."

Dr. Madden read the story with increasing excitement. The Africans had gained their freedom only to fall into the hands of the Americans. The Spaniards were demanding their return to Havana for trial before a Spanish court of justice. The newspaper suggested the demands would be met. They might be brought any day to a Havana jail.

Dr. Madden thought of all the misery he had seen in General Tacón's jail, of the hours he had spent there in the section called the *Gallera* by the officials, *un infierno de inmoralidad* by the Cuban people, the *Infierno* by the prisoners, innocent or guilty, confined there. The misery the Africans had undergone already would be nothing to that of the *Infierno*.

Before he left Consul Trist's office, Dr. Madden had made up his mind: He would leave his post in Havana, leave the snubs and sneers he had suffered there trying to find justice for unfortunate Africans, leave the hopelessness that never failed to force itself on him, leave Havana, where he had lost his fight for thousands—go to America, where he might help a handful.

Once the decision was made, it was easy enough for him to get the approval of his superiors, easy enough to mail his regrets and farewell to Governor General Espeleta, easy enough to dodge the formal hypocrisy extended departing Englishmen, members of the Court of Mixed Commission. . . .

XI

MEN OR PROPERTY

W. S. Holabird, United States Attorney for the District of Connecticut, was still indisposed at his home at Winsted when Ingersoll brought him the account of Judge Judson's hearing on board the *Amistad*. In a sitting room serving as a law office, a room cluttered with the books and papers of a law practice, Ingersoll waited while the old man read the documents, and then gave a more detailed account of the Africans and their condition. Every word, every deferential gesture made his own ambition clear: to follow Holabird in office.

"I fear the Abolitionists will stir up an unwarranted amount of excitement over the case," Ingersoll warned.

"Any excitement over niggers is unwarranted," Holabird snapped.

"The Spaniards seemed displeased with Judson's decision," Ingersoll continued. "They demanded possession of the schooner and slaves, and assistance in returning them to Havana."

"That would have been the wisest course, no doubt."

Over wine and food the two men discussed the case, unraveling as they could the legal entanglements, briefing it on their partial knowledge of the law of nations. Then when there was no more they could say, Ingersoll prepared to return to New Haven.

"Will you report to me any developments in New Haven?"

Holabird asked. "Much will depend on counsel employed by the Abolitionists."

When Ingersoll had gone, Holabird re-examined the documents and wrote a summary of the case to John Forsyth, Secretary of State of the United States. The particulars of the case as he had them from the documents were easy to state, his own diffidence more difficult.

"I *suppose* it will be my duty to bring them to trial," he wrote, "unless they are in some other way disposed of." Then he added hopefully, "Should you have any instructions to give on the subject, I should like to receive them as soon as may be."

During the remainder of that day and the day following, rumors of Abolitionist activity in behalf of the Africans reached Winsted. There was talk of mass meetings, of open interference to rescue the blacks from New Haven jail and send them on to Canada. Late intelligence from Hartford was that Governor Ellsworth of Connecticut himself had offered to serve as counsel for the Africans.

Whatever truth there was in the rumors, it was apparent that the Government was not likely to have the support it held in the Prudence Crandall case, that the anti-slavery movement was growing. Holabird, an appointee of an already shaky administration, a political hack who looked to his superiors rather than to himself in difficult cases, wrote a hurried letter to Felix Grundy, Attorney General of the United States.

"The Abolitionists," he said, "have already got up a great excitement on the subject. They seem determined to make capital out of the matter. They have organized with reference to the subject and have employed an army of counsel. I wish you would give me your opinion and instructions on the subject."

Holabird grew more uneasy in mind as the complications developed. He felt pushed into prosecuting a case for which he had neither the strength nor the heart—a case that should be settled in Washington. He dreaded the excitement and emotionalism of a jury trial—when not the *Amistad* Africans but the question of slavery would be on the stand. He doubted that the charge of murder could be proved against the Africans, that a jury could be found in Connecticut that would convict them.

It was with considerable relief that he received a caller the following day: Señor Antonio G. Vega, Spanish Consul at Boston, a man obviously schooled in protocol in Madrid, Havana, Washington, a royalist unperturbed in a democratic New England village.

The Spaniard was formal and to the point. "I have just received a copy of a letter which Señor Ángel Calderón de la Barca, Envoy Extraordinary and Minister Plenipotentiary of Her Catholic Majesty, the Queen of Spain, has addressed to your Secretary of State, Mr. John Forsyth, concerning the case of the schooner *Amistad*. Señor Calderón has instructed me to confer with you, as your Government's representative in Connecticut, on the matter. Are you aware of the facts in the case?"

"Only those in the reports of the hearing held by Judge Judson."

"I have not seen those reports, but I have talked to Señor Ruiz and Señor Montes."

Over glasses of wine he repeated the entire story as he had heard it from the two Spaniards.

"Ah, they have suffered much at the hands of those black beasts," he added. "They are indeed grateful to Lieutenant Gedney and Lieutenant Meade for their most providential rescue. Her Catholic Majesty herself would have every reason to be grateful to America *if* the Africans had been duly turned over to Señor Ruiz and Señor Montes to be sent to trial before a proper tribunal and by the laws of Spain, to which they are subject."

"I am personally of the opinion—"

Holabird got no farther in stating his opinion.

"It was most generous," Señor Vega continued, as if he had to get through a rehearsed speech, "of the officers of the

Washington to rescue Señor Ruiz and Señor Montes and protect their property. I must, however, protest the admittance of their salvage claim before an *incompetent* court. Don Ángel has demanded the immediate delivery of the schooner and every article found on her, including the slaves, without payment of salvage, or any other charges except those allowed in the Treaty of 1795."

"I am not aware of the terms of that treaty," Holabird fumbled.

"In that case, I will leave with you the copy I brought." Señor Vega took a printed document from his dispatch case.

"You will, of course, want to read the entire document. May I, however, take the liberty to point out the articles most pertinent to the case of the *Amistad?* I shall begin with Article 8."

Holabird leaned forward as if to ask for the document itself, but Señor Vega began reading:

"In case the subjects and inhabitants of either party, with their shipping, whether public and of war, or private and of merchants, be forced, through stress or weather, pursuits of pirates or enemies, or any other urgent necessity, for seeking of shelter and harbor, to retreat and enter into any of the rivers, bays, roads, or ports belonging to the other party, they shall be received and treated with all humanity, and enjoy all favor, protection, and help; and they shall be permitted to refresh and provide themselves, at reasonable rates, with victuals and all things needful for the subsistence of their persons, or reparation of their ships, and prosecution of their voyage; and they shall no ways be hindered from returning out of the said ports or roads, but may remove and depart when and whither they please, without any let or hindrance."

The Spaniard paused and studied the effect of his reading on Holabird.

162

"A man as astute as yourself," he said, "will see that the article I have read applies specifically to the *Amistad*. You cannot doubt that."

"On first reading it seems so."

"Then may I read Article 9. It is even more applicable to the case."

Again Holabird listened while Señor Vega read:

"All ships and merchandise, of what nature soever, which shall be rescued out of the hands of any pirates or robbers on the high seas, shall be brought into some port of either State, and shall be delivered to the custody of the officers of that port, in order to be taken care of, and restored entire to the true proprietor, as soon as due and sufficient proof shall be made concerning the property thereof."

Without waiting for Holabird to comment, Señor Vega said, "I believe Señor Ruiz and Señor Montes properly established their claims by the papers Lieutenant Gedney found on board the *Amistad*."

Holabird thumbed through his papers and found the *traspasos* and the translations Lieutenant Meade had made of them.

"Do you mean these?"

"I do. They have the official seal of Her Majesty's Government in Havana. No one can doubt their authority. There is also the question of salvage, on which Article 10 has specific instructions."

Again he read from the treaty.

"When any vessel of either party shall be wrecked, foundered, or otherwise damaged, on the coasts or within the dominion of the other, their respective subjects or citizens shall receive, as well for themselves as for their vessels and effects, the same assistance which would be due to the inhabitants of the country where the damage happens, and

shall pay the same charges and dues only as the said inhabi-
tants would be subject to pay in a like case; and if the
operations of repair should require that the whole or any
part of the cargo be unladen, they shall pay no duties,
charges, or fees, on the part which they shall relade and
carry away."

With the air of a man who has closed an argument, he handed the document to Holabird.

"I am sure that Judge Judson was not aware of the stipula-tions of the Treaty of 1795, otherwise he would not have entertained a claim of salvage against the *Amistad* and her cargo. He would have recognized that the matter was one for your General Government to negotiate."

"Has the Judge since received copies of the Treaty?"

"Not from me. I thought it best to present my case to you. I am instructed by Don Ángel to persuade you that the United States District Court of Connecticut is in this case incompetent, and that the case should in no way be consid-ered within its jurisdiction."

"What do you want me to do?"

"Convince Judge Judson of those facts. This case involves much more than the monetary value of ship and cargo. The crime is one of those which if permitted to pass unpunished would endanger the internal tranquillity and safety of the Island of Cuba, where the citizens of the United States not only carry on considerable trade, but where they possess terri-torial properties which they cultivate with the labor of Afri-can slaves. If this crime goes unpunished, these blacks will hear of it—for there are plenty of American Abolitionists to tell them—will lose no opportunity for attempting revolt. The dread of the repetition of these acts could be expected to take possession of the minds of the people residing in Cuba and Porto Rico. Then, instead of the harmony and good feel-ing existing between them and the people of the United States, sentiments of a different nature would be awakened. How can the man who promotes or advocates discord in fami-

164

lies expect to be regarded with benevolence? How can one who acts in such a manner pretend to the title of friend?"

Holabird drew back at the mention of American Abolitionists. Had he not already anticipated trouble from that quarter? But the Spaniard had not finished on that subject.

"No one is ignorant of the existence of a considerable number of persons who are employing all the means which knowledge and wealth can afford for emancipating the *Amistad* slaves, at any price. It is evident from the excitement which this occurrence has produced in the public mind, from the language used by some of the public papers in relating it, from the exertions certain persons have commenced in favor of the revolted slaves, for whose defense they have engaged some of the ablest lawyers in Boston, New Haven, New York—"

"I have read the papers," Holabird interrupted.

"Then you know that Señor Ruiz and Señor Montes have only one recourse—to apply at enormous expense to a foreign court for the restoration of their property."

"What of Señor Calderón's request to Mr. Forsyth?"

"We have some hope there. Your Secretary of State was in Madrid for some years, settling the Florida treaty. He won a high regard for himself in Her Catholic Majesty's Government, and with the Spanish people. In fact, his wide black hat, cutaway coat, and square-toed shoes became the American symbol for many Spaniards. He is not insensible to the necessity for friendship between the United States and Spain. He will not be insensible to Señor Calderón's demands—"

"Which are?"

"That the *Amistad* be immediately delivered up to her owner, together with every article found on board at the time of her capture, without payment being exacted for salvage; that it be declared that no tribunal in the United States has the right to institute proceedings against, or impose penalties upon, the subjects of Spain for crimes committed on board a Spanish vessel and in the waters of Spanish territory; that the Negroes be conveyed to Havana to be tried by the

Spanish laws which they have violated; that if, in consequence of the intervention of the authorities of Connecticut, there should be any delay in the delivery of vessel and slaves, the owners may be indemnified for any injury that may accrue to them."

Returning the papers to which he had been referring to his dispatch case, Señor Vega rose to pace about Holabird's study.

"I am instructed to say that in return Her Majesty's Government agrees to a concession—that, for the protection of United States property, slaves that have escaped to Cuba will be extradited."

Having stated his Government's case and observed with satisfaction its effect on Holabird, Señor Vega departed for Boston.

After he had gone, Holabird studied the articles of the Treaty of 1795. His conclusion was that the Africans of the *Amistad* could be regarded in only one light: as property. As such they had no rights in the courts of the United States.

The following day he wrote a second letter to John Forsyth, saying that he had examined the case more fully and arrived at the opinion that neither his nor any other district of the United States could have jurisdiction over the *Amistad* Africans. Without mentioning Señor Vega's visit, he summarized the Spaniard's opinions as his own. Then he requested Forsyth to see if by the Treaty of 1795 the vessel and blacks could not be delivered up to Spain before the court could sit. That would rid the Administration of a vexatious question.

For two days Holabird labored half-heartedly at preparing the case against the *Amistad* Africans. Then Forsyth's reply stopped his labors. Forsyth, finding himself remarkably in agreement with Holabird, had called other Cabinet members for consultation. They were all clearly of the opinion that the case was covered by the Treaty of 1795 Then Forsyth had passed Calderón's letter on to President Van Buren for his decision. Holabird felt with relief that at last the case

would be settled at the Executive level. Forsyth had indicated as much by concluding his letter with, "In the meantime you will take care that no proceedings of your circuit
court, or of any other judicial tribunal, places the vessel,
cargo, or slaves beyond the control of the Federal Executive."

In his elation at this turn of events, Holabird showed
Forsyth's letter to friends in Winchester. He sent word of it
to Ingersoll at New Haven and begged him to come immediately for consultation. Unwittingly he had thrust the club
of authority into a hornet's nest. . . .

Abolitionists from Boston to Philadelphia cried indignation at this obvious attempt of the Executive to influence the
Judiciary. They heaped abuse on Van Buren as a fence-strad-
dling opportunist, on Forsyth, the slave-owning ex-Governor
of Georgia, on Holabird as the cringing tool of a pro-slavery
Administration.

"An honest attorney," they said, "a free man, would have
replied to the Negro-driving Secretary of State that in Connecticut there is no process known by which men are kept
in prison at the pleasure of the Executive."

Friends of the Africans begged Governor Ellsworth to act
in the name of the State of Connecticut if the interference
continued. Anti-Van Buren men, looking to the next election, hoping to get the campaign for Harrison going like a
prairie fire, pointed to this as one more evidence that the
man from Kinderhook was playing puppet to his party.

In Boston John Quincy Adams openly attacked the Administration for attempting to apply pressure on the courts;
in New Haven Roger Sherman Baldwin prepared a writ of
habeas corpus, hoping to forestall the Executive; in New
York Sedgwick and Staples wrote a letter to President Van
Buren himself.

"We assert," they said, "that neither according to law of
this, nor that of their own country, can the pretended owners
of these Africans establish any legal title to them as slaves.
They were bought by Ruiz and Montes directly from the

slaver. We put the matter on the Spanish law, and affirm that Ruiz and Montes have no claim whatever under the Treaty of 1795. These Negroes have only obeyed the dictates of self-defense, and liberated themselves from illegal restraint. It is this question, sir, that we pray you to submit for adjudication to the tribunals of the land. It is this question that we pray may not be decided in the recesses of the cabinet, where these unfriended men can have no counsel and can produce no proof, but in the halls of Justice, with the safeguards that she throws around the unfriended and the oppressed. . . ."

Men or property?

That question still remained, but it was overshadowed by this new attack on Constitutional principles—an attack that roused men to action regardless of their sentiments on slavery. . . .

XII

PALAVER AT HARTFORD

Marghru was awakened at dawn by Mrs. Pendleton, who came to the children's room carrying a candle in one hand and a bowl of porridge in the other. "Marghru, Ka-le, Teme, Kene," she called them by name. Then she put the porridge on a stand and told them to put on their clothes and long woolen stockings.

While they were eating, she went out. In a few minutes she came again, this time bringing a pair of roughly cobbled shoes for each child. The children looked at the shoes and began laughing. Mrs. Pendleton urged them to put them on. They sat on their bed and pulled the shoes over their rough woolen stockings. Then Mrs. Pendleton showed them how to lace and tie them. Marghru had hers tied first and sat stroking the stove-black leather. Then, when Mrs. Pendleton had gone again, they hobbled about the room getting used to the shoes, trying to imitate the sturdy clump, clump of her step.

While they were still stepping exaggeratedly and laughing at every step, Colonel Pendleton came for them and took them to the compartment on the second floor of the jail, where all the Africans able to walk were shuffling about painfully in new shoes.

"Where you take us?" Burnah asked Colonel Pendleton.

"To Hartford for the trial."

Burnah was not sure he understood.

169

"Palaver?" he asked.

"Yes, palaver," Colonel Pendleton assured him.

Burnah explained Colonel Pendleton's words to the others.

"Cinqué? Cinqué?" they asked. Would Cinqué go with them?

Colonel Pendleton shook his head and tried to explain to them that Cinqué would be brought up by stagecoach Monday. Burnah was unable to understand fully. His words to the other Africans filled them with ominous forebodings. Were they being taken away to death? If so, why was Cinqué being left behind? Why were the two sick men in the hospital cell not going? The children began weeping and begging to be left in jail.

Colonel Pendleton lined them up in a column of twos. There was one missing. He called their names from a sheet of paper, and shouted "Foone." But Foone did not answer. Colonel Pendleton and his wife searched through the jail till they found Foone hiding in a hall closet. They dragged him out shivering with fright, chattering in Mendi, and made him take his place in the column.

Burnah said, "Foone say Foone go home."

Then Colonel Pendleton marched the captives out of the jail, past the Tontine Hotel, to the Farmington Canal Basin near Long Wharf. In their new shoes they hobbled and halted, making laughter for the Saturday morning crowds gathered to watch them go.

He marched them onto a waiting canal boat and seated them in two rows on benches facing each other on the upper deck. Then he made each wrap himself in a white blanket against the morning chill. They looked like strange white birds with shiny black heads.

A boatman hitched three white horses one behind the other to the boat. He mounted the horse nearest the boat and shouted farewell to the crowd gathered on the dock. The captain blew a blast on his boathorn and the horses moved slowly along the towpath. The children laughed in amazement. They had seen boats driven by oars and sails, but never by anything like the three beautiful white horses.

Out of New Haven they went, through fields and woods, up the valley, past Sleeping Giant Mountain. The air was cool and crisp, the green of the hills tinged lightly with the yellow of maple, the red of dogwood. All along the way the boatman blew his pleasant-sounding horn. Word had passed around that the African cannibals would pass that way. At villages and drawbridges crowds gathered to watch them pass, murderers and pirates on their way to trial. "Are they guilty? Will they kill them?" they asked each other.

The boat stopped in Bristol Basin at Plainville and Colonel Pendleton ordered them to step from the upper deck to the dock. Marghru watched the others go. Then she stooped down and dusted her shoes with the hem of her skirt. Her skirt drawn up to her ankles, her new shoes showing, she stepped proudly after the others.

Colonel Pendleton shouted for the crowds to stand back. Then he marched the Africans to wagons waiting to take them the remaining fourteen miles to Hartford.

Along the road people stood near their farmhouses to watch the strange procession pass. In Hartford hundreds of people lined the road leading to the jail in Meeting House Yard. Among them were men who had traveled as much as a hundred miles to see the Africans and attend their trial. With them, as with the people all the way from New Haven, the question was "Will they be put to death for murdering the Captain?"

From the wagons they marched to Hartford jail. There they were lodged in a large room, around which were cells filled with white and colored prisoners. The room was entirely bare, and the Africans huddled together in the middle and settled on their blankets. Afraid to talk, afraid to answer the prisoners who jeered from their cells, they waited through the night.

On Sunday visitors from white churches came and held services in which they prayed and sang. The Africans did not understand; they sat mutely through hymn and prayer. Then the jailer opened the door to visitors, charging them twelve and a half cents each to see the cannibals. All afternoon the people filed through. As their numbers increased, the Africans became more alarmed. Was this the ritual before the execution?

The next day Cinqué arrived with Norris Wilcox. The Africans welcomed him with shouts and laughter and much cracking of fingers.

"Cinqué! Cinqué!" the children shouted and clung to his hands.

Somberly he told them that he thought their time to die had come. But when they told him the wonders of their boat trip to Hartford, he lost his serious mien. Then, sitting on the floor with the others gathered around him, he described his trip from New Haven in the stagecoach. Soon he had them laughing. For the moment they were eager children alive to the wonders of civilization—not a gang of desperate criminals awaiting trial for murder and piracy.

Lewis Tappan arrived in Hartford the morning announced for the trial, tired from the overnight boat trip from New York to New Haven and the stage trip from New Haven to Hartford. When he came to the State House, where the Circuit Court was to meet, he saw posted on the door a notice of libel, signed by United States Marshal Norris Wilcox, enumerating various articles found on board the *Amistad*, including the Africans among the other effects. A group of men idly read the list.

"What if they are decided to be property?" Lewis Tappan asked the men. "Consider the sight of them placed on a block on the Green in front of the State House."

Here and there were men roughly dressed for the trek West, men who had pulled up stakes in Connecticut and Massachusetts to settle claims in Michigan, Illinois, Iowa, Kansas, men who would take the slavery fight into new territory. His words set them to thinking. The cry of the slave auctioneer had been stilled in Hartford: it must be stilled across the land.

Tappan found that Circuit Court had already opened. Judge Smith Thompson not having arrived, Judge Judson presided and delivered the charge to the Grand Jury. He avoided bringing up the *Amistad* case, but intimated that Judge Thompson would have something to say about it on his arrival. Having no interest in the case on contracts being heard by Judge Judson, Tappan went to see for himself the projects he had begun in behalf of the Africans.

He went first to the City Hotel, where he found Amos Townsend in his room.

"Are your plans ready?" Tappan asked.

"They are. We have places to hide them in Farmington till we can start them north."

"And men to help take them from Wilcox and Pendleton?"

"About twenty. We could have taken them easily on the road from Plainville to Hartford."

"That was too early. We still must give the courts a chance at justice. If they fail, then we can kidnap—nay, we must. We commit murder if we allow them to be returned to Cuba."

"This is strange business for a man of your years and wealth."

"I have seen much in those years. I have seen my house burned, my family abused. I have seen wealth tightly held slip through the fingers like sand. I know there are only two things to be desired—freedom on earth, peace in heaven. That is enough for an old man to know."

Tappan rose, took Townsend's hand, and studied his face intently. Townsend was young, barely past his majority, but Tappan had placed much faith in him. Now, when the testing had come, his grip was firm, his eyes steadfast.

"I know you will not fail these poor unfortunates," Tappan said.

Tappan then went to the jail, where he had to push his way through the crowd milling about, waiting to pay their fee and see the cannibals. He found the captives huddled fearfully on blankets in the middle of the large room. Spectators broke out of line, filled half the room. White and colored criminals looked through their bars and jeered at the crowds. The children clung to Cinqué.

When Cinqué saw Lewis Tappan, he rose and took his hand in the American manner.

"Massa, Massa," he said. "White man friend."

Marghru pulled at his hand, held up her new shoes for him to see. Laughter from the spectators woke Tappan to new wrath.

"Why are these Africans on exhibition like animals?" he shouted at the Hartford jailer. "Why are the children in jail at all? They are not implicated in the criminal charge."

Leaving the jailers and spectators open-mouthed at his anger, Tappan went in search of the lawyers he had hired to defend the Africans. Surely the little girls would be released on a writ of *habeas corpus* and removed from the evil influences of a common jail.

He found Baldwin, Staples and Sedgwick at work in the counsel chambers of the State House.

"We have no time to lose," Tappan told them. "The Spanish Government has demanded the prisoners. Our Government will doubtless surrender them if they can—and quickly. Van Buren wants to be rid of the case before it can become an election issue. Have you prepared a writ of *habeas corpus?*"

"Yes."

"Have you prepared a separate one for the little girls?"

"No."

"I advise you to prepare one immediately so we can present it to the Court at the earliest opportunity. It may be we can get the whole case argued on a *habeas corpus* writ. If the Government does try to surrender them, we may have to use other measures. The great danger is that Wilcox will take them away at night and put them on some ship for the Spaniards."

174

"Have you taken precautions?"

"Amos Townsend is keeping watch on Wilcox. He has recruited some twenty trusted men to guard the jail day and night—to kidnap the Africans if they must. If we could get them out on bail, the distance to Canada could be covered—"

On Thursday afternoon the Court Room was crowded with spectators—men, women, children—mostly whites, with here and there a black face gleaming from the New England paleness. Outside on the tree-lined Green, in the shadow of the classical State House, while they waited for the doors to open, they had argued themselves hoarse over the Africans, and divided themselves emotionally on the question of slavery as effectively as the Mason-Dixon Line divided the North from the South. Now, with the stillness of an audience waiting for the curtain to rise on a great tragedy, they waited for the trial to open.

It was known that Judge Thompson would preside, Judge Judson having quitted the bench of the Circuit Court to open the District Court for the filing of libels by all interested persons. It was known also that the Court would hear argument on a writ of *habeas corpus* on the three little girls. Judge Thompson had stated at the filing of the writ that all matters regarding the case might come up at the hearing. The fate of the Africans might be settled that afternoon.

Lewis Tappan worked his way through the crowd and found Simeon Jocelyn near the front of the Court.

"I have just come from the District Court," he whispered. "Gedney and Meade filed their libel praying for salvage. Have you heard what value they place on the Africans?"

"No."

"Twenty-five thousand dollars."

"They wouldn't bring it at auction—in New Orleans or anywhere else."

"Ellsworth filed a libel for Captain Green of Sag Harbor and Hungerford filed for Ruiz and Montes."

175

"A sorry business for Governor Ellsworth to be engaged in."

"I thought so too, but he has to maintain his private practice. His income from the State is not enough. And he has shown himself friendly to the Africans' cause. Holabird's position is much worse—representing the Administration. He filed a claim on two distinct grounds—that the Africans had been claimed by the Government of Spain and ought to be retained till the pleasure of the Executive might be known, and that they should be held subject to the disposition of the President to be retransported to Africa under the Act of 1819. In either case, control would be in the hands of the Executive. Holabird seems closely linked to Judson in this affair."

"And Judson?"

"As pro-Administration and anti-Negro as ever. The only worthwhile thing he said at the hearing was that there was no power by which the District Court could sell men, women, and children. Perhaps he has come to realize the anomaly of trying to sell slaves in a free state—"

His speech was broken by Colonel Pendleton and the three little girls, entering the Court Room through a side door. At the sight of the staring people the little girls held on to Colonel Pendleton and wept as though they approached the executioner's stand. Colonel Pendleton offered them apples and tried to quiet them. They wailed louder. Lewis Tappan took Marghru's hand and helped Colonel Pendleton to seat them.

When the Court Room was quiet again, Ingersoll read Marshal Wilcox's return to the *habeas corpus* writ. Then he spoke to the Court.

"Your Honor, I present for your consideration a warrant in behalf of the United States against certain persons named therein for murder and piracy, alleged to have been committed on board the *Amistad*. On that warrant these three girls were ordered to recognize in the sum of one hundred

176

dollars each to appear as witnesses, in default of which they were committed to New Haven jail."

A sympathetic wave swept the audience. Heads leaned toward heads. Whispers rippled against the brown-stained walls. These little girls witnesses to murder and piracy! One hundred dollars bail? Who would expect them to have one hundred dollars?

Ingersoll, unaware of the indignation his comment had caused, continued.

"Lieutenant Gedney of the *Washington* has presented a libel for salvage, in which these girls were seized as *part of the cargo* of the *Amistad,* as appears by the return of the Marshal on the warrant issued by the District Court."

"Cargo indeed," the whispers ran.

"Bales of goods!"

"Bolts of cloth!"

"Has the Marshal forgot we are in Connecticut?"

Judge Thompson rapped for order. Ingersoll went on speaking, undeterred by the spectators.

"Señor Montes, a Spanish gentleman, has presented a libel claiming these girls as his slaves and valued at thirteen hundred dollars. He has claimed that these slaves were legally purchased in the Island of Cuba, where slavery is allowed. He has claimed that according to treaties existing between the United States and Spain they ought to be delivered up to him, without loss."

At the mention of Señor Montes, the spectators turned to stare at the old man, sitting comfortably, brazenly with Señor Ruiz and Señor Vega, surrounded by the American lawyers they had employed to defend their claims.

"The District Attorney of the United States has presented a claim stating that the proper representative of the Queen of Spain has demanded the restoration of these persons as the property of Spanish subjects. As the Attorney on behalf of the United States he is asking this Court to try the issue on the claim of the Spanish Minister, and if it should appear that they should be given up, to make an order accordingly.

But if it should appear that they were illegally imported into the United States, I pray that the Court make an order to enable the President to send them back to Africa under the Act of 1819, which provides that Africans taken on board American vessels engaged in the slave trade may be sent back to their native land by direction of the President."

When Ingersoll sat down, the counsel for the Africans conferred quickly with Tappan and Jocelyn. The *habeas corpus* writ had brought the whole case into argument. In spite of their feverish preparations they were not ready. Their only recourse, they agreed, was to request Judge Thompson to adjourn Court until the following morning.

The spectators, led to expect more of the session, were loath to leave. They collected in groups, arguing for the Spaniards, against the Spaniards, for the Africans, against them. Then when Simeon Jocelyn announced a *God palaver* with the Africans in jail, enough to fill the large room went over and joined in the hymns and prayers.

When the Court opened on Friday morning the three little girls, wrapped in their white blankets, occupied a bench directly in front of Judge Thompson. Theodore Sedgwick, chosen by the defense to reply to the Marshal's return, looked at them long enough for the drama of the situation to take effect, swept the audience briefly with his eyes, and then addressed Judge Thompson.

"Your Honor, these three little girls are not now and never have been slaves, or the property of Don Pedro Montes. They were born at some place in the Senegambia District in Africa. Last April they were seized by Don Pedro Montes or his agents or some other persons and illegally put on board a Portuguese or Spanish vessel, and carried to the Island of Cuba, in the dominions of the Queen of Spain, contrary to the laws of nations and nature, and contrary to the laws of Spain."

His voice, resounding, filled with emotion, pity, made the

Fig. 8 Building in Farmington, Connecticut, used as quarters by Africans. (Courtesy of the Village Library of Farmington, Connecticut.)

Fig. 9 Kitchen directory listing names of the Africans. (Courtesy of the Village Library of Farmington, Connecticut.)

Fig. 10 Portrait of Josiah Willard Gibbs. (Francis Bicknell Carpenter, "Josiah Willard Gibbs," Yale University Art Gallery.)

spectators lean forward. At last they were to hear some oratory—not the flat monotone of Ingersoll.

"When they arrived at Cuba, they were secretly and privately landed and taken to a secret place, from which they were taken at night by Don Pedro Montes or his agents and put on board the schooner *Amistad*. After being at sea for two or three months they were brought to the port of New London, where they were seized by the Marshal of the District of Connecticut and imprisoned. The importation of these three little girls from Africa was contrary to the laws of Spain, as appears from the decree of the King of Spain, issued in December, 1817, prohibiting the African slave trade, and the further ordinance of the Queen of Spain of November, 1838, directing measures to be taken to carry into effect the decree of 1817—"

"What proof have you of these allegations?" Judge Thompson asked.

"Your Honor, I have here an affidavit signed by John Ferry, a native African, who has seen and conversed with these little girls. He affirms that they are native Africans, from seven to nine years of age, and that they can speak neither Spanish nor Portuguese."

He looked at Señor Montes and Señor Ruiz sitting with their counsel.

"Perhaps some Spanish gentleman would like to address them in his own language?"

The spectators laughed. Ingersoll was on his feet in an instant.

"Your Honor, if the Court please, I would make the suggestion whether your honors will go into this inquiry, on the writ of *habeas corpus*, while the merits of the case are pending before another tribunal, the District Court. In the cause now pending before that Court these important and intricate questions are to be settled. Will this honorable Court, on a writ of *habeas corpus*, take the whole case out of the hands of the District Court, in this summary manner, instead of taking the case by appeal, if they shall be dissatisfied with the decision of the District Court? Manifest injustice might thus be done. Questions may arise in the course of these trials involving the faith of treaties and the rights of individuals wherein great injustice might be done if they are decided in this summary way—"

Thinking this a move by the Administration to keep the case within Judge Judson's jurisdiction, Baldwin sprang to his feet with an objection.

"May it please the Court, the gentleman has gone forward and presented a preliminary question upon which he asks the honorable Court to dismiss the *habeas corpus*. The grounds on which this writ is brought are that they are illegally held under the process of the Court of the United States, which has no jurisdiction over them, and that they are held in custody not as *persons* but as *property*—as mere chattels to be kept in custody till other parties, litigating questions in which they have no interest, can come to a conclusion of their case. This may take one year, or five years."

"These persons are held under commitment to appear as witnesses in a criminal case," Judge Thompson reminded him.

"If the Court please," Baldwin replied, "we propose to offer surety for their appearance—"

Baldwin's speech was interrupted by the entrance of the Grand Jury into the Court. Obviously perplexed, the Foreman read a statement of facts in the *Amistad* case which sounded like a summary taken from Hyde's articles in the New London *Gazette*. Judge Thompson accepted the statement, and then announced that instructions to the Grand Jury would be given at the afternoon session.

Baldwin waited for the Grand Jury to file out. Then he resumed his quiet, scholarly examination of the case.

"Here are three children, between the ages of seven and nine, who are proved to be native Africans, who cannot speak our own language or the Spanish language, or any language but their own native African. Does not this honorable Court see they cannot be slaves? How is it that our

180

Courts are called upon, on the mere suggestion of Lieutenant Gedney, or of these Spanish gentlemen, to treat them as slaves? Do our own laws tolerate the African slave trade? Have they not for years regarded and treated all engaged in it as pirates—enemies of the human race? Do they not brand them with infamy? Are we to set aside our laws at the request of these Spanish gentlemen?"

Ingersoll tried to object, but Judge Thompson overruled.

"What claim to salvage upon these children has Lieutenant Gedney? What claim has an officer of the United States Navy for reducing to the condition of slavery men and children whom he found free in fact? Is this a duty imposed by law on our Naval officers? Are they to come into our Courts and claim a reward for restoring free Africans to slavery? This is what Lieutenant Gedney asks this Court—to say that he has performed a meritorious service, not in saving the lives of these persons, but in saving these slaves to these Spanish gentlemen.

"Here is the cargo of a vessel in the hands of thirty or forty Negroes claiming to be free. They are brought into the State of Connecticut and libeled as property. What is the Judge to do? Is he to issue his warrant, directing the Marshal to sell those persons as property? Let us carry out the warrant, and I think it will appear that the District Judge had no idea of including the persons as part of the cargo. Suppose an application had been made for an order to sell the property as perishable—for some of these poor Africans have died since they were taken. Suppose those Spanish gentlemen had claimed that, like other property, the persons were to be sold. His Honor, Judge Judson, remarked when he saw the return of the Marshal yesterday that there was no power in the District Court to sell men, women, and children."

"If that be so," Judge Thompson said, "they are not taken nor held at all under the process of that Court for salvage, and it is unnecessary to argue that question. The simple question before this Court is whether there are any legal questions pending to justify the Court in holding them."

Baldwin knew he had won an important point. So did friends and enemies in the audience. But there remained still the libel before the District Court to hold them on the claim of the Spanish Minister, and that of Don Pedro Montes, claiming them as property. He attacked the claim of Montes first.

"I ask on what pretense Don Pedro Montes can come into this Court and ask us to reduce these persons to slavery. Where did he get possession of them? Who brought them to him? They were brought to Cuba by pirates, in violation of the laws of Spain. Don Pedro comes here himself as a man who is encouraging this foul traffic. How much better is the man who purchases stolen property than the one who steals it? But here are stolen men, brought in by pirates, purchased by this man—how much better is he to be regarded in this Court than if the original slaver had been brought here? Would the Court allow the claim of the man who stole these human beings from Africa, if he should come here and ask the Court to restore his property? I think that upon every principle these persons must be declared free, and that they cannot be sent back to the District Court because that Court has no jurisdiction over them."

Baldwin's quiet, impassioned plea brought hope that Judge Thompson would settle the case immediately. But Ingersoll raised new questions on the enigma of slavery in America.

"We have been told," he said, "that these persons cannot be considered as property because this is a free country. We are before a Court acting for a peculiar kind of government. In a part of these States slaves are recognized as property. It is idle for the gentleman to stand here and say they are *persons* and therefore not *property*. The suggestion that Don Pedro Montes ever engaged in the African slave trade, or knew persons engaged in slave trade, or knew that these persons have been brought from Africa is utterly unfounded and entirely gratuitous. The Attorney of the United States has with great propriety filed his libel that, if under the treaty with Spain, we are bound to restore them, the public faith should be unimpaired; but if not, such an order should be made under the laws of the United States as will enable them to return to Africa. We think this Court will not, in this summary manner, take the case out of the District Court."

At the conclusion of his argument, Judge Thompson adjourned the Court for noon recess—a recess in which counsel for the Africans hurriedly assembled fresh arguments in behalf of their clients.

When the afternoon session opened, every inch of space in the Court Room was taken. Word had passed around that Cinqué and some of the other cannibals would appear in their own defense. The spectators were disappointed to see only the little girls, wrapped in their blankets, staring with finger-in-mouth wonder. Only Marghru, who had overcome her fears somewhat, returned the smiles of the ladies near her.

When the Grand Jury filed in, the Court Room became quiet, tense, waiting for the Foreman's address to Judge Thompson, waiting for Judge Thompson's decision. The question of jurisdiction was to be settled immediately. They would soon know whether the Africans would be tried for murder.

"The general rule of the law," Judge Thompson said, "is that the Courts of the United States have jurisdiction only of offenses against the laws of the United States. In addition, there may be offenses committed against the laws of nations, of which the courts of all nations have jurisdiction."

His voice droned, but his words were magic.

"These persons were apprehended within the District of New York; and, therefore, under no circumstances could these persons be tried for murder and piracy in the District of Connecticut. The offense was committed on a Spanish vessel, with a Spanish crew and commander, a mere coasting vessel on the Island of Cuba. The Courts of the United States have no more jurisdiction than if the offense had been committed on Cuban soil. I have no hesitation in telling you that, under the statement of facts presented, this Court has no jurisdiction; and that there is not enough by which you could found an indictment."

His decision stirred the spectators to excited whispering, handshaking. The Africans would not be tried on capital charges. Connecticut would not witness the execution of Cinqué. The Grand Jury filed out. Before the excitement could die down, Staples rose to address the Court, to press the advantage gained.

"Your Honor, I was prepared to speak of the order which held these three little girls as witnesses on charges of murder and piracy. But that question has now been disposed of. The last ground on which they may be detained is the libel of Don Pedro Montes through the District Attorney. As to the claim of the District Attorney, he acts here in some manner in aid of the movements of the Minister of Spain. How, we know not."

His words aroused fresh excitement. There had been rumors of Holabird's duplicity, but no one expected open charges in the Court Room. It was a bold move by the defense. But those who expected to measure the effect on Holabird's face were disappointed. He sat with his head slightly bowed, his hand on his cane.

"He also acts for the Executive of the United States on the supposition that these Africans may fall into his hands," Staples continued. "On that subject the law is perfectly clear. If these slaves were not brought in here by American citizens, or in American vessels, the President of the United States has nothing to do with them. This is the case of a Spanish vessel, forced in by necessity. Has the Spanish Minister anything to do with this case? I think not. When the owner is present making his claim, no minister can interfere. Don Pedro Montes sits in this Court, thus disposing of the claim of the Spanish Consul and Minister. Likewise, where the claimants are present, the President has nothing to do with

184

the case, regardless of the articles of the treaty cited by the Spanish Consul."

Holabird was the center of attention. Surely he would speak now, answer his attacker. But he remained with his head bowed, his hand on his cane. After a pause which gave Holabird ample opportunity to speak, William Hungerford, counsel for Señor Montes, addressed the Court.

"Your Honor, whether this man could or could not acquire property in these slaves is the question. If slavery is allowed in Cuba, he could become owner of them. It seems to follow as necessary and right that we stand on the common law of that country, which is that slavery is recognized as legal and proper. There could be no difficulty, therefore, in acquiring property in the persons of Africans brought into Cuba. With the treaty arrangements on the subject of slave trade, we have nothing to do. In addition, we are told that these persons cannot come before this Court—that this Court has no jurisdiction. If I understand the treaty between this Government and Spain, it is obvious that we are bound to surrender all property to the Spanish claimant. How is it to be done? They do not have to be sold as property. They can be surrendered to the Spanish claimants by the President, or by an order from this Court. I see no difference."

Consideration of his argument was interrupted by Holabird, who at last rose to address the Court.

"I stand here," he said, "to contend that these blacks are freemen—that they have been brought within the jurisdiction of the United States, and may be holden to abide the decision of the proper authority, and if found to be, as I suppose, native Africans, they may be sent to their own native land. On that contention I filed the libel in behalf of the United States."

What new ruse is this? friends of the Africans asked themselves. Was it to get possession of the blacks and then surrender them to the Spaniards? Was it purely political—a public acknowledgment by the Administration of Abolitionist strength—a vote catcher for the coming election? While they puzzled, Staples answered for the defense.

"The District Attorney reminds me of the saying, 'Save me from my friends, and I will take care of my enemies.' It is contended that these Africans are property. If they are property why cannot they be sold as such? Why cannot they have a slave market in the city of Hartford, and sell by auction these forty Africans! Why? Because it would be too revolting—because it would not be borne. As to the claim set up by the District Attorney for the United States, I am suspicious that the Spanish Minister had more influence with this officer than did the President of the United States himself."

Holabird refusing to reply, counsel for all claimants suddenly closed their arguments, and Judge Thompson recessed the Court briefly before giving his decision on the writ of *habeas corpus.*

"My feelings," Judge Thompson said to a packed Court Room, "are personally as abhorrent to the system of slavery as those of any man here, but I must, on my oath, pronounce what the laws are on this subject. The true question then is as to the law, and not as to any of the questions involved in the case. The important question is as to the place of seizure. It seems to be agreed by the counsel on both sides that the seizure was actually made in the District of New York. If that be the case, this District Court has no jurisdiction of it whatever. If it should be decided that the District Court here have no jurisdiction, they can decide also that the cause be transferred to the District of New York. The Court would in that case send vessel and cargo to that Court. No benefit would arise to them in being removed. However, I shall direct the District Attorney to go with a member of the defense counsel to Montauk Point to investigate the facts and determine if possible where the seizure was actually made. The Court does not undertake to decide that these persons have no right to their freedom, but leave that matter in litigation in the District Court, subject to appeal. I therefore deny the motion for the writ of *habeas corpus*."

"Do you mean to say," Baldwin asked heatedly, "that a foreigner coming here with a slave can call upon the United States Courts to enforce the claim of the foreigner to that slave?"

"I do not feel called upon to decide that abstract question," Judge Thompson snapped. "The Court is adjourned."

Baffled, dissatisfied, uneasy, the people filed out of the Court. There had been no clear-cut decision—no assurance of justice. The question of Executive interference rankled them. The Africans would not be tried in Connecticut for murder, but they might still be turned over to the Spaniards by the President. If not, the case might be kept in court until justice would be lost.

Lewis Tappan joined other friends of the Africans at the counsel table.

"I presume," Baldwin said, "the Court would allow the prisoners to be discharged on giving bail."

"That would have to be on their appraisment as property," Tappan replied. "I will not consent to that. I'd rather see them remanded to the jail in New Haven. At least that will show the people of Connecticut the extent of their entanglements in the guilt and dangers of slavery."

Lewis Tappan left the State House with John Ferry and went to the jail to tell the Africans that they could not yet go free—that the system of slavery still had them bound.

When he was admitted he heard excited chattering from the Africans and the voice of Thomas Gallaudet trying to quiet them.

Gallaudet, founder of the first school for deaf and dumb in Connecticut, a thin-faced man with narrow spectacles and hair like pigs' bristles, had worked out a sign language for conversing with the Africans. During the afternoon he had been trying to discover their idea of a Supreme Being as the judge and rewarder of human actions. He had directed their attention to natural objects: the sun, moon, stars, wind. They answered that they understood all these things and that Ngil-li was above all.

Then Gallaudet conveyed the idea of murder by cutting the throat and asked if Ngil-li would punish for that also. When they caught the meaning, they cast their eyes down and refused to talk to him any more.

"Beware of him," Cinqué told them. "He is from the Spaniards and wants a confession of what happened on the schooner."

That had started the uproar. When Cinqué saw Lewis Tappan, he ran forward and clasped his hands. Then he pointed to Gallaudet and drew his hand across his throat. The Africans threw themselves to the floor, crying and begging Tappan for deliverance from Gallaudet.

With the help of John Ferry, Tappan explained Gallaudet's purpose to them. When they were quiet again, he explained that they were not yet free, that they would soon go on the canal boat to New Haven jail.

While he was still with them, Roger Sherman Baldwin came to the jail.

"I have just learned," he told Tappan, "that Lieutenant Meade has filed a damage suit for fifty thousand dollars against you in Boston because you publicly suggested that he took the doubloons from the trunks at Montauk."

XIII

NEW ENGLAND DURESS

Cinqué watched without anxiety as Colonel Pendleton marched his comrades out of the Hartford jail, leaving him alone on his blanket in the large room. Lewis Tappan had promised they would all meet again in New Haven. New Haven jail seemed a pleasanter place than the one in Hartford. There at least he could buy a cup of wine from the bar, with money given him by his white friends.

Cinqué did not have long to wait in Hartford. United States Marshal Wilcox came to take him to New Haven on the afternoon stage. The stagecoach was filled with white passengers, among whom Cinqué recognized Amos Townsend, Lewis Tappan's friend. Because of the objections of some passengers to riding with a colored man, Cinqué was not allowed to ride inside. He climbed up to the seat beside the driver, a man as black as himself.

When Cinqué spoke to him in Mendi, the driver laughed. "How come you use that talk on me?" he asked.

Then, knowing Cinqué could not understand him, he told his own story, his voice shaded with condescension toward the bush African. He had been born in South Carolina, trained as a house servant, and brought to New Haven to serve white guests stopping at The Pavilion. Now he was a citizen of New Haven, a free man of color, in good standing with passengers on the Hartford stage.

When the stagecoach stopped at the City Hotel in Hartford, the driver handed the reins to Cinqué and alighted to help passengers. Cinqué sat with the reins in his hands, imagining himself a free man with beautiful horses to drive and the splendid clothes of a coachman. He took a handful of silver coins from his pocket and studied them. Would they be enough to buy the driver's long black coat and beaver hat?

On the way to New Haven the driver allowed Cinqué to hold the reins on easy stretches of road. As rigs go it was a poor one, and the road was narrow, but Cinqué's mind was on the splendor of himself guiding the horses as the coach lumbered along.

"Look at the black prince," people said to each other from the roadside. He did indeed look like a black prince, proud and arrogant on his stagecoach throne.

His triumph did not extend into New Haven, as the driver took the reins outside the village and guided the horses to the regular stage stop at the Tontine Hotel. It was a pleasant afternoon, the sun setting clear, a fine blue from autumn fires enveloping the town, the smell of leaf smoke refreshing after the dust of the road.

A crowd had formed a ring on the Village Green, and from his stagecoach seat Cinqué could see Grabo, Kimbo, Bato, and Ka-le playing an African leaping game, while the other Africans and Colonel Pendleton watched in a body. When Grabo turned a somersault, the crowd laughed and cheered. Cinqué was impatient to be among them. When the stage stopped, he leapt to the ground and kept some paces ahead of Norris Wilcox across the Green.

Cinqué called to his friends in Mendi, and the circle parted to receive him. The Africans shouted "Cinqué!" and stopped their game. Cinqué walked to the center of the ring and turned a somersault. The crowd cheered. He was much better than Grabo. Their applause set him going. He jumped, wheeled, turned handsprings backward and forward, walked on his hands, all with a grace of movement and rhythm that caused the white spectators to shower him with coins. He turned a cartwheel, stopped, drew himself to full height, and with great dignity stepped back among the Africans while Ka-le and Kimbo gathered the coins and brought them to him.

The sun having set, Colonel Pendleton stopped the games and herded them back to jail. They trailed across the street and through the tavern, where a few men drank wine by the light of whale-oil lamps. Instead of returning Cinqué to the cell with the common prisoners, Colonel Pendleton took him to the second-story cells with the others. He left the connecting doors open and they all gathered in one cell to talk over the change brought about by their trip to Hartford.

Mrs. Pendleton came to the cell calling "Antonio! Antonio!" She found him in a cell alone. "Antonio," she said, "you will work with me in the tavern and kitchen."

Then she took Kimbo and Foone with her to help Antonio bring back supper for the Africans.

While they were eating, Cinqué held up a silver coin to Antonio and said "Rum." Antonio took the coin and a few minutes later brought him a tin cup of wine. Once started, Antonio made the trip from cell to tavern with frequency until his pockets were well filled and the Africans were in a deep sleep.

The following afternoon Norris Wilcox distributed new suits of warm clothing to the logy, irritable Africans—clothing ordered by Judge Thompson as a part of the better treatment for the Africans while they awaited trial before the District Court. After he had gone, they dressed themselves and Cinqué sent Antonio to the bar for wine.

Many trips later, Mrs. Pendleton had Kimbo and Foone bring a big boiler of potatoes to the cell. Each African was allowed two on his pewter plate. Cinqué sat looking at the brown skins. Then he made signs for Mrs. Pendleton to peel them for him.

"Peel banana," he commanded in broken English.

191

"I don't peel potatoes for niggers," she said. "Peel it yourself."

Angered at her use of *nigger*, Cinqué spoke to her sharply in Mendi. She stood her ground, and ordered him to peel his potatoes. Afraid of this white woman who talked like a man, afraid to show weakness before his comrades, Cinqué turned to Foone, cuffed him on the head, and told him to peel the potatoes. Foone peeled the two potatoes and laid them on Cinqué's plate. Cinqué took one and bit into it. Finding it dry and like sawdust in his mouth, he made signs to Mrs. Pendleton that she should bring gravy.

"Hunger needs no sauce," she said. "Eat your potato and shut up."

Not looking at him, she went ahead with her task of dividing out food.

Cinqué cuffed Foone again and sent him to the jail kitchen for a bowl of gravy. When Mrs. Pendleton saw Cinqué with the bowl of gravy, she took it from him and placed it outside the door beyond his reach. Cinqué again made signs that the potatoes and gravy should meet.

She shook her head angrily. "You're drunk," she screeched, "dog drunk. What you need is a blacksnake whip across your shoulders."

Cinqué threw his plate of potatoes at her feet and stalked to his bunk, sulking.

A few minutes later Mrs. Pendleton was reporting the incident to her husband's customers, among whom were the editor of the *Columbian Register* and a popular phrenologist.

"The Abolitionists are filling him with stubbornness and pride," she complained.

Slight as the incident was, these critics of the Africans expanded it to make Cinqué a savage beast. They fanned indignation with the story that he had threatened a white lady. They used it as an argument against Abolitionists. They used it as argument for turning the Africans over to their Spanish masters, who would know how to treat them. As they talked, the editor's mind was busy shaping the details for the New York press.

The phrenologist used it as payment on a professional grudge. "This will show Fletcher up," he said. "This will show how false his analysis of Cinqué was." He turned to the editor. "Will you ask him in your paper to determine whether his bad behavior grew out of his benevolence, veneration, conscientiousness, comparison, or form—his bumps which Fletcher designated as large—or the effect of appetitiveness and indulgence?"

There was no good word for Cinqué around the bar that night. Even the mildest of his critics said, "He is a child and the Abolitionists are spoiling him."

Professor Gibbs, hearing these stories, was convinced that most of the misunderstandings lay in faulty communication. With a good interpreter the Africans could be persuaded to forsake their pagan customs, to adapt themselves to the New England way of life. John Ferry, inadequate from the first, had returned to New York. His search in New Haven had ended in failure. There was nothing left but to take the boat to New York and comb the water front for a person who could speak Mendi.

For two days he wandered along the docks on East River from the Fulton Slip to the Battery looking for colored men who would respond to his raised fingers and careful counting: *eta, fili, kiau-wa*. . . . Everywhere he met incomprehension, or laughter from Negroes proud of their ability to speak English.

"Why don't you try the *Buzzard?*" a ship's captain he met at Coenties Slip asked. "She's a British slave patrol schooner . . . laid up in Quarantine, with two prizes."

Early the next morning Professor Gibbs hired a boat and went to Quarantine below New York. Ahead of him lay the green bluffs of Staten Island, behind him the Dutch houses of lower Manhattan. In Quarantine he found three schooners riding easily at anchor. Two, the *Eagle* and the *Clara*, flew the American flag. *H.B.M. Buzzard* proudly floated the British Union Jack.

As his boat drew near, Professor Gibbs saw some Negro youths mending sails on the *Buzzard*'s deck. Impatiently he held up a finger and called out *"Eta."*

The word brought the Negroes running to the rail.

"You speak Mendi?" one of them asked in English.

"No," Professor Gibbs shouted. "Do you?"

"Yes, sir. I am from Mendi."

While they called numerals back and forth, Professor Gibbs' boat came near and he excitedly grasped the rope from the *Buzzard*'s rail.

"What is your name?" he asked.

"James Covey."

"Who is your Captain?"

"Captain Fitzgerald. Will you speak to him?"

A white man joined the Negro boys looking down from the schooner.

"I am Captain Fitzgerald, at your service. Will you come aboard?"

His men lowered a rope ladder. With some steadying from below and tugging from above, he arrived on deck, looking rumpled, awkward, unsteady on the swaying deck.

"I am Professor Josiah Willard Gibbs of Yale College," he said to Captain Fitzgerald. "You may have heard of the *Amistad* case."

"I have indeed."

"The *Amistad* Africans are in jail in New Haven, and I am looking for an interpreter. This boy," he pointed to James Covey, "says he is Mendi."

"I believe that is right, James?"

"Yes, sir."

"How did you learn English?" Professor Gibbs asked him.

"I was born in the village called Gho-rum in the Mendi country and lived there with my father and mother. When I was a child I was kidnapped and sold at the factory of Don Pedro Blanco. When we were three days from Gallinas we were captured by a British schooner and taken to Sierra Leone, where I was placed in the asylum for liberated Africans. There I went to school to the missionaries and studied the English language."

"Do you write English?"

"As well as I speak it."

"How old are you?"

"Eighteen."

"How long have you been on the *Buzzard?*"

"I took him on board when I arrived at Sierra Leone last October," Captain Fitzgerald intervened.

Professor Gibbs turned to Captain Fitzgerald.

"Would it be possible to take him to New Haven long enough to get the full story from the *Amistad* Africans?"

"Certainly, sir. We cannot possibly get clearance for sailing within three weeks."

While James Covey went below to prepare for the trip to New Haven, Captain Fitzgerald took Professor Gibbs to his cabin for tea and talk. Not often during his stay in New York had he found a sympathetic ear. The nature of his work made Americans shun him along the water front.

"This is a rotten affair," he said when they were seated over their tea, the Captain sun-reddened and rough, the Professor pale and scholarly. "This American attitude toward the slave trade."

"I don't understand—"

"You would not, unless you had seen what I have seen." His voice had a compelling tone. "Perhaps I should tell you my story, if you have the time."

"I cannot get a boat to New Haven until afternoon."

"It's a long story, and not a pleasant one. I left England last October for the Slave Coast with a crew of fifty men. At Sierra Leone I added twenty blacks. Then I joined the dozen other British cruisers in the slave patrol. It was the dry season and there was work for all of us. My first prize was a Sandy Hook pilot boat, the *Circe*. She had sixteen men on board, all Spanish and Portuguese. As she had no Negroes on board,

I had to release her, though she was proceeding from Gallinas to Núñez, obviously in search of a cargo. That was before I knew how close Sandy Hook is to the heart of the American trade," he added bitterly.

"Then, after a brisk fight, I boarded the Spanish brig *Emprendedor*. She had four hundred and seventy slaves and had left Gallinas that morning. I took her to Sierra Leone and placed the slaves in an asylum."

"Is that the usual procedure with recovered slaves?"

"Yes—at least for those taken on Spanish vessels. The case is judged by the Court of Mixed Commission. Then the slaves are kept in Sierra Leone and taught the English language and a trade. Some of them get back to their own tribes, but the danger of recapture is great."

"Is Sierra Leone a good place for them to stay?"

"Better than Cuban sugar plantations or Texas cotton fields. Out on patrol again, I boarded the *Eagle*, though she was flying the American flag. She had a Spanish crew and an American master, Captain Joshua Littig of Baltimore. She had no slaves on board, but was loaded with rice, copper boilers, and lumber for constructing slave decks. She had Spanish papers and a power of attorney signed by Consul Trist in Havana giving Captain Littig power to sell or dispose of schooner and cargo. I concluded she was a slaver and the American flag a foil, but did not detain her at the time."

"Have you authority to board vessels flying the American flag?"

"Only if we have reason to believe they are using the flag falsely. A few days later I boarded the *Clara*, Captain Hooker master, off the River Núñez. She had no slaves aboard, but was equipped for the trade. She had Spanish papers but flew the American flag. Captain Hooker, an insolent, unreasonable man from New York State, threatened to have the United States Government protest the boarding. In spite of his threats, I took her under sail for Sierra Leone. On the way, we fell in with the *Eagle* again, still without a slave cargo but under American colors. Determined to put a stop to this prostitution of the American flag, I decided to bring both schooners to New York and prosecute their masters."

"Have you been successful?"

"Less than I expected. I lodged complaints in the proper courts against Hooker and Littig. Then I went to Washington. Through the influence of Mr. Fox I was permitted to see President Van Buren and give a personal account of the part American ships play in the slave traffic. Van Buren treated me like an impostor. He refused to accept the prizes, saying that he considered them Spanish vessels in spite of the fact that they flew the American flag. It was futile talking to him."

"What became of the suits?"

"Some Abolitionist papers took up the case. Hooker committed suicide rather than face the charges. Littig has been indicted, but I doubt if there is enough sentiment against him to secure a conviction."

"What will you do now?"

"The American Government will not let me dispose of the prizes here. As soon as I get clearance I will take them to Bermuda and try to get them condemned."

"Then will you return to the Slave Coast?"

"Yes. I have been away too long."

"Do you feel so strongly for black men?"

"Yes. Any humane man must, once he has seen them on the slave deck. But it is also a profession with me. I get five pounds sterling for each slave I present to the Court of Mixed Commission. The months I have lost have been expensive."

Their talk was interrupted by James Covey, coming to report that he was ready to travel. Professor Gibbs took Captain Fitzgerald's hand warmly.

"This has been most enlightening," he said, "and I am embarrassed for the use to which the American flag is put. How long may I keep Covey?"

"A week, ten days. I can arrange leave for as long as you need him."

On the boat to New Haven that afternoon Professor Gibbs and James Covey labored over a Mendi vocabulary.

Early the next morning Professor Gibbs walked across the Village Green from Yale College with George Day and James Covey. Before leaving New York, he had taken Covey to Lewis Tappan and reported the results of his visit to the *Buzzard*. They had agreed that a school for teaching the Mendis the English language and Christian moral doctrine should be started at once. With the approval of the Friends of the Africans, Professor Gibbs had employed George Day, a Yale divinity student, as the teacher.

They arrived at the jail and asked to speak to the Africans.

"They are at breakfast," Colonel Pendleton replied. "Can you wait till they have finished?"

But the Africans had seen James Covey standing in the passageway. They shouted to him in Mendi, and when he responded in their tongue, they began laughing and shouting like children. They rushed past Colonel Pendleton and dragged Covey inside the cell, storming him with questions about home.

When they had calmed down somewhat, Professor Gibbs began an orderly interrogation of Cinqué, and, with the remarkably good assistance of James Covey, established full details of his story. When he had finished, Cinqué expressed a wish.

"If you were in my country and could not talk with anybody, you would want to learn our language. I want to learn yours."

"We want to teach you," George Day assured him. Then he turned to Colonel Pendleton. "The Committee for the Africans have decided to establish a school—with your approval of course—and have engaged me as the teacher."

"It is agreeable with me so long as it does not interfere with their work. Perhaps you know they will be moved to Westville soon. This building is to be torn down to make way for a new city hall. Mrs. Pendleton has undertaken to teach the little girls housework. I expect to occupy the men part of each day working about the buildings and on the farm at Westville. I can set aside two hours each day for schooling."

"That will be acceptable for teaching them to read and write English," Professor Gibbs said, "if we can have evening periods for instructing them in the Bible and Christian principles."

It was arranged then that, until the removal to Westville could be accomplished, George Day would teach them at the jail from ten to twelve each morning for five days a week. Then in the evenings and on Sundays friends of the Africans could meet in the jail for *God palaver.*

A routine, once established, soon palls. Two hours in the morning chopping wood, cleaning rooms, polishing shoes for Colonel Pendleton and his family; two hours of struggling with the peculiar sounds and difficult script of English; a brief time at play on the Village Green with spectators laughing and pitching coins; a longer time at afternoon chores— then the long evenings when the Africans squatted, native fashion, in their cell while New England ministers and divinity students prayed, sang, lectured them on how to be good children of God, a God mysterious, indeterminate, never once seen in the shape of a fetish.

James Covey, left behind indefinitely when the *Buzzard* sailed for Bermuda, took his work with George Day seriously, devoutly. Together they labored at shaping pagan minds to a New England mold. Mission trained himself, a zealous convert to Calvinism, Covey wrung every possible moral meaning from prayers and sermons and hymns. At the same time, he was exact in conveying Colonel Pendleton's commands to the Africans.

Then in the times when they were left alone, when even James Covey left them, they tried to throw off the severity of jail and New England, tried to recapture for a brief time the freedom of an African village, where the gods were less strict, the devils more benign.

On such a night Colonel Pendleton had joined the villagers in a political rally on the Green. All day long carpenters had worked erecting a log cabin across from the jail. When darkness came, men gathered carrying lighted torches. A band struck up a Tippecanoe march and soon a torchlight procession was circling the log cabin, shouting their battle cry, "Tippecanoe and Tyler too."

The Africans, watching the torches, hearing the incessant thump of the drum, began talking of home, of the family and friends they had left behind, recalling their celebrations at planting time and harvest. They called Antonio, and for the money they had, he brought them a gallon jug of rum from the bar.

As they drank, their talk grew faster and louder. The drum outside stopped, the marchers cupped their ears to political speeches. Konoma, near the door, began beating a low rhythm on the wall with his bare hands. Then Cinqué began singing a song of home—the song that lives in every heart, every language around the world, the song that makes a red rock in Ambon, a *nipa* hut in Luzon, a brick cottage on Long Island the symbol of what is most precious on earth.

The longing for home grew more intense, the rhythm increased, and soon they were dancing, slowly at first and then in wild gyrations that shook the jail.

Mrs. Pendleton came running through the passageway with Antonio at her heels. Whale-oil lamps threw her grotesque shadow across the grotesque pattern of dancers.

"Stop that heathen racket," she shrieked.

They kept on with their singing and dancing. She grabbed the jug—empty now—from Foone's hands.

"Stop! Stop!" She threatened them with the jug, swung above her head.

They laughed at her without missing word or beat.

"If you don't stop, I'll send for Colonel Pendleton."

By now they could not stop. When she slammed the door behind her, they laughed louder, leapt more wildly.

A few minutes later the door jerked open again and Colonel Pendleton faced them, a long leather whip in his hand.

"Stop it, stop it," he shouted. A few stopped and slunk away into the shadows of the cell. But Cinqué, Grabo, Kimbo kept on dancing and singing defiantly, while Konoma stamped a rhythm with his rough boots.

Colonel Pendleton was shouting at all the "heathern niggers," but he had chosen Cinqué to bear the punishment. When Cinqué danced by again, Colonel Pendleton wrapped the stinging whip around his shoulders.

"Stop it, you black devil," he shouted.

The cut of the whip brought Cinqué to a quick halt. Again he faced a white man, and the white man held a lash. Again the Wuja was crying in his ears, "Kill the white man!" Don Pedro Blanco, Captain Ferrer, Colonel Pendleton—their faces merged in a whirling mass of hate. He raised his hands to strike, and then dropped them. He could not fight back, and his comrades would suffer because of him. But this was no time to flinch. Proudly he faced Colonel Pendleton and waited for his punishment.

Seeing Cinqué had given in, Colonel Pendleton let words and whip fly.

"I give you meat."

Crack!

"I give you clothes."

Crack!

"Everything you have, I gave you all."

Crack!

"And this I get for gratitude. You insult my wife. You defy my word. You disturb the peace with your heathern yelling. . . ."

For them, for him the orgy suddenly passed. He let the whip drop and faced a quiet, defeated group of black men.

"I am sorry for you," Kin-na said. "You do not think of God."

Colonel Pendleton raised his hand to slap him, but thought better of it. Instead, he placed Cinqué in solitary confinement and locked their cells for the night.

Then he went down to his tavern to face a group of Abolitionists drawn from the Green by the noise, a group quieter than Colonel Pendleton expected. They had heard too much to be indignant, enough to know chastiser and chastised were weak human vessels.

They could not make Colonel Pendleton promise not to whip the Africans, but they did make him promise not to sell them any more liquor.

XIV

VOICE OF THE TOMBS

Dissatisfied with the results of the decisions at Hartford, distrusting what the Executive might do with the Africans, Lewis Tappan and Roger Sherman Baldwin decided that a delaying action was necessary. The logical step was to have the Africans bring charges against Ruiz and Montes in a civil suit—in Connecticut if possible, in New York if the Spaniards were found there. It was a desperate measure, for a court might declare them slaves, and a slave could have no remedies by civil action against his master.

Their decision was made imperative by the change in Spanish ministers at Washington. The imperious Calderón had been replaced by the more imperious, more arrogant Chevalier de Argaiz. He was a little man with a fiery temper and a royalist's scorn for the ways of democracy. His manner of speaking to the President of the United States shocked even the enemies of Van Buren. He repeated the demands made by Calderón on Secretary of State Forsyth in a tone that made the friends of the Africans fear the Administration would accede to his demands. They had to work fast. At any moment the case might be dropped in the District Court, and Van Buren would be free to surrender them to the Spaniards.

Lewis Tappan, in New Haven, took affidavits before Samuel J. Hitchcock, Judge of the New Haven County Court, from Cinqué, Fuleh, and Foone, charging assault and battery and false imprisonment. Then he traced the Spaniards from Hartford to Boston to New York.

To make the litigation as complicated as possible, and to test the question of whether the Africans were to be regarded as free or slave, he had Staples and Sedgwick present the affidavits to different courts. Judge Inglis of the Court of Common Pleas granted one process, Chief Justice Jones of the Supreme Court granted the other.

On October 17, 1839, Lewis Tappan accompanied Deputy Sheriff Joseph Keen to the Spanish Hotel at 65 Fulton Street, New York, where they found Señor Ruiz and Señor Montes enjoying an excellent noon meal with the manager. At the sight of Tappan, who had become a familiar figure to them at Hartford, the Spaniards rose quickly, a look of aversion on their faces.

"*Cabrón,*" Ruiz flung at him.

"You are under arrest," Keen told them, "on charges entered by the Africans of the *Amistad.*"

"At the instigation of this man?" Ruiz demanded.

"That I cannot say—"

"It must be so. Otherwise, why would he be here?"

"I have no wish to argue. I am instructed to arrest you and give you an opportunity to arrange bail before I take you to jail."

Ruiz, less debonair in anger, explained to Montes what was wanted. Both men abused Tappan in Spanish, but they offered no protest to the arrest.

Tappan told Keen to offer to accompany them to the Spanish Consul or to any of their friends who might furnish bail.

"We will go to Señor Granja," Ruiz told them.

From the Spanish Hotel they went to the office of Señor Granja in Liberty Street. There Ruiz and Montes, with the full indulgence of Joseph Keen, described the nature of the suit to Señor Granja, a Spanish merchant of considerable means.

"The bail will be set at one thousand dollars each," Keen informed them.

"I will go bail in any amount," Señor Granja immediately offered.

Keen left Ruiz and Montes at liberty in the office of Señor Granja and went to the Sheriff's Office to verify the acceptability of Señor Granja for bail. Tappan took a chair in a corner and resigned himself to the flood of abuse rising from the Spaniards.

When Keen returned, he found Mr. Purroy, counsel for the Spaniards at Hartford, joined with them around Señor Granja's desk, adding his blame of trouble-making Abolitionists.

"Your bond is acceptable," Keen reported.

"Then if you will permit me to have consultation with my clients," Mr. Purroy said to Keen.

Keen and Tappan stepped outside for half an hour. Then Mr. Purroy called them in again.

"My clients have concluded to go to jail," he told them.

Ruiz looked at Tappan with cold hatred, and then turned to Keen.

"I have seen your common jail that you call 'The Tombs,'" he said. "It is an ugly, dreary place—not the kind of residence for Spanish gentlemen. We will go to your jail. There we will enlist more sympathy for ourselves among right-thinking people. Our voices will be heard ten times as far—from prison."

"Señor Granja is entirely acceptable as bail," Keen reminded him.

"We will go to jail," Ruiz insisted. "We will see if your National Government will not interfere."

Tappan turned directly to Ruiz. The bitterness against these Spanish slave traders he had held inside him so long suddenly burst forth.

"If I could have my wish," he said, "I would send both of you to Africa with the blacks and let you be tried before a tribal court. Cinqué's father is a judge. I would have him judge your case—your crimes against black men."

The Spaniards laughed a hard mocking laugh.

205

"Come," Ruiz said gaily, "let us be led to jail."

Ruiz and Montes led the way, followed by Keen and Tappan and then Granja and Purroy. They came to the jail, which had been in use no longer than a year. Gloomy as it was, it was a show place, admired as a splendid work of art, the purest specimen of Coptic architecture outside Egypt. But, inspired as it was by a picture of an Egyptian tomb in a popular travel book, it was called "The Tombs" by those who found themselves locked inside.

A puzzled turnkey opened the cell block and watched Keen lead the two immaculately dressed Spaniards inside. Tappan, on his first visit to the jail, took in details quickly. The building was oblong, about fifty feet wide and three times as long. There were four tiers of cells, assigned, as he learned, according to the prisoners' ability to pay for special privilege. In the first tier, thieves, drunkards, women of the street rattled bars and shouted curses. Boy prisoners played games in the cell-encircled court. On the second tier, at a point from which they could see all one hundred and forty-one cells in the jail, a group of evangelists were singing the opening hymn of their afternoon jail service.

Keen took the two Spaniards to a cell in the fourth tier—a cell obviously reserved for affluent prisoners. In contrast to the gloomy exterior, this compartment was comfortably furnished with beds, chairs—extra ones for visitors—pictures, and clean linen. Here they could be comfortable, read, entertain their friends, order any food or drink they wished to pay for —all a part of the indulgence the Sheriff had ordered. They were above the noise of the first tier, but the thin voice of the evangelist raised in supplication over lost sheep made the jail another kind of *Infierno* for the Spaniards.

With Ruiz and Montes in jail, Lewis Tappan set about getting stronger support for the Africans' cause. He wrote letters begging for donations, he talked before churches and Abolitionist societies.

To Ellis Gray Loring in Boston he wrote: "If the judges

are firm there will be no difficulty. But they fear losing their popularity. How easy it is for them to blind themselves to justice if the rights concerned belong to a black man."

Publicly he denounced the legal profession, the men who, if they were really devoted to the Constitution, could press the fight for humanity.

"How few lawyers there are," he thundered from the Broadway Tabernacle pulpit, "who possess a high character for learning, eloquence, moral and physical deep feeling for the oppressed, and great weight of character."

To Simeon Jocelyn, in the privacy of his office, he spoke his concern for the counsel they had employed for the Africans.

"Sedgwick has learning, physical courage, a respectable character. But he does not argue cases well. His words drop soft like water when they should be molten steel."

"He is better than Staples—showed to better advantage at Hartford at least," Jocelyn reminded him.

"As a man, yes. Staples has shown that he does not feel the foundation principles of human rights. He has never been stirred to fervor for the cause of black men. I have tried to kindle a fire under him, but the heat dies away before any effect can be felt."

"Then we must depend on Baldwin."

"In the District Court of Connecticut only. He will be unable to come to New York. In this case we have to depend upon Sedgwick and Staples."

Lewis Tappan was at his desk in the warehouse going over details of the case with Sedgwick and Staples when Señor Vega arrived from Boston.

"I have come to you—the persecutor of Señor Ruiz and Señor Montes," Señor Vega said to Tappan. "Only you are responsible for their being arrested and lodged in a common jail."

"My responsibility is to the helpless Africans—"

"Few Americans think so. They recognize your action for

what it is—a ruse to further complicate matters. Who is this *Pipi* named in Cinqué's affidavit?"

"Señor Ruiz."

"Then I accuse you of having had them falsely arrested. There is no person called *Pipi*. Señor Ruiz is familiarly known as *Pepe*, as persons named José around the world are called. Thus it appears that through your ignorance a *Pepe* has been imprisoned instead of a *Pipi*, which I believe the law does not permit."

Tappan looked at Sedgwick and Staples for help. They could give none, neither knowing the Spanish language or Spanish customs of giving nicknames.

"I have here a copy of a letter the Chevalier de Argaiz has sent to Mr. Forsyth," Señor Vega continued. "He is well aware of how flimsy are the charges against Señor Ruiz and Señor Montes. He is also aware of the difficulty the Africans will have in proving their cause. The courts in the State of New York cannot possibly have jurisdiction. The Africans in the deposition declared their state of slavery by admitting having been sold. He is aware that in no country and in no period in history has a slave enjoyed civil rights."

His words aroused Tappan to angry protestation, but Sedgwick signalled him to remain quiet, to hear the Spaniard out.

"The Spanish Minister," Señor Vega continued, "has asked President Van Buren himself to release Señor Ruiz and Señor Montes and to indemnify them for the losses they have suffered—"

"Who will indemnify the blacks?" Tappan demanded.

"The Chevalier de Argaiz," Señor Vega continued smoothly, ignoring Tappan's question, "has appealed to President Van Buren in consideration of Her August Majesty, the Queen of Spain, as the head of one government to another. She has only recently been made happy by the termination of a Civil War and the assurance that her August Daughter will be allowed to succeed her to the throne. To keep *her* happy, and not to make her suffer with the sufferings of Señor Ruiz and Señor Montes, the Chevalier de Argaiz has asked Mr. Forsyth to free these gentlemen on writs of *habeas corpus*. It will make Her August Majesty happy."

Tappan was unable to hold his anger longer. "Anything for that false woman in Madrid," he exploded bitterly.

"It is apparent," Sedgwick interpolated more calmly, "that the Spanish Minister is not aware of the processes of the United States Courts. President Van Buren could not interfere if he wished."

"The Spanish Minister spoke of that in his letter. He cannot understand a government in which the Chief Executive must bow to the will of an inferior court. He questions the authority of the Chief Executive under such circumstances. In short, he questions what you call *democracy*."

Long after Señor Vega had gone, Tappan, Sedgwick, and Staples puzzled over what to do in case the President intervened. Then they set to work on affidavits which would prove that, whether he was called *Pipi* or *Pepe*, José Ruiz was the object of the suit.

Judge Inglis held the preliminary hearings in chambers, neither the Spaniards nor the Africans being present. It was a prosaic hearing, with counsel for both sides presenting their claims cautiously, and a more cautious Judge deferring his decision until he could give more time to the case.

A week later Lewis Tappan went to hear Judge Inglis give his decision on the Spaniards' application for common or nominal bail. It had been a discouraging week for the friends of the Africans. Mobs had threatened Tappan and Jocelyn on the streets. Crowds hissed Tappan when he arrived at the Court, the same crowds that had cheered Ruiz and Montes.

Tappan heard the decision and then caught the boat to New Haven to report developments to Roger Sherman Baldwin. It was pleasant to sail along a shore bare with the first touches of winter, pleasant to walk the quiet streets of New Haven, with no angry voice but the wind in bare elm trees raised against him, pleasant to sit before a fire with Baldwin.

Before coming to Judge Inglis' decision, Tappan reported the discouraging news that had come from Washington.

"Forsyth has written to the Chevalier de Argaiz to inform him of President Van Buren's stand in the case. He has given the Spanish Minister to understand that under the constitution of the United States the Executive has no authority over the Judicial branch. He therefore could not interfere in the processes of the courts. That sounds good for the political record. Actually, he has offered Ruiz and Montes assistance. He assured them that under the laws the courts afford them all the necessary means of securing their freedom and whatever indemnity they are entitled to. He has gone a step farther. He has instructed Benjamin Franklin Butler, United States Attorney for the District of New York, to place himself at the disposal of the Spaniards, to offer advice and aid in securing their release and indemnity."

"Such counsel has not been offered to the Africans of the *Amistad*," Baldwin said. "What is Butler's response?"

"Butler is another Van Buren man. He has assured the Spaniards that he will render all the aid in his power."

"The Executive's actions might easily influence a Judge."

"Easily, if the Judge is pro-slavery and a party man. Van Buren had to give an infamous pledge on the subject of slavery for the support of his party. A very free man would have rejected it with scorn. Now is the collar about his neck. In the South can he vote as a free man? No, no. He is a thorough party man. and how can a party man be free? Or a party Judge? How can he show justice to a handful of unfortunate Africans?"

"Has this latest Van Buren strategy reached the papers?"

"Only one or two anti-slavery papers. The pro-slavery papers are too busy denouncing the arrest and persecution of the Spanish gentlemen, guests of the American people. Have you seen William Cullen Bryant's editorial on the subject in the *Evening Post*?"

"No."

"He says that if Señor Ruiz and Señor Montes refused bail

and went to jail to excite public sympathy, the shift will hardly help them. I believe the Spanish gentlemen realized the wisdom of his remark. At least they applied for discharge on bail."

"And the decision?"

"Judge Inglis ruled that since Señor Montes according to the affidavits was not implicated in the charge of assault and battery except as a witness, his bail should be nominal. Bail for Señor Ruiz should be reduced to two hundred and fifty dollars."

"Are they released?"

"Señor Montes has taken up residence again at the Spanish Hotel. Señor Ruiz was remanded to jail. He apparently still hopes for intervention by the United States Government."

"Did the ruling take into consideration their status as free or slave?"

"Judge Inglis did not undertake to settle that question at this hearing. He simply indicated that at this time they suffer under no disability that would make it impossible for them to sue for damages for personal injury."

Though Tappan did not know it, on the same day Chief Justice Jones of the Supreme Court had rendered a decision on the same grounds. He held Señor Ruiz to bail in the sum of two hundred and fifty dollars. He thus affirmed the jurisdiction of the Court in the right of the Africans to have their freedom and the extent of their injury sustained and passed upon by a jury.

The Chevalier de Argaiz himself came to New York for what was expected to be the final hearing in the case of Señor Ruiz. He called first on Benjamin Franklin Butler, United States Attorney for the District of New York, who impressed the Spanish Minister with his affability and willingness to help Señor Ruiz. But he had been unable to devise a scheme by which Señor Ruiz could go entirely free without due process of law through the Court.

"It should be easy to prove the illegality of his arrest," the Chevalier de Argaiz argued.

"I have a note from Mr. Vail, Acting Secretary of State, on the subject," Butler said. "The Government has instructed me to do anything within my knowledge to help the case. But I can see nothing the Government can do. The Courts of the United States, according to the treaties with Spain, cannot take jurisdiction in criminal action. But they are bound to take action in civil suits."

Butler accompanied the Chevalier de Argaiz to the hearing before Judge Inglis. The case had aroused enough curiosity for the Court Room to be filled. At the bar was Señor Ruiz, looking pale and tired, irritated beyond endurance by confinement and hymns and preaching.

At the request of Mr. Purroy, Señor Ruiz was allowed to speak in his own defense.

"Your Honor," he said, "it is necessary only to point out the facts in the matter to a person of your sagacity and penetration."

Briefly he outlined the circumstances of his purchase of the Africans. Then his defense developed into an attack against Lewis Tappan. In English at times, more frequently in Spanish, he flayed Tappan for his part in the *Amistad* affair, for trying to come between another man and his property. The attack was violent, abusive, but still no objection came from bench or counsel. He blamed Tappan for keeping the matter open, for arousing strife between the United States and Spain. He went into an attack on democracy, and ended with a question on the enigma of slavery in the United States. Apparently the Chevalier de Argaiz had drilled him well in what to say.

When he had finally finished, Sedgwick rose. "In view of the attack we have just heard, Your Honor, I request that Mr. Tappan be allowed to speak."

The request granted over Mr. Purroy's objection, Lewis Tappan stood before the court, the lines in his face deepened by sadness and hurt. He looked at Judge Inglis, and then at the Spaniards.

"I am altogether a free man, I think. I fear no man—court no man. I speak my honest opinions on all subjects, publicly or privately, whatever abuse or loss of money it may cost. Like my Divine Master, I have made myself of no reputation. I desire no office—will wear no man's collar. What I have done for these poor friendless Africans I had to do. I hope to have the love of part of the community, if need be the hatred of the rest, but I crave the respect of all."

His voice broke; he returned to his seat. The Court Room waited in silence while Judge Inglis read his decision. The case of Señor Ruiz would be held over, but he could go free on bail. Señor Montes was entirely free.

That same day Señor Montes, a tired and broken old man, left the Spanish Hotel and walked alone to the docks, where the schooner *Texas* waited to take him to Havana. He went gladly, willing to leave to the hands of others the fate of three little girls and one boy. His voice had not prevailed beyond "The Tombs."

XV

DON ESCRÚPULO

Outward bound, the schooner *Texas* passed a Yankee trader from Havana, bearing a cargo of molasses and one passenger, Dr. Richard Robert Madden, for New York.

Dr. Madden stepped from the trader with the manner of a man suddenly given his freedom. In Havana his figure had been too well known, his hatred of slavery too widely publicized. Wherever he had gone, Cubans had despised him for his interference. They were weary of the English conscience forever in their midst. Even the voyage to New York on the Yankee trader had been unpleasant. He suspected her of aiding slave traders, the captain of being a slaver. He resented the cool silence with which he had been treated on board. But now he was in New York—free. His eyes would be spared the sight of Africans being sold at auction, his ears the sounds of screams from the *Infierno*.

He stopped to make a purchase from a vendor at the dock and to ask his way to Lewis Tappan's office, the address of which he read from a letter. Then he walked the short distance to the Tappan warehouse in Hanover Square.

The two men had never seen each other before, but they clasped hands like long lost friends.

"Am I too late to help the *Amistad* Negroes?" Dr. Madden asked.

"Not yet. The case is to be heard at an adjourned meeting

of the District Court of Connecticut on the third Tuesday in November."

"Good."

"You will testify in their behalf?"

"Gladly, and give the Court a picture of Cuba that will make even a Negro hater hesitate to send them there."

"God grant you can outweigh the testimony of Ruiz and Montes. Do you want to see the Africans first?"

"If it is at all convenient."

"We will go to New Haven tomorrow, and from there to Hartford. What else do you plan? Could you be persuaded to go to Washington to see Van Buren? Perhaps you could exert some influence on him through the British Minister."

"Sir, when I was here last I went to see General Jackson. I discussed with him the results of emancipation in the British West Indies. Old Hickory appeared much interested. 'General Jackson,' I told him, 'the sooner you adopt a similar measure in the United States the better.'

"The President burst out laughing, and addressing guests on either side, said, 'This gentleman has just come from the British West Indies, where the British have been emancipating their slaves. He recommends me to make myself famous by following their example.' Their laughter stirred him to say more.

" 'Come here, Donaldson,' he said to his private secretary, 'put the poker in the fire, bring in a barrel of gunpowder, and when I am placed on it give the red poker to the Doctor. He will make me famous in the twinkling of an eye.' "

Dr. Madden waited for Lewis Tappan to appreciate the anecdote.

"Then," he continued, "General Jackson scolded the Abolitionists bitterly for the trouble they were making. I doubt whether Van Buren will be more friendly. I fear he is a weak man, trying desperately to hold on to the power that is his by chance. I fear he has made up his mind to yield to the demands of the Spaniards. Or at least I gather that from the papers in Havana. I will see him nevertheless, and urge Mr.

Fox to take what measures our Government may feel wise. From there I will go to England. I will press the matter upon Queen Victoria and see what measures she will take through the American Ambassador to the Court of St. James. I have met Andrew Stephenson. He is strongly pro-slavery, and may be difficult to interest in the *Amistad* Africans."

"Stephenson belongs too much to the Administration," Tappan said. "But surely the young Queen will be touched by the suffering of these poor Africans."

Dr. Madden took from his pocket the knife he had bought from a vendor at the docks. It was a Bowie knife, with the handles finished in white bone.

"Have you seen one of these?" he asked.

Lewis Tappan took the knife in his hand and turned it slowly. "Death to Abolition," he read in black letters on the white bone.

"Our country is in a dreadful situation," he said. "Slavery is the worm at the root of the tree of liberty. If the worm is not killed, the tree will die. How can we kill slavery when the strength is so great on the other side?"

Madden and Tappan were a strange pair in New York and on their way to New Haven. Madden was Irish Catholic, and a scholar who had studied languages and customs in a dozen countries. He was a writer with numerous books to his name, a judge who had handed down significant decisions in slave cases in Sierra Leone and Havana. Tappan was a deacon in the Broadway Tabernacle, a Yankee merchant with puritanical New England upbringing.

Tappan found Madden lacking in piety, a profane man who did not hesitate to take a glass of wine, a man who poked fun at Tappan's abstemiousness. Madden gave Tappan a book of his poems on prayer, but Tappan was unable to associate the poems with their author.

When they arrived at the New Haven jail, they found the Africans at school, reciting to Professor Day with James Covey acting as interpreter. After shaking hands with Dr.

Madden, Professor Day asked him to speak to some of the Africans. He stepped up to Foone.

"*Salaam Aleikoum,*" he said. "Peace be to you."

Foone stared at him a moment, and then with his palm touching his forehead, bowed low.

"*Aleikoum Salaam,*" he replied devoutly.

"With you be peace," Dr. Madden translated for the others. "Some of these people are Mohammedans," he continued.

Day and Tappan looked as if a fiercer devil had crossed their path.

"We thought them all pagans," Day exclaimed, "not infidels!" New problems of religion impinged themselves on this young teacher who had never knowingly faced a Mohammedan before. "But we must bring them all to Christianity."

Dr. Madden's words had created equal excitement among the Africans. They gathered in groups and chattered their raucous tongue. Then he went among them saying, "*Allah Akbar.*" "God is great." To this prayer a third of them answered.

"I am fully convinced that these Africans are *bozales,*" Dr. Madden told Lewis Tappan. "I have spoken with many like them in Sierra Leone. It is not unusual to find Mohammedans among the peoples in the interior."

Then he called James Covey and had their individual stories repeated to him. Of all the stories, he lingered over Cinqué's longest.

"I have seen a man as magnificent as he is in the barracoon at *Misericordia*—the same manly bearing, the same marks of Berber blood. It may be that I saw him there. . . ."

Baldwin and Townsend came to visit Tappan and Madden at their rooms in the Tontine Hotel.

"Only six of the *Amistad* Africans and Antonio will be taken to Hartford for the trial," Baldwin said.

"That will be enough, if we can arrange to have them

plead their own case," Tappan replied. "How will they travel?"

"By stagecoach."

Tappan turned to Amos Townsend.

"Our plans are ready," the young man said. "I will follow them in another vehicle. We have men posted along the way and in Hartford to see that they are not stolen away before or after the trial. Our previous plans with the friends at Farmington will be carried out if we must resort to the Underground Railroad—"

"We want no unnecessary violence," Tappan cautioned him.

Townsend left the group and went to make arrangements for transportation for Tappan and Madden to Hartford along the route the Africans would take.

"There are some new developments in the case," Baldwin told the others. "Our request to have the case transferred to the District of New York will doubtless be denied. Holabird has been to Culloden Point to investigate and will testify before the Court that the schooner was taken on the high seas."

"Will Holabird argue the case himself?"

"I doubt it. He claims ill health and has written to Forsyth for more counsel and more money to pay for help in prosecuting the case. He went to see Van Buren in Albany and got his personal approval for extra counsel. He will no doubt place the case in the hands of Ingersoll."

"Isn't it rather unusual that a District Attorney can go directly to the Chief Executive in a case?" Tappan asked.

"It is, but there are many unusual aspects of this case."

"I trust Ingersoll even less than I trust Holabird," Tappan continued, "and Judson least of all."

"They complement each other remarkably well. Holabird has tried another ruse. He has put pressure on Gedney and Meade to withdraw their claims to salvage, and with some success. He told them that it was the wish of Van Buren to surrender the Africans to the Spanish Minister and have

218

them returned to Cuba. The only obstacles to such an action were the suits for salvage of Gedney and Meade and of Captain Green of Sag Harbor. Gedney and Meade both offered to withdraw their claims on condition that the Africans would be immediately returned to Havana—"

Tappan sprang to his feet to fight this new threat, but Baldwin continued talking.

"Fortunately I heard of the subterfuge in time to go to Sag Harbor and see Captain Green. He is an old sea captain wise in the ways of the slave trade. When I explained circumstances to him, he agreed not to withdraw his claim. Holabird has been to Sag Harbor twice to see him, but he remains steadfast. He is determined to bring the case to court. No doubt Gedney and Meade will refuse to withdraw their claim when they hear of his action."

"I have disturbing information from Washington," Tappan told them. "Through my brother, the Senator there, I have learned that Attorney General Felix Grundy has rendered an opinion on the Africans—to the effect that the United States has no jurisdiction over the case and that they should be released to the Spaniards as soon as they are free of the courts. He and Van Buren are aware of the storm such an opinion would raise, and have decided to keep it secret until after the trial at Hartford. My brother was unable to get a copy of the decision."

That evening three stagecoaches left the Tontine Hotel for Hartford. In the first were United States Marshal Wilcox, Colonel Pendleton, and the seven blacks. In the second, Amos Townsend and a group of determined men with weapons. In the third, Tappan, Baldwin, and Madden, the two Americans probing deep into the heart and mind of the Irishman, letting their own provincial minds be stirred by the breadth of the world this man had seen and known. Their great regret was that James Covey had been left behind, ill. Even if they could get Cinqué before the Court, his words would be lost without an interpreter.

The adjourned term of the District Court opened its session at ten in the morning of November 20 before Judge Andrew T. Judson. Baldwin took his place at the counsel table for the Africans, six of whom were seated behind him, their faces black and shining above their prison shirts. At another table sat Señor Vega from Boston and Mr. Purroy from New York. General Isham appeared for Gedney and Meade, and Governor Ellsworth, looking detached and correct, appeared for Captain Green. Montes was absent, now well on his way to Havana. So was Ruiz, still in jail in New York. Tappan and Madden took seats among the spectators crowding the City Court Room.

Baldwin was allowed to open.

"Your Honor," he said, "I deny that the District Court of Connecticut has jurisdiction in this case. The Africans of the *Amistad* were captured on the shore of Long Island in the State of New York, and therefore are not liable to trial in Connecticut. I further deny that they have ever been slaves. They are free men, and as such ought to be set at liberty. I will present evidence to prove that these Africans, or a part of them, were seized on shore and are therefore entitled to trial by jury."

General Isham called for testimony from Gedney and Holabird, who gave detailed accounts of their investigation into the location of the schooner when she was captured.

"I made careful examination," Holabird said, summing up, "and found that the schooner was lying clearly and decidedly upon the high seas. She was about three-fourths of a mile from shore and in three to four fathoms of water."

"The question now," Judge Judson said, "is as to the jurisdiction of the Court. The situation of the *Amistad* has to be settled by proof, and the evidence must be confined to the simple question, whether the seizure was made in the District of New York or Connecticut. You," he said to Baldwin, "may call your witnesses to the stand."

Baldwin first called Captain Green of Sag Harbor, who testified that the schooner was not more than thirty rods from shore. Then he called Peletiah Fordham, who agreed with Captain Green. An older man than Captain Green, a man of humorous face and sharp eye, he was allowed to stray beyond the question of the exact location of the schooner. He told of their traffic with the blacks, of their arrangements with Captain Green, and of the two trunks.

"Joseph Cinqué lifted one trunk," he said, "and I heard the money rattle. Me and another nigger lifted the other trunk and then I heard some more money. . . . So we determined to have the vessel at all hazards, forcibly if we can, peaceably if we must."

His last remark quickened the spectators to laughter. Judge Judson had to rap with his gavel to restore order.

Then the people looked at each other with questions in their eyes. How much gold was really on the schooner? Who got it? Where is it now? The Spaniards had testified to at least eight thousand dollars in doubloons. Remembering Lieutenant Meade's slander suit against Lewis Tappan pending in Boston, they kept quiet, while their distrust of Gedney and Meade grew.

Baldwin turned the question to how many Africans were on shore. If they could prove that most of them were, they still might stop the trial on a question of jurisdiction—have the case transferred to the District of New York, away from the rule of Andrew T. Judson.

Green and Fordham testified to more than twenty, Meade to eight. Green pointed to Burnah. "Call that nigger," he said. "He speaks English."

Instead of Burnah, General Isham called Antonio to the stand. With the craftiness of a politician, Antonio surveyed the Court Room. He saw Lieutenant Meade with an encouraging smile on his face. He saw Señor Vega and the lawyer for the Spaniards. He had heard Lieutenant Meade testify to eight. The clerk read the question to him and Meade translated it into Spanish.

"How many blacks were on shore at Culloden Point?"

"Eight," Antonio said confidently. Meade's smile was more

221

friendly, more encouarging. "Five went off in the *Amistad's* boat and three in the brig's."

Then Baldwin called Burnah. He was dressed now in woollen pantaloons and shirt. He had made a turban from a red shawl and wound it about his head. The clerk swore him to an oath he obviously did not understand. Then the clerk read the question.

"How many blacks were on shore at the time of capture?"

Frightened, bewildered by the many white faces before him, Burnah looked at the clerk blankly. He could not understand so much English.

"Have we no interpreter at all?" Judge Judson asked sharply.

Again Baldwin explained that James Covey was ill in New Haven and John Ferry had been dismissed as incompetent.

The clerk tried to convey the question with signs. Burnah shook his head that he did not understand. Then Lieutenant Meade repeated the question to Antonio in Spanish. Antonio spoke to Burnah in a mixture of English, Spanish and African.

Counsel for both sides leaned forward, waiting for his words.

"Eight," he said hesitantly.

The cause was lost. Without an interpreter it was futile to call the other Africans. The testimony of Antonio and Burnah was allowed to stand.

With the confidence of one who feels victory within his grasp, Holabird rose to press the Government's claims.

"Your Honor, the Spanish Minister has officially presented a claim to the Government of the United States, setting forth that the *Amistad,* cargo, and slaves, the property of Spanish citizens, were taken possession of by a public armed brig and brought to the jurisdictional limits of the Court under cir-cumstances such as to make it the duty of the Government to cause the property to be restored to the true owners with-out delay, as required by the treaty stipulations with Spain.

I pray that if the claim be well founded, the Court will make such order of the disposal of vessel, cargo, and slaves as would comply with our obligations to Spain and preserve the faith of the Government."

The effect of his speech on Judge Judson was apparent. Here was a bold statement of the position of the Chief Executive in the case—a position no doubt outlined by Van Buren himself in his meeting with Holabird at Albany. Judson had only to give an order and the case would be closed, the Africans moved out of reach of the Abolitionists.

But before the sound of the speech had died away, Baldwin was on his feet, pleading earnestly for a short postponement until James Covey could recover sufficiently to serve as interpreter—until Cinqué himself could be heard through Covey. The Spaniards had been given every privilege. Had the blacks not the right to be heard?

The decision turned not on Baldwin's plea, but on General Isham, who, being called home for an emergency, had to ask for postponement. Judge Judson, with an air of tiredness, postponed the case until the next meeting of the District Court of Connecticut, in New Haven on January 7, 1840.

"How can Dr. Madden be heard?" Baldwin asked. "He cannot remain in America until January."

"He can testify by deposition at two this afternoon, if it is generally agreeable," Judge Judson replied.

A small tense group gathered in the City Court Room that afternoon to hear and take the deposition of Richard Robert Madden. He, a high representative of a high culture, sat in the chair the primitive Burnah had occupied that morning. He had traveled a thousand miles to help bring justice to a group of ignorant Africans, and that devotion to justice was not lost on at least some of those present. Quietly, patiently he waited for his time to speak.

Facing him was District Attorney Holabird, heavy of body, heavy of mind, his concept of justice shaped by the prejudices of the nation in which he lived.

223

With the skill of a man long experienced in giving and taking testimony, Dr. Madden told of his work on the Court of Mixed Commission in Sierra Leone and Havana and of his recent visit to the captives in New Haven jail. Then, taking a translation of the *traspasos* from the *Amistad,* he turned it in his hand while he explained the use of *bozal* and *ladino* among slave traders in Cuba.

"From my conversations with the Africans of the *Amistad* I am sure they are *bozales,* and that the application of *ladino* to them on the passport was a fraud on the part of the House of Martínez and those working for it."

"Have you ever visited a Cuban barracoon?" Holabird asked.

"Many times—in Havana, in Matanzas, in Santiago de Cuba."

"How many are in Havana?"

"Six or seven."

"When did you visit one last?"

"On September 24. I went to *Misericordia,* the barracoon in which the *Amistad* Africans were held prisoner. It is kept by a man named Riera. Riera being away, I talked with his major-domo, who told me the captives of the *Amistad* had been purchased in that barracoon by a man from Puerto Príncipe."

A slight rustle ran through the audience. His testimony might have bearing on the case. Dr. Madden noticed the increased interest and continued speaking in a carefully controlled voice.

"When he spoke to me of their fate the major-domo said, *'Qué lastima.* . . . What a pity it is.' Surprised at what I thought was a show of humanity on his part, I asked what he meant. 'What a pity it is the loss of so many slaves,' he said. 'They will surely be executed in the United States.' "

Holabird could see that the testimony of this one small, quiet, man had created much sympathy for the Negroes. Over and over he repeated his questions in the cross-examination, trying to make the witness appear incompetent, trying to establish some excuse for throwing out his testimony. On statement after statement he raised objections, but Judge Judson allowed the testimony to stand, with the provision that admissibility would be decided later.

Later, later, always later, the friends of the Africans thought, while they struggled harder to keep up the fight, while the Africans themselves shivered in the New Haven jail.

His testimony ended, Dr. Madden left the Court with Lewis Tappan. On the stage to New Haven, the boat to New York, they talked of what more Dr. Madden could do to help the Africans.

"I will see Van Buren," Madden said. "I cannot believe it will help, but I will see him. It will be a polite meeting, with whatever pleas I make quietly brushed aside. But I will see him. And I will see Fox. He will hear everything I have to say."

"And when you get to England?"

"When I get there I will make my report to the Queen. I doubt not she will direct a message to Van Buren. When England and Spain are in the balance, perhaps Van Buren will see the weightier side."

XVI

"GIVE US FREE"

Winter, cold, cheerless, shivering winter, with snow piled high on the Green, with ice forming in pails in their quarters at night, tried souls and bodies of the *Amistad* Africans. They talked and dreamed of dry warm December nights in the Mendi country—harvest time at home. Afraid to dance a harvest dance, they sang their harvest songs lower than the wintry wind in the elm trees outside. They begged to go home before the next rainy season.

"Wait for the palaver here in January," Lewis Tappan told them. "Then you will be free to go home."

On the sly they bought wine from Colonel Pendleton's tavern to warm their blood. They also got more blankets, and spent day and night wrapped in them. Still they complained of the cold. It was a time of misery and despair for them. Better to die, they said, than remain forever cold.

"Better for them to go to Havana as slaves than bear a New England winter," friends of the Spaniards said.

While they shivered in jail, their friends worked for their defense, making preparations that at times seemed futile because an order from the President could end their work and send the Africans off to Havana.

News from Washington trickled through to New Haven. Judge Judson's decision for delay had created dissatisfaction in the offices of the President. Both Van Buren and Forsyth had expected the trial at Hartford to end the vexing problem—that it would be closed and forgotten by the time serious campaigning for the Presidency opened. They had expressed concern that Judson had ignored their instructions in the matter. He must have been aware of what its continuance might mean in the November elections. In New Haven, friends of Van Buren publicly asked him to deny that he had tried to influence Judson, and waited in vain for the denial.

Lewis Tappan brought Baldwin a copy of Attorney General Grundy's opinion on the case, released at last at the request of Van Buren. It was a decision to stir the friends of the Africans to violent measures. He found that since not all the owners of the schooner were in the United States, a delivery could not be made to them. The case had become an argument between two governments, and should be settled by an agent of the Government rather than by a Court. The Negroes had been charged with infraction of a Spanish law, and should be tried before Spanish courts. He could see no withholding of justice even if the Negroes were not slaves. In his opinion, the only thing possible was to surrender them to the Spanish Minister, for transportation to Havana.

"My brother reports that Van Buren and Forsyth are highly pleased with Grundy's opinion," Tappan told Baldwin. "It should please the Chevalier de Argaiz and all those who sympathize with Señor Ruiz."

But it did not please the Abolitionists and friends of the Africans. It was an opinion designed to placate the Spanish Minister, and they could find no humanity in it. . . .

Señor Vega called on District Attorney Holabird at the Tontine Hotel in New Haven, where he had gone to prepare his prosecution of the Africans.

"I have seen the Chevalier de Argaiz," he said. "He is now confident the case will soon be settled amicably. Indeed, he has thought so since the Attorney General's opinion. The United States Government seems aware of our rights—"

"All proceedings to date on the part of the United States," Holabird reminded him, "have been on the assumption that Señor Ruiz and Señor Montes alone were aggrieved, and that their claim to property was founded in fact and justice—"

"But the case remains in the hands of a minor judge in an inferior court."

"No doubt Judge Judson will declare his court incompetent when the hearing opens. That is the will of the Chief Executive, I am sure."

"So the Chevalier de Argaiz was informed when he called on Secretary of State Forsyth on December 29. The meeting between them was entirely amicable, and Mr. Forsyth informed the Minister that there was no doubt as to the decision of the Court. The Africans will be surrendered to the Spanish Minister."

"I have been so informed."

"The Chevalier de Argaiz has written to Mr. Forsyth to ask further assistance of the United States Government. As you know, if the Negroes should be released to the Spanish Minister, he could not possibly transfer them to Havana. The *Amistad* is unfit to make the voyage, and it would be difficult to hire a vessel to take them. He has asked President Van Buren to transport the Africans to Cuba in a Government vessel. I am sure the President is aware that such an action would earn the gratitude of Spain, and at the same time the Government would save itself the trouble and expense of keeping the Negroes in prison longer."

Holabird studied the Spaniard's face for a moment and then spoke in a confidential tone.

"I had more recent information by the New York boat today. The President has acceded to the Spanish Minister's request. He has asked Mr. Forsyth to make all arrangements for the vessel, and for Lieutenant Gedney and Lieutenant Meade to go with the Africans to Havana to give their testimony against them. These orders are secret, and I have to pledge you to secrecy."

"On the word of a gentleman."

"Mr. Forsyth wrote to Secretary of the Navy, James K. Paulding, ordering him to have the vessel to convey the Africans to Havana anchored off New Haven when the trial opens. We fear that the Abolitionists will try to steal the Africans. He has ordered their removal from New Haven as quickly as the trial is over."

"And Señor Ruiz?"

"I believe it is the plan for Señor Ruiz to be released on bail and to proceed to Havana by a private vessel. I have been instructed that the United States schooner *Grampus*, Lieutenant Paine commanding, will convey the Africans to Havana."

"The Chevalier de Argaiz has no doubt been informed."

"I presume so. At least Mr. Forsyth wrote him saying the President had acceded to his request. The President was more readily inclined to do so because the Africans, having claimed they were not slaves, would have an opportunity in the Spanish courts to prove the truth of their allegations. . . ."

"What can we do now?"

"We can only wait for Judge Judson's ruling that the District Court of Connecticut is incompetent. . . ."

Lewis Tappan, torn between duty to the unfortunate blacks and duty to his daughter, dying of tuberculosis in New York City, bade his daughter await death firm in her hope in Christ, and shuttled back and forth between New York and New Haven. Obsessed by the necessity of freeing the Africans, he told their story to strangers on the New Haven boat, to customers in his warehouse, begged money for their defense, braved taunts and stones on New York streets in search of friends for the anti-slavery fight.

He could trust Roger Sherman Baldwin to prepare the legal arguments, but legal arguments were not enough in a case in which fear and prejudice outweighed any feeling for justice, in which the President of a nation placed foreign and party pressures above the rights of slaves. In spite of attempts to suppress it, news of Van Buren's letter to Judson had spread. In bitterness, friends of the Africans quoted Forsyth's instructions to Holabird: "You will take care that no proceeding of your circuit court, or of any other judicial tribunal, places the vessel, cargo, or slaves beyond the control of the Federal Executive." No legal argument would prevail if Judson chose to accept the orders of the President.

Rumors came from Washington that the *Grampus* had been ordered to New Haven to transport the Africans to Havana. Lieutenant Gedney and Meade carelessly let it be known that they were going to Havana to bear testimony against Cinqué. Lewis Tappan heard these developments in New York and rushed off to New Haven again. Strong measures had to be taken by the friends of the Africans.

On instructions from Tappan, Amos Townsend organized a hundred men to kidnap the Africans and start them on the Underground Railroad north if it appeared they would be sent to Havana. Townsend manned a sloop and anchored her in New Haven harbor to await the arrival of the *Grampus*. Men of New Haven and Farmington and Hartford came to his aid, among them Leonard Bacon, the minister, and Nathaniel Jocelyn, the painter. The sloop could not hope to win out in a fight with a man-o'-war, but the Africans might be rescued on Long Wharf or in boats. Friends of black men were alerted, underground stations were kept open. New Haven people anxiously awaited the trial that might end in battle.

The night before District Court opened, Lewis Tappan took James Covey with him to the jail. In a cell alone with Cinqué, their faces shadowy in candle light, Lewis Tappan instructed him on the coming palaver.

"The *Grampus* arrived in New Haven harbor tonight," Tappan told him. In detail he gave her size and complement —formidable compared with the sloop that opposed her. "She is under orders to take you and your friends back to Havana to stand trial—"

"No—no go to Havana," Cinqué pleaded. "Cinqué afraid to go to Havana." He drew his hand across his throat.

Tappan tried to console him.

"It is better for you not to go to Havana. You will no doubt be killed. We must try to save you. Mr. Baldwin will try to have you appear as a witness in your own defense. Do you understand?"

Cinqué nodded yes.

"He will also call for Grabo and Kimbo—perhaps some of the others. You must speak to save yourselves—to go home to Africa, not back to Havana. It will be better for you to speak first. Then if they speak, they must agree in every part with what you have said. Do you understand?"

Cinqué took his hand. "Yes, massa."

"I will not tell you what to say. God will tell you that."

When Lewis Tappan left the Tontine Hotel the next morning to go to the Court, he saw Captain Green and Peletiah Fordham on the steps, looking dogged and determined to have the case settled in their favor. Tappan crossed the Village Green to the stately, classical temple of justice called the State House. Yale law students, dismissed from classes to attend the trial, crowded the doors. In the Court Room spectators from as far away as Boston and New York argued with each other for standing room, most of the seats being taken by women.

The hearing opened with Antonio's testimony. Still crafty, still believing it advantageous to him to help the Spaniards and not the Africans, he testified that they had plenty of food on the *Amistad,* and that they were never mistreated. He testified that Cinqué had killed Captain Ferrer, and would have killed him had Burnah not intervened.

At the mention of Cinqué, the spectators turned again to stare at him, squatting on his haunches as he would have in the palaver room in Mani, wrapped around with a white blanket that covered him entirely except for his head, surrounded by a dozen other Africans all wrapped in blankets,

231

all staring at the white people impassively. To these New Englanders, Cinqué appeared a dull, ignorant heathen, hardly worth the storm raised over him.

When Antonio finished, District Attorney Holabird read a summary of facts relating to the case assembled by Señor Vega, Spanish Consul at Boston. He emphasized the point that there was no law in force in Cuba prohibiting the importation of slaves from Africa, and that the Court of Mixed Commission at Havana had jurisdiction only over cases of slaves captured at sea. Meticulously he showed that the *Amistad's* papers were in the usual form and genuine. Friends of the Africans watched him build the Government's case on a structure furnished by the Spanish Minister.

Counsel for Lieutenants Gedney and Meade presented their case, claiming that they were entitled to the highest rate of salvage, and that the salvage would be enhanced if the slaves were held as property according to the laws of Spain. He apparently failed to see the absurdity of trying a slave case under slave laws in a free state. Meade being absent, Gedney sat alone, his eyes straight ahead, his face slightly flushed at whispered gibes around him.

Governor Ellsworth, counsel for Captain Green, followed, and claimed salvage for arresting the Negroes on Long Island and rescuing part of the property. At the mention of the trunks filled with doubloons, the Yale students broke into laughter. Judge Judson silenced them on the protest of Gedney's counsel. Then Governor Ellsworth argued that neither the pilot nor a national ship could claim salvage for performing a duty. He said that if the Government should let the Africans go free, his client would be content. If not, his client claimed the right to participate in salvage of vessel and cargo. He insisted that Captain Green had no wish to realize gain from the Negroes themselves.

Captain Green fixed his black penetrating eyes on Gedney, looking at him as if he searched his very soul and found the answer to how they could demand salvage on the bodies of human beings—the answer, greed. The effect was not lost on Gedney, nor on the spectators.

In the afternoon Sedgwick spoke for the Africans. After reviewing the facts of the case as he had them from the Africans, he argued that Ruiz and Montes had no claim to ownership of the blacks.

"The papers they have," he shouted, "wouldn't prove ownership to a horse or a dog."

Judge Judson had to rap the audience to silence.

"There is no tribunal this side of Algiers," Sedgwick continued, "that would deprive human beings of their liberty on such proofs as have been produced in this Court."

Holabird had prepared well for this argument.

"If Señor Ruiz and Señor Montes have been engaged in illegal slave traffic, it is the duty of the United States Government to return the Africans to the Spanish authorities in order that justice may be obtained. But that is not the province of this Court. The Africans should be held for such action as the United States Government may feel proper. This is a problem of international diplomacy to be handled only by the President of the United States."

Judge Judson studied Holabird's face intently. The spectators stared at the Judge. How would he react to this blatant interference from the President? Would he remain a party man, or would he strike for the Constitution he had sworn to uphold?

But Holabird was insensitive to the questions he had raised, to the resentment against him personally. He had his eyes on Cinqué. The friends of the Africans had brought him into Court to speak. Well, let him speak. Let this dog-faced monkey make fools of the Abolitionists. Seeing that Covey was near enough to Cinqué to interpret, Holabird thundered,

"Who killed the Captain?"

Covey interpreted rapidly.

"Who killed the crew?"

Before Covey could finish, he was shouting again.

233

"Did you kill the Captain? Did you kill the cook? Did you threaten to kill this Creole boy? Did you torture Señor Montes?"

As question after question poured in upon him, closer and hotter, not mock questions like those of the Wuja but real questions that meant life or death to him, Cinqué gradually rose, propelling his weight upward with the strength of his legs, keeping his arms folded, his body erect. Then he threw the blanket aside and stood wearing the red flannel shirt and white pantaloons he had worn when he was on the *Amistad*.

The sense of wrong, of injustice, wreaked upon him and his people, of his absolute right to break all bonds and fight for freedom, overpowered him. All hesitation overcome by the storm of feeling, indignation animating every feature, he began slowly, eloquently to tell the long story from the time he was kidnapped in Mani and sold to Don Pedro Blanco to the night of the mutiny on the *Amistad*. At first James Covey kept pace with him, throwing his words like bullets at the audience, but as his feelings increased, Cinqué spoke more rapidly, more passionately, letting the words roll from his lips like a torrent. The audience no longer needed James Covey. They knew by the look on Cinqué's face, the gestures of his hands thrown forward in a striking motion or drawn to his throat like a noose that he was justifying his fight for liberty. His voice rose to a crescendo in Mendi, and then broke on English.

"Give us free! Give us free!" he shouted, entreated, implored.

Overcome by this outburst as if it were lightning from heaven, Judge, lawyers, spectators were unconscious of the impropriety of such an exhibition in a court of justice. Then Holabird saw the effect of Cinqué's words.

"I object," he shouted angrily. "Take this man out of Court. He will have an unfair influence on decisions."

"Objection sustained," Judge Judson ruled, but the effect had already been created. Not a man in the Court but knew

234

he had seen greatness in this man they called savage, cannibal, nigger, beast. . . . Lewis Tappan bowed his head in
thankfulness. Judge Judson's face seemed somehow softer.

When the Africans had been removed from the Court
Room, Roger Sherman Baldwin presented his plea in their
behalf, in a speech lasting nearly three hours. He was calm,
scholarly in his review of the whole ground of testimony,
in his analysis of the treaties binding Spain and the United
States and Spain and Great Britain. He was acid in his comments on Lieutenants Gedney and Meade, who claimed
human life for gain.

"I trust," he concluded, "the Court and Government
would rejoice to be rid of this embarrassing question. The
course of the Government in surrendering these unhappy
Africans to the Spaniards can lead only to their death in
Havana. I trust the Court will free itself from all pressures,
and act only in the interest of justice for these unfortunate
people. For them, justice lies in being returned to Africa, to
their families and homes, free to pursue their own way of
life. As for me, I can do no better than repeat the words of
Cinqué, 'Give us free!' "

When he had finished, Judge Judson sat for a moment
shading his face with his hand. Then, without looking up,
but in a voice deeply agitated, he adjourned Court until
the following Monday morning.

Meanwhile, the *Grampus* lay waiting in New Haven Harbor.

When District Attorney Holabird arrived at his room at
the Tontine Hotel, he found Lieutenant Paine of the United
States Navy waiting for him. Paine showed him the warrant
signed by President Van Buren himself ordering Marshal
Wilcox to deliver the Africans over to Lieutenant Paine.

"This warrant is not valid," Holabird pointed out immediately. "It states that the Africans are held in custody on a
process now pending before the Circuit Court. This is the
District Court. The Abolitionists could make much of that."

"What can we do?"

"Get a new warrant."

"Do we have time?"

"From Friday to Monday. Ingersoll can make it, if we get him started at once."

Holabird wrote a hasty letter to John Forsyth and enclosed the warrant for correction. Ingersoll took the night boat for New York.

"We must not let the Abolitionists know of this," Holabird warned. "They have stirred up too much trouble already."

On Monday morning Lewis Tappan took a cold walk toward Long Wharf to get a good look at the *Grampus* riding at anchor. Not far away was a sloop, her sails half set, waiting any signal from land to help rescue the Africans. On the water front, around the Green, near hotel and jail, men assembled by Amos Townsend waited for the Judge's decision. If the decision went against them, they were ready to take justice into their own hands.

Long before time for Court to open, a crowd gathered at the State House. They had seen the *Grampus* in New Haven Harbor; they knew relatives and friends manned the sloop nearby. They knew Van Buren's stand, and that Ingersoll had gone to Washington on a mysterious mission. They knew that more than the lives of a handful of Africans was at stake: a nation was on trial.

"Will the Africans be delivered to their masters, or to the Spanish Government, or will they be set free?" they asked one another.

More soberly, they asked, "What will happen when our courts are no longer free? When the President can order a Judge what decision to render?"

Ingersoll came from Long Wharf and pushed his way through the crowd to Holabird. He handed him the document.

"It is corrected," he whispered.

236

Holabird passed the word along to Lieutenant Paine, waiting in the Court Room with an armed guard from the *Grampus*. Friends of the Africans tensed themselves for the fight that now seemed inevitable.

Judge Judson, his thin face impassive, opened his Court to an audience that squeezed into every space. Enemies of the Africans, friends of the Africans—but the Africans themselves were absent. Cinqué's speech had aroused too much emotion, Judge Judson had ruled. What greater feeling might be built up when he reached the end of his decision?

Judge Judson cleared his throat. The spectators rustled forward and then settled into stillness. The paper in his hand trembled slightly, his voice rang out.

"The District Court of Connecticut has jurisdiction, the schooner having been taken possession of, in a legal sense, on the high seas."

His words brought consternation to the audience. Both sides had hoped he would decide otherwise. But he was continuing.

"The libel of Thomas R. Gedney and others is properly filed in the District Court of Connecticut. The seizers are entitled to salvage and an appraisement will be ordered. One third of that amount and cost will be decreed just and reasonable."

Señor Vega whispered an angry protest to Holabird, but Holabird ignored him.

"Green and Fordham of Sag Harbor, who claim to have taken orginal possession of vessel and cargo, cannot sustain their claim, and therefore their libels be dismissed."

Captain Green looked at Captain Fordham. "What about the doubloons?" Captain Fordham asked in a whisper that brought a rap from the bench.

"Ruiz and Montes, through the Spanish Minister, have established no title to the Africans, as they are undoubtedly *bozal* Negroes, or Negroes recently imported from Africa, in violation of the laws of Spain."

Señor Vega rose to protest. but Judge Judson motioned for him to remain silent. He stood glaring at the Judge.

"The demands of the Spanish Minister to have the question tried in Cuba cannot be complied with, as by their own laws it is certain they cannot enslave these Africans, and therefore cannot properly demand them for trial."

These words brought the spectators to their feet in excitement.

"Antonio, being a Creole, and legally a slave, and having expressed a strong wish to return to Havana, is to be restored to his Spanish owners under the Treaty of 1795."

He stopped and looked around the room. His hearers knew he had come to the most important decision of all: What to do with the Africans?

"The decision is that these Africans be delivered to the President of the United States under the Law of 1818 to be transported to Africa, there to be delivered to the agency appointed to receive them and conduct them home."

His words stirred the spectators to shouting, some in anger, some with prayers of thanksgiving that justice was at last to be done to the poor Africans. Judge Judson rapped his gavel, but the spectators would not be quieted. His words adjourning the Court were lost in the roar. Only a few thoughtful ones studied the Judge's face, trying to find the reason for his decision. Had Cinqué really stirred him to compassion? Had he at last rebelled against White House pressure? His impassive face revealed no answer as he left the Court Room to make his way back to the quiet home in Canterbury.

Holabird remained behind, trying, in a loud voice, to explain to Señor Vega that the case was not yet over—that he had instructions from the White House to appeal the decision to the Circuit Court.

Lewis Tappan made his way to the captives in jail as fast as he could go. When he arrived, Cinqué and six of the other men were together in a cell. Tappan grasped Cinqué's hand. Tears stood on his cheeks and his voice shook.

"You are free! You are free!" he cried. "Free to go back to Africa once more."

The word was like magic. Cinqué threw himself at Tappan's feet. The others fell beside him, all reaching out their hands to touch the boots of this great friend of black men. They wept with joy, their words became an incoherent jumble of native language and the English so recently learned.

"Massa," they said, "white man massa!"

When they had subsided somewhat, Tappan had all the others brought in and the news told them. Again there was a scene of wild rejoicing through which the names of African villages and African loved ones rang. Then Tappan told them what returning to Africa meant. They had been away many moons, they had learned the ways of white men.

"Would you like some of your American teachers to go with you?" he asked.

"Yes! Yes!" they cried.

He pointed to Mr. Griswold, who was standing to one side.

"Would you like Mr. Griswold to go?"

Cinqué leaped to his feet and went running to Mr. Griswold. He threw himself to the floor again.

"Go, go," he begged. "We will take care of you. We will let no one harm you."

Two visionaries who glimpsed the ideal and weighed not the cost of achieving it, Lewis Tappan and Griswold sat down to talk with the Africans of how a great missionary movement could be undertaken with these Africans as a nucleus. They saw visions of white men and women tramping darkest Africa, setting up churches and schools, converting, educating, healing. . . .

Amos Townsend and his men watched the *Grampus* slip silently out of New Haven Harbor. The tenseness had gone, but they still had to watch. While they watched, Nathaniel Jocelyn worked at his heroic portrait of Cinqué.

XVII

WESTVILLE WAITING

Their elation lasted less than a wintry afternoon. Roger Baldwin came to the jail with word that Holabird had already begun his appeal on the decision, under instructions from the Secretary of State. Holabird, a thorough party man, unable to understand Judson, another thorough party man, had let his language pass beyond the bounds of good taste, had threatened Judson with party reprisal, openly for lingering spectators to hear. Judge Judson's only response was to set January 24 as the date for hearing the plea for appeal.

What course could the case take on appeal? If the Circuit Court upheld the District Court, the Africans would be free. If the Government carried the case to the United States Supreme Court, as Holabird had openly threatened to do, their lives still remained in the balance.

People knew well the pressure that had been put on Judge Judson to surrender the Africans to the President for transportation to Havana. Judson had refused, for reasons he still kept to himself. Pressure would be placed on Judge Smith Thompson of the Circuit Court. Friends of the Africans feared he might yield. If he should reverse the decision, the Africans would go to the Spaniards. If not, the case would go to the United States Supreme Court, where Judge Thompson would again be among the presiding judges.

With depressed spirits Lewis Tappan tried to explain to Cinqué and his companions what this appeal meant. They could not understand about the palaver, but they knew what more months of waiting in jail meant.

"We want to go home," they repeated. "Merica cold."

That night Tappan and Baldwin asked for their release on bail, but their request was denied.

News of Judge Judson's decision spread quickly north, south, west. Public opinion was sharply divided on the decision. But public opinion was against keeping the Africans in jail longer.

"Let the courts work at justice as they will," people said, "those waiting should not be kept in prison."

In Washington the decision sent John Forsyth running for new instructions from Van Buren. The President was in a state of pique at having his wishes overruled, and of worry at possible repercussions among Southern voters. He had sounded sentiment north and west, and felt that pro-slavery forces still held the balance of power in free states. He dreaded facing the Spanish Minister, who could be expected to call within twenty-four hours.

Holabird met Señor Vega in New Haven for further conference on the case.

"I have heard from Mr. Forsyth again," Holabird reported. "He has been instructed by the President to make an appeal and carry the case to the Circuit Court, on the part of the decision relating to the *Amistad* Africans and the part related to salvage. The decision relating to Antonio will not be mentioned. It is well enough to let it stand. He will be returned to Havana."

"That is acceptable to the Chevalier de Argaiz," Señor Vega replied. "But the Chevalier is greatly dissatisfied with the remainder of the decision. How is it that in your country the wishes of the President can be ignored?"

The President's son John visited New York and Albany, speaking openly of the President's great dissatisfaction with the decision.

"My father feels," he said, "the case has great and impor-

241

tant political bearing of which Judge Judson has taken no notice."

Enemies of President Van Buren, political and personal, took issue with him openly on the case. Papers published statements that Van Buren had written Judson personally while he had the *Amistad* case under consideration, urging Judson to return the Africans to the Spaniards. "Such flagrant interference of the Executive with the Judiciary strikes at the roots of our system of government," the papers editorialized. Ingersoll of New Haven immediately wrote the President asking him to refute the charges, or at least to let his friends refute them before they became political fodder. He published his letter, and then burned with shame when no refutation came.

Tappan and Baldwin tried to gauge the extent of the President's embarrassment, and decided it might be great enough for him to be willing to negotiate with them directly to have the Africans freed. The President, they decided, might thus be able to extricate himself from a difficult situation. They arranged to place their negotiations in the hands of Tappan's brother Benjamin, Senator from Ohio.

After denying Senator Tappan an audience for weeks, Van Buren suddenly asked him to call.

"I saw the President this morning," Senator Tappan wrote Lewis. "He is firm in his decision to appeal to the Circuit Court. You may suppose that although he is altogether willing the business should take the course pointed out by the District Judge, it would not do to sanction the erroneous principles of that decree. Not to appeal would be to accept them by acquiescence."

Stopped on that course by the President's fence straddling, Tappan and Baldwin began preparations of alternatives on Judge Thompson's decision, scheduled for September 17.

Tappan and Baldwin had grown closer in their long fight for the Africans. Staples and Sedgwick, on the other hand, had drifted from them, though they had both agreed to remain as counsel through the Circuit Court hearing. It was obvious they were no longer ardent fighters in the cause.

"They do not appear to have dug deep into the great question, either as moralists or lawyers," Tappan told Baldwin.

One phase of their proof in the case had to do with the treaties between Spain and Great Britain on the slave trade, which Judge Judson had refused to accept as evidence because they were translations and not authenticated. Baldwin wrote Forsyth for authentication, requesting immediate reply but not expecting to receive it before the case was called.

Another question faced the friends of the Africans: What would they do in case Judge Thompson should dismiss the appeal instanter on the ground that the Spanish Minister had intruded when the parties litigant did not do so? Señor Ruiz had been released from "The Tombs" on bail and had gone to Havana. It was unlikely he would return for the hearing. Friends of the Africans were willing to let their suit against him lapse.

Under the circumstances, Tappan was sure the case could not go to the Supreme Court, no matter what the President wished. If that proved true and Judge Thompson entertained an appeal, he would have to decide finally. If he should decide against the Africans, Baldwin had to be ready with a writ of *habeas corpus*. Amos Townsend and his group had to be ready as well with their underground system to take them north.

In August, 1840, the Africans, except the three little girls, who were left to work for Mrs. Pendleton, were taken to Westville. There, at the foot of West Rock, they had the advantage of a large enclosed yard for outdoor exercise. They also had classes in reading and writing and religion, taught by Professor Day and his associates at the Yale Divinity School. They studied hard and worked hard, with Cinqué constantly driving them. He used the argument that all would be punished for the mischief of one. He also told them that they would all receive more favor if they worked hard.

Colonel Pendleton put them to work cutting wood and working in the fields. Life became dull and irksome. Visitors were rare, and there were no more gifts of coins and snuff, and no chance to buy wine.

"Tell the Merica people," Kinna said to Lewis Tappan, "that we very, very much want to go home."

They resented their isolation, with so few Americans to talk to.

"You no talk Mendi," they said. "I no talk Merica—me sick, nobody talk to me."

They found contradictions between the teachings of George Day and the behavior of Americans. Colonel Pendleton took advantage of their willingness to work. He kept them going hard from early morning to late at night. He even made them wash their own clothes on Sunday.

"Me no like work on Sabbath," Konoma told him.

"What does a nigger care for Sunday?" Colonel Pendleton retorted.

At times the retort was with a whip.

The Abolitionists were growing in numbers and strength. Their violent decade—the decade of Crandall, Garrison, Lovejoy, and Whittier—was over. At last they could hold meetings, publish papers without organized resistance. An Abolitionist might get eggs or stones thrown at him, but no longer in the North and East did whole communities rise against them. They had their members in Congress, and could bring pressure in the Legislative branch of government.

At a request from anti-slavery members, the main documents of the *Amistad* case were presented in House Document 185. The Congress was at last vitally involved in the case. Tempers rose to a high pitch. Southerners and pro-slavery members fought the introduction of the documents, but the Abolitionists won the fight.

244

A storm centered around the official translation of the Spanish *traspasos*. Someone had translated the word *ladino* as *sound*. The whole issue of whether they were *ladino* or *bozal* Negroes was negated by that translation.

Lewis Tappan, in New Haven for a conference with Baldwin, caught the error.

"Forty-nine *sound* slaves," he read to Baldwin from the document.

"That changes the complexion," Baldwin said. "It is a neat side-stepping of the issue on when they were brought from Africa."

"Who could have committed the fraud?" Tappan demanded.

"It will take a Congressional investigation to find out. Our only hope is to present the case to John Quincy Adams. His position in the House is our only advantage."

When Adams received word of the mistranslation, he demanded a complete investigation.

"I cannot suppress such a scandalous mistranslation," he shouted in anger on the floor of Congress. "On that word the lives of thirty Africans depend."

Then he asked leave to present two petitions. One was on the *Amistad,* and counter to the rule that abolition petitions should not be entertained by the House. Objections were raised against his reading it, but he read, shouting to make himself heard above the pro-slavery din. The House refused to receive the petition, and Adams left the Capitol, a saddened man, to try to get his petitions published in the *National Intelligencer.* How else could he inform the people?

One year to a day from the first trial in Hartford, on September 17, Judge Thompson read his decision upholding the District Court. District Attorney Holabird heard the decision and immediately appealed the case to the Supreme Court, as he had been instructed by Van Buren and Forsyth.

The friends of the Africans knew they had to gird themselves for one last fight.

The Supreme Court would not meet until January, weeks after the November elections, but the effect of the appeal, friends of Van Buren hoped, would be to allay doubts of pro-slavery voters. On election day Van Buren could count in votes how valuable the fight had been to him.

Wearily Lewis Tappan and Roger Sherman Baldwin made the trip from Hartford to New Haven to pick up the threads of the case, to prepare for the last fight. Sadly Tappan told the Africans at Westville that their waiting was not yet over —that they must spend another bitter winter in New Haven. So many had died already. How many will die before we are free? they asked him.

In New London, Marshal Wilcox sold the *Amistad* under a process from the District Court. The schooner soon lost her identity in a busy New England harbor. Only her name remained as a symbol.

In New Haven, rumors spread that Colonel Pendleton had decided to keep Marghru as a slave for Mrs. Pendleton, and had offered Teme and Kene for sale as soon as the litigation was over. Whether the rumor was to be believed or not, those who came and went at the County House could see that the Pendletons had many personal services from the three girls and Antonio.

XVIII

OLD MAN ELOQUENT

The appeal before the Supreme Court a certainty, the friends of the Africans met in New Haven to plan their fight. Lewis Tappan, harassed by financial worries, distressed by the illness of his daughter, which had now reached terminal stages, was the dominant figure in the little group in Baldwin's office. Simeon Jocelyn and Joshua Leavitt supported him in his purpose to fight with every legal measure, and if legality failed, to steal the Africans away and send them to freedom in Canada.

Staples had asked to be relieved, on the grounds that his own business was too pressing. Tappan was not disposed to retain him longer, being dissatisfied with his showing, regretting his lack of moral conviction, his lack of fire.

"Who will take his place?" Jocelyn asked.

Baldwin and Sedgwick would stay on to the termination of the matter. At least Baldwin would. Sedgwick had stayed away from this meeting, perhaps to show his unwillingness to continue the fight. Tappan, fearing to trust him in a battle before the Supreme Court, expressed little regret at his absence. But there must be someone to assist Baldwin. Who could best assist in preparing and presenting an impassioned plea for freedom?

"Rufus Choate of Boston would serve," Leavitt suggested.

"Mr. Choate is a good man and an able lawyer," Baldwin said, "but in precarious health and might not be persuaded to go. If he did, he might break down at a strategic moment. His appearances before the Supreme Court have been relatively few in his old age."

"At the moment I can think of no other," Tappan said. "We must ask him. In the meantime, we must consider arguments before the Court—"

"The Supreme Court may reject the appeal," Baldwin interrupted, "on the grounds that no United States Court has jurisdiction. Or it may reject it on the grounds that the controversy over the Africans has now resolved itself to a question of property. If so, the Africans would not be valuable enough for the Supreme Court to consider."

"How much would they have to be valued at?"

"To confer jurisdiction of the Supreme Court, they would have to be valued at two thousand dollars each. I am sure they are not. Cinqué might bring two thousand dollars on a Boston market—or in New Orleans—but what of the others, the children included?"

"Should we have an appraisal made?" Tappan asked.

"Yes, in case the question comes up—with proper affidavits from reliable appraisers."

"Will you get them?"

"Yes."

"You will include all necessary expenses in your fees."

This without question of what kind of man a reliable appraiser of human flesh might be.

When they had finished all details of business, the men were still reluctant to go. Late October chilled the night, but a heavier chill lay on their hearts. Would all their work for the Africans be in vain? Would the Chevalier de Argaiz still have the satisfaction of delivering Cinqué and his comrades to a Cuban court?

"I have the name of the man who should carry the defense to the Supreme Court," Baldwin said out of the silence.

The others stared at him, waiting, asking only with their eyes.

"John Quincy Adams."

The name broke the gloom that had descended upon them.

"I have thought of him," Tappan said. "He has written much in defense of the Africans. He tried to introduce a resolution in Congress on their behalf. But he too is an old man—older than Choate. He has not argued a case before the Supreme Court since before he was President."

"That does not matter," the others argued. "If you could persuade him, his years, humanity, eloquence will surely make justice prevail."

They agreed that John Quincy Adams should be asked, and Lewis Tappan was appointed to ask him. Their meeting broke at midnight. Then Lewis Tappan went to pace the Village Green, already phrasing the arguments that would persuade a former President to fight against a President who had failed his trust.

On the morning of October 27, 1840, Lewis Tappan and Ellis Gray Loring took a carriage from Boston to Quincy to put their request to John Quincy Adams. On the nine-mile drive they had plenty of time to regret that Rufus Choate had rejected their plea to appear as counsel for the Africans. His health was indeed feeble, and he obviously lacked the strength to present an argument in Washington. They also had plenty of time to think up arguments to persuade Adams. Tappan carried two scrapbooks on the *Amistad* case on his lap, and as they rode along, they reviewed the long struggle.

The old man was at his desk in his study when Tappan and Loring were shown in. Loring, who had known him for years, presented Tappan.

Tappan found him looking older than he had expected, but showing remarkable vigor and vitality in his hand grip. The bald head, tufted white sidewhiskers, white hair falling on his collar, stooped shoulders made him seem more than seventy-three. But Tappan found his eyes sharp, piercing, his voice calm and steady.

Adams drew three chairs before the open fire, his own at an angle facing his two visitors. Tappan looked at the old flint and steel on the mantel long enough to reassure himself, and then got immediately to the subject.

"You are aware that the case of the Africans of the *Amistad* is to be heard before the Supreme Court?"

"I am, and I regret the case should have been held on so long. I feel the error lies in Judge Thompson's original charge to the grand jury. The Africans should have been indicted for piracy and murder—if a grand jury could have been found that would indict them—and after being acquitted, they should have been set free."

"But Judge Thompson did not think the Africans had been guilty of piracy and murder," Loring objected, in a tone that launched them into controversy.

Tappan, seeing that their views differed on legal points no longer involved in the case, and fearing the result of an argument, hastened to make his request.

"Mr. Staples has retired from the case," he said, "and we are in need of someone to replace him. That is why we came to see you. We want to place the burden on your shoulders."

Adams rose and stared out the window, leaving his two guests to find answers in the fire. After a silence that left Tappan and Loring uncomfortable, he returned to stand before them.

"I am aware of the honor you are bestowing upon me, but I must excuse myself on the plea of my age and the oppressing burden of my duties as a member of the House of Representatives."

"We would not require much of your time—"

"And I must plead my inexperience in the forms and technicals of arguments before judicial tribunals. It has been more than thirty years since I argued a case before the Supreme Court of the United States."

The burden of persuasion was on Tappan.

"We are not disposed to argue experience or inexperience," he said earnestly. "We only implore you to speak out for these unfortunate Africans. It is a matter of life and death. Your presence there might prevent their being sent back to Cuba for the justice of a Spanish court."

"I am an old man—"

"Full of wisdom and humanity," Tappan broke in. "You have heard Cinqué's story; you have seen portraits of his noble face. Would you send him to death in a Havana prison?"

Adams turned to the window again to hide the agitation in his face. Tappan and Loring remained silent. When they thought he must have forgot them, he turned and faced them. His words were low, his voice steady.

"With the blessing of God and if my health permits, I will argue the case before the Supreme Court."

The two men grasped his hands and all three stood in an attitude of prayer.

"I will implore the Almighty God," the old man continued, "so to control my temper, to enlighten my soul, and to give me utterance that I may prove myself in every respect equal to the task."

While the fire crackled on, the three men sat making plans for the defense. It was agreed that Roger Sherman Baldwin would write the brief and present the first argument, and that he should submit to Adams his brief and all the legal aspects of the case at his command. They agreed also that Sedgwick would not be asked to assist in presenting the case before the Supreme Court. Adams would more than compensate for the loss of Sedgwick and Staples.

Tappan left his scrapbooks with Adams. Then he and Loring took their leave, firm in the belief that justice would at last prevail in their fight.

Two weeks later, at five in the morning, John Quincy Adams walked to the station to get the half-past-five train to New Haven. The cars had brought him to Hartford from Boston the afternoon before. Now they would take him to New Haven in time for breakfast. The coaches were cold

251

and dirty, but he found them immeasurably superior to the stagecoaches he had ridden over the same route since his youth. What progress civilization had made in those years! Half the way to New Haven his mind was occupied in turning various aspects of that thought to light, analyzing it for a possible paper or talk.

In New Haven he walked to the Tontine Hotel and took lodgings and breakfast. Soon after breakfast Roger Sherman Baldwin called on him at the Hotel and invited him to his office in his home. There until after noon Baldwin went over the case with him, giving him copies of briefs and arguments. But there were imponderables no brief could take into consideration.

The election was over, and Van Buren had lost. The Whigs, with their log cabins and hard cider, had swept Harrison into office. But the case would come before the Supreme Court before Van Buren relinquished office.

"He may no longer try to interfere," Adams suggested.

"On the other hand, I feel he might use the case as a fiendish kind of revenge. There has already been much pettiness in this case; there could be a great deal more. You may have heard of Tappan's recent strife with Holabird."

"No."

"During the trial before the District Court, Judge Judson refused to accept a translation of the Treaty of 1817 between England and Spain as authentic. I immediately wrote Forsyth asking him to verify the document for trial purposes. After months had passed without reply, Tappan took the matter up with both Holabird and Forsyth. Forsyth, it seems, had written to Holabird that the document was valid. But when Tappan went to Holabird, he claimed not to have heard from Forsyth. Only recently Holabird wrote to Tappan that he had at last found the letter in question from Forsyth. It had been in his office at Winsted without having been opened. Or that is his story. Incidents like that and the one involving the translation of *ladino* should warn us that duplicity is still possible."

252

"We are getting to the heart of the question involving the mistranslation," Adams assured Baldwin.

But the two men could see much to despair of in the actions of pro-slavery men, or of men who saw gain in surrendering the Africans to the Spaniards.

In the afternoon Baldwin took Adams to Westville to see the Africans. United States Marshal Wilcox and Colonel Pendleton accompanied them. During the two-mile ride, Adams put Wilcox and Pendleton through a rigid inquisition on their treatment of the Africans.

The men, now thirty-six altogether, were all confined in one room about thirty feet long and twenty feet wide. There were thirty-six crib beds, ranged in rows on either side. Their quarters were even less comfortable than those in the jail, as Baldwin quickly pointed out to Pendleton.

"Cinqué! Grabo!" Baldwin called.

The two men left their woodchopping and came to the room. They shook hands with Adams and greeted him in forced English. It was a meeting of primitive man and the finest product of civilization.

"These are the two chief conspirators," Wilcox said.

It was apparent they had not understood his words. They bowed to him, smiling as if he had paid them the highest compliment. Their teachers had prepared them for meetings with friends of Lewis Tappan.

"We read," Cinqué said, his manner dignified, his face proud with achievement.

Colonel Pendleton brought a Bible and asked Cinqué and Grabo to read. Laboriously they spelled through a few verses of the New Testament. These men, Adams thought, accused of piracy and murder, were like children with a hornbook.

Then Pendleton gave Ka-le a slate and told him to write a few words for Mr. Adams. Painfully he wrote "Ka-le," "Mendi," and "Merica."

"How fast do they learn?" Adams asked.

"Not fast at all," Colonel Pendleton answered.

"I should think not, huddled as they are, and having no other persons to talk to but themselves. Yet it seems to me that Cinqué and Grabo have very remarkable countenances."

"They learn no better than the others."

"And the two light ones? The two that are almost mulatto bright?" Adams pointed to two men withdrawn to a corner.

"No better than the others."

Adams took careful note of the clothing, bedding and utensils furnished the Africans.

"Not what they ought to be," he said to Wilcox. "Will you not accept help from their friends?"

"We think it better not to. The feeling is too great now. It might rise beyond control if Abolitionists were allowed to come with their gifts."

Adams took Cinqué's hand. "God willing, we will make you free," he said.

"God is good." Cinqué offered a sentence memorized in his lessons.

Then Adams brushed his hand lightly over Ka-le's fleece and walked out of the room.

Back at the Tontine, he worked the remainder of the afternoon on the speech he had promised to deliver in New Haven that night—on the progress of civilization. His visit to Westville had provided many new aspects to consider.

November passed into December. In a few days the holiday spirit would descend on Washington, sending Government officials hurrying home for Christmas with their families. But there was no holiday spirit for John Quincy Adams. He had given his word to defend the *Amistad* Africans before the Supreme Court in January—no more than three weeks off. There was no turning back, though daily his agitation increased, daily he felt himself less worthy to defend these worthy men.

The night was dark and cold—the kind of night that sent men and women scurrying for warm fires in lighted rooms. They barely noticed an old man walking through the streets

of Washington, head bowed, eyes fixed on the ground, oblivi-
ous to everything except the thinking that tortured him.

All afternoon Adams had spent reading the documents in
the *Amistad* case and reviewing the work he had accomplished since his return to Washington. His efforts had been
great, the results futile and disturbing.

His first visit had been to Attorney General Henry Gilpin,
Van Buren's appointee after the resignation of Felix Grundy.
He had requested Gilpin to ask President Van Buren to consider the expedient of having the case dismissed by consent
and without argument.

Gilpin saw the President immediately.

"The President," Gilpin reported, "has decided that the
Amistad case should not be concluded without argument.
The Spanish Minister insists that the men be delivered to
him as slaves and transported to Havana."

"Is the President willing to stand on the insistence of the
Spanish Minister? Is he placing the wishes of the Spanish
Minister ahead of justice for thirty-six people?" Adams
asked.

"He would not want to incur criticism at this point.
Furthermore, a motion to dismiss the case was made in the
Circuit Court and refused."

Adams was not to be put off easily.

"I deny the right of the Spanish Minister to claim the
Africans as property. The pretended owners have claimed
them and not appealed from the decision. How can the Spanish Minister claim them?"

"I doubt if the President will yield to your consideration."

It was apparent that Gilpin considered the interview over.
But Adams had still another request to make: If the case
could not be dismissed, could it be taken up in the first week
of the Court's sitting? Adams made the request to please
Baldwin, who had pressing matters at home—made it against
his own better judgment. He felt that if the case could be
held beyond the date when Harrison would take office, the
question of interference with the courts might be avoided.

From Gilpin, Adams went to Secretary of State Forsyth. He found Forsyth smarting from comments flung at him over the falsification of the *traspasos* by the State Department translator.

The investigating committee, through hearings at which they interrogated all the persons connected with the printing of House Document 185, had determined that a proofreader named Trendholm had made the alteration.

"I did not know the meaning of the word *ladino* as applied to Negro slaves," Trendholm had testified. "I supposed it must mean *sound*. It is usual in printing for the proofreader to correct manifest errors. I had no intent or reason to falsify the document."

It had been impossible for the investigating committee to pursue the matter further, and they published their findings. But enemies of the Administration continued to accuse Forsyth of personally directing the falsification.

Forsyth, when Adams saw him, had just finished reading comments made by Judge William Jay, comments that questioned deeply the Secretary's honesty and integrity. Angered and hurt, he would not listen to Adams' arguments in favor of dismissing the case without argument.

"I am determined to pursue the appeal to the Supreme Court," he said. "Let the Abolitionists find their answer there."

Recalling all his efforts, Adams could see no opportunity not taken. Now, walking the dark streets past midnight, he knew the case would go before the Supreme Court. The danger came to him as it had come often in the last decade —the course of the United States led directly to civil war. In speaking for Cinqué, he added his voice to rumbling thunder.

In his anguish, he talked to himself as he walked.

"How shall I," he asked himself over and over, "find means to defeat and expose the abominable conspiracy—Executive and Judicial—of this Government against the lives of these wretched men? How shall the facts be brought out?

How shall it be possible to comment upon them with becoming temper—with calmness, with moderation, with firmness, with address, to avoid being silenced, and to escape the imminent danger of giving the adversary the advantage in the argument by overheated zeal? Of all the dangers before me, that of losing my self-possession is the most formidable . . ."

His wanderings had taken him past the Capitol, now dark and quiet. There, in the room on the first floor where the Supreme Court met, he would make his plea.

"Let me not forget my duty," he prayed.

Christmas came and went; Adams sat before his study fire waiting for the British Minister, Henry Stephen Fox, to call. Adams reread the letter from Fox asking for an appointment, saying he had been instructed by his Government to inquire in behalf of the *Amistad* Africans. Dr. Madden had reported the case well. The story of the Africans had caught the imagination of the young British Queen.

Adams was interrupted by a knock at the door.

"Come in," he said, expecting Mr. Fox to enter.

The door opened and a lady, carefully dressed, heavily veiled, entered the room. Surprised, Adams sprang to his feet and advanced toward her.

"I am Miss Margaret Monroe Stewart," she said. "You do not know me, but I have often seen you on your way to the Capitol."

Adams was pleased with her soft voice, her pleasant manner. He took her hand and tried to lead her to a chair. But she remained standing.

"I have come to you, sir, with a plea," she said.

"Yes."

"My sister is the wife of Lieutenant Gedney."

Adams could not entirely hide his surprise. Why should Gedney have anything to do with him?

"He is very sick," she continued, "and, my sister fears, not of very sound mind. I have come to entreat you that, in argu-

257

ing the case before the Supreme Court, you will not bear hard upon Lieutenant Gedney. He has suffered much on account of the Africans. She fears if you are harsh, it might kill him. I know it will kill my sister—"

He has suffered much. The words stuck in Adams' mind, made black and bold against the pages he had read of the Africans' suffering. *He has suffered much.* Adams saw Cinqué in the slave hold, saw him raising the sugar cane knife to kill the captain. Saw him murder for freedom. Saw him poorly quartered and clothed in a cold New Haven jail. But for the libel of Gedney, Cinqué might now be at home in Africa.

But here was a woman pleading for compassion—compassion for a man who had harmed Cinqué so much. Adams was forced to ask himself the question, What would Cinqué gain by a public condemnation of Gedney?

"I assure you, madam," he said after pausing to consider, "that I will have due consideration for the condition of Lieutenant Gedney."

Adams closed his teeth on words struggling for utterance. The woman touched his fingers, and with a smile of gratitude was gone.

Before he had time to ponder over this unexpected visit. Mr. Fox was shown in. Having met before, having established a basis of mutual respect, the two men shook hands. Adams was immediately aware of the other's agitation.

"It is rumored," Fox said without ceremony, "that the Supreme Court will deliver the Africans up to the Spaniards."

"I have heard the rumor."

"Can anything be done?"

"What have you in mind?"

"As I told you in my letter, Her Majesty's Government has asked me to speak in behalf of the Africans. Dr. Madden has touched the hearts of Englishmen deeply with their story. How can I best pursue the matter?"

"Have you had correspondence with Secretary of State Forsyth on the case?"

"None at all."

"Then I recommend that you direct a note to him expressing Her Majesty's wishes."

Fox stared at Adams intently for a moment.

"I really came to ask your help in drafting that note," he said simply.

Adams provided paper and quills. Together they worked over the letter—in which Her Majesty's Government stated emphatically that it had proof that the *Amistad* Africans had been illegally transported from Africa to Cuba and feloniously reduced to slavery; in which the provisions of the Treaty of 1817 between Great Britain and Spain were summarized; in which the interest of Her Majesty's Government in the subsequent welfare of the Africans was made known.

While Adams dictated, Fox set down a plea that Forsyth and Van Buren could hardly ignore.

"These unfortunate Africans have been thrown by accidental circumstances into the hands of the authorities of the United States. It may probably depend upon the action of the United States Government whether they shall recover the freedom to which they are entitled, or whether they shall be reduced to slavery, in violation of known laws and contracts publicly passed prohibiting the continuance of the African slave trade by Spanish subjects. Under these circumstances Her Majesty's Government anxiously hopes that the President of the United States will find himself empowered to take such measures in behalf of these Africans that will secure their liberty, to which without doubt they are by law entitled. . . ."

When the letter was finished, Adams read it through carefully.

"This should have more weight," he said, "than the Chevalier de Argaiz's latest peremptory note. He claims the Africans as property. He insists that they be charged as assassins as well. How will he reply to questions raised herein?"

Washington was already filled with early arrivals for the

259

inauguration. Tippecanoe clubs from East and West set up log cabin headquarters on the streets. Men carrying miniature log cabins and cider jugs marched through the streets to bands playing the "Tippecanoe Slow Grand March." The Whigs for the moment seemed untouched by the gnawing question of slavery.

On Saturday morning, January 16, Adams and Baldwin went to the Supreme Court, Baldwin to file a motion for dismissal as they had agreed, Saturday being the day for such arguments. Baldwin was steady and sure in his purpose. Adams was like a schoolboy called upon to deliver a speech. More than thirty years had elapsed since he had appeared before the Supreme Court. Though Baldwin was to present the main argument, Adams felt unsure and not half prepared. He entered the Court with a heavy heart, full of undigested thoughts, sure of the justice of his cause, deeply desponding his ability to sustain it.

As the Justices filed in, Adams stood reviewing his associations with each: Chief Justice Taney, whose impeachment he had once proposed; Justice Smith Thompson, who had served in Adams' cabinet; Justice John McLean, who had been Adams' Postmaster General and had betrayed Adams to Jackson; Justice Barbour of Virginia, whom Adams had never liked and had once described as a "shallow-pated wildcat, fit for nothing but to tear the Union to rags and tatters."

Chief Justice Taney opened the Court and announced that the Court thought it best to postpone the *Amistad* case to await the arrival of Justice Story. It was desirable for a full Court to be present for the hearing.

The postponement gave Adams momentary relief, but the suspense was scarcely less distressing than the ordeal itself. Together he and Baldwin went to call on Mr. Fox, who had sent word of his reply from Forsyth.

"The letter is less than we expected," Fox said to Adams. "I fear the President has used our position as a rebuttal of criticism. Forsyth says, 'You must be aware that the Executive has neither the power nor the disposition to control the proceedings of the legal tribunals, when acting within their appropriate jurisdictions.' "

"It is no more than I expected," Adams said.

Mr. Fox read the remainder of the letter aloud.

" 'You have doubtless observed from the correspondence published in a Congressional document that it is the intention of the Spanish Minister to restore these Negroes, should their delivery to his Government be ordered, to the Island of Cuba, whence the vessel in which they were found sailed; where they will be placed under the protection of the Government of Spain. It is there that questions arising under Spanish laws, and the treaties of Spain with Great Britain may be appropriately discussed and decided; and where a full opportunity will be presented to the Government of Her Majesty, the Queen of Great Britain, to appeal to the treaty stipulations applicable to the subject of your letter.' "

Adams took the letter and read it through again slowly. Then he turned to Baldwin.

"Our defense is all the Africans have left. May God give us strength to carry it through."

Adams and Baldwin went to a committee room in the Capitol. When they were alone, Baldwin took a letter from his papers and handed it to Adams.

"This letter from Cinqué will show how much depends on us," he said.

Adams took the letter and spelled out the poorly formed letters:

"Mr. Baldwin

"Dear Friend

"I wish to write you a letter because you have been so kind to me and because you love Mendi people. I think of you very often. I wish to tell you one thing about Mr. Pendleton, how he do to Mendi people, and, when he came here with chains, he put them on some hands and he whip them too hard. . . . Mr. Pendleton says they tell you lie; Mendi people not go to Mendi. . . . We do bad, and when we came to Westville, and he came and whip plenty of them and it is not better for us and he do bad to Mendi people. We forgive him and he curse and he whip us. . . . And all love you very much and, dear friend, I pray for you and I love your very much indeed, and your Cinqué."

With that as a goad, the two lawyers set to work building their defense.

XIX

RESOLUTION IN WASHINGTON

On the morning of February 18 John Quincy Adams rode to the Capitol in his carriage, with Congressman Smith from Indiana as his guest. The old man talked little, his mind being preoccupied with the *Amistad* case. The British Government had formally asked the Spanish Government in Madrid to release the Africans and prosecute Ruiz and Montes, a course the Spaniards were not likely to follow, but an interesting one for Adams' speculations.

When they arrived at the grounds they found a crowd assembled in the front yard of the Capitol, not for a demonstration for Tippecanoe and Tyler but to witness a test firing of Colt's new repeating firearm.

"This new-invented instrument," Adams said to Smith, "is claimed to be capable of discharging twelve times a musket in as many seconds."

"When is the firing to take place?" Congressman Smith asked a man with a real jug of cider.

"It was announced for a quarter to eleven."

"Should we stay and watch?" Adams asked. "It is only five minutes."

They alighted from the carriage and Jeremy Leary, the coachman, turned the carriage out the drive. John Causten, the colored footman, sprang to his perch, his eyes wide with excitement as he looked back at the crowd.

Adams and Smith walked toward the place of the demonstration.

"Fire!" an order rang out, and a burst of gunfire roared and echoed against the buildings, sharp and startling in the cold air.

Adams' carriage had not yet reached the street. The horses took fright at the noise and broke into a run. Leary jerked the reins and shouted, but they would not be reined. "Help!" people shouted from the streets and from passing carriages. But there was no help. They jammed the carriage against a messenger's wagon, broke the whiffletree, tore their harness apart, upset the carriage, and ran on in frenzied flight. The impact threw Leary and Causten to the ground.

Adams and Smith ran to them, but others were ahead of them.

"Leary is seriously hurt," one of the men said to Adams.

Causten was stretched on the ground, crying, "Take me to my uncle."

Some of the colored men in the crowd, knowing him and where his uncle lived on Capitol Hill, took him away. Others carried Leary to one of the lower rooms in the Capitol, where he lay groaning in great agony.

"Send for a priest," he begged Adams.

Adams sent for a priest and also for four doctors. A Naval surgeon happened by at the moment. Adams saw him and caught his arm.

"Will you examine this man?" he asked.

The surgeon gave a superficial examination.

"I believe he has received only a severe contusion of the back," he announced.

He tried to make Leary comfortable, but the injured man kept clawing at his lower clothing and groaning with pain. The surgeon made further examination and discovered a more alarming wound in the bowels. He then ordered the man removed home immediately.

The priest arrived, confessed him, and administered the rite of extreme unction.

Adams hovered over his coachman until he was lifted into a wagon furnished with mattress, pillows, and blankets and taken away to his home.

Then Adams, shocked by the accident as well as troubled over the fate of the *Amistad* Africans, walked alone in the Capitol western yard. There Roger Sherman Baldwin found him a little later.

"The Mississippi case is closed," Baldwin told him. "Daniel Webster, with our consent, will speak on a case involving a similar question. The question is whether a State of the Union can constitutionally prohibit the importation of slaves within her borders as merchandise. Should we consent to the delay?"

"Yes, though I doubt if it will enhance our arguments."

Relieved of the necessity of arguing the *Amistad* case that day, Adams went to the House for a time, and then to the Supreme Court Law Library, still in search of arguments in favor of the Africans. The search was well nigh futile. Except for the case of the *Antelope*, with a relationship that was oblique at best, he found nothing that supported the claims of the *Amistad* Africans—no precedent was set.

He worked diligently until seven in the evening, and then went by Capitol Hill to see Causten, whom he found bruised and sore but not seriously injured.

"Thank God you are all right," he told Causten. "I fear Jeremy is in a serious condition."

Jeremy Leary was indeed in serious condition when Adams saw him. His lips formed agonized prayers, and he had no word for his old friend, who sat by his side until late at night.

The next afternoon Adams walked home from the Capitol in gathering darkness. He had stayed to hear Daniel Webster argue the second Mississippi case, and then stopped by the House for another hour of work. He arrived at home after six and went immediately to Jeremy Leary. He knew the end was near. At six thirty Leary died, almost without a groan. . . .

After a troubled, sleepless night, Adams walked to the Capitol with spirit humbled to the dust, with heart melted in sorrow, with mind confused and agitated. The case of the *Amistad* Africans had been fixed to open that morning. How could he plead their cause well when he was so sore and distraught?

He found Baldwin at the Capitol.

"Leary is dead," he said. "Would you consent to apply to the Court to postpone the case until Monday?"

But Baldwin was concerned with cases waiting for him in Connecticut.

"I must refuse," he said. "I must return home as soon as possible."

Together they walked to the Supreme Court chamber on the ground floor of the Capitol. They found the arched room crowded with spectators drawn to the trial by the publicity it had been given. Visitors for the inaugural, men in rough Western dress, here and there a woman or an Indian, mixed with the Washington audience to pack the space to the book-lined walls. People unaccustomed to the splendor of Washington pointed to the colored bas-relief of Justice holding the scales and that of Fame crowned with the rising sun—neither so honest or inspiring as the plain marble bust of Chief Justice Marshall to the right of the fireplace.

When the Court opened and the case was called, Adams rose to his feet facing the Judges, who sat in robed dignity behind their mahogany desks. The light from the east windows, somewhat softened by transparent curtains, fell almost too full on his head and shoulders.

"My friend and servant, Jeremy Leary, died last evening," Adams said. "The funeral is set for three this afternoon. As a personal favor I request the Court to suspend proceedings from two P.M. today till Monday."

"Certainly," Chief Justice Taney answered for the Court.

Adams and Baldwin had supposed that upon their motion

to dismiss the case the opening and closing would be with them. But Chief Justice Taney presented a contrary ruling.

"The question of jurisdiction being blended with the merits of the cause," he announced, "the opening and closing will be with the Attorney General upon the appeal from the Circuit Court."

Adams retired to his desk within the bar. Attorney General Gilpin stepped to the place within the light and began making a statement of facts, beginning with the registry of the *Amistad* and including all the documents of House Document 185. A restless audience heard him through these documents, all of which they had read in newspapers, and wondered that the Government should have chosen so colorless a man to present its case. With relief, they filed out of the Court when it adjourned at two.

At four Adams walked in the procession to the new Roman Catholic Church of St. Matthew's for the funeral of Jeremy Leary, a procession consisting mainly of members of the Roman Catholic Temperance Association, of which Leary had been a member. Adams joined his wife in a pew and sat with bowed head while Father Donelan read his text:

"Yea, speedily was he taken, lest that wickedness should alter his understanding, or deceit beguile his soul."

Adams saw the ritual of the Mass, heard the priest's words, but his mind was preoccupied with thoughts on the transiency of life, the certainty of death, the final reckoning. He found himself measuring his own sense of faithfulness by the faithful Jeremy Leary.

After the burial in the new cemetery belonging to the Church, Adams rode home with his wife and Mrs. Smith, but he was too deep in grief to join in their conversation.

On Monday morning Adams walked to the Capitol with a thoroughly bewildered mind—so bewildered as to leave him nothing but fervent prayer that presence of mind would not utterly fail him at the trial. The pattern had been broken by the death of Jeremy Leary—more time was needed to set it right.

The night before, at almost the last hour, he still had not prepared his argument, but he had arrived at the solution of an extemporaneous discourse accommodated to the argument of the Attorney General, scarcely yet unfolded, and also to Roger Sherman Baldwin's, still to come. Late in the evening he had begun indexing the documents he expected to use and attempting to arrange his notes into haphazard coherence.

Now, on Monday morning, with the trial facing him, he realized that nine-tenths of what he had written was waste paper—to be thrown out.

The Court opened to as varied an audience as America could muster—an audience in which the merely curious mingled with hot-headed defenders of both sides of the slavery conflict. But some of the chief actors in the long fight were not present. Ruiz and Montes had settled down to business in Cuba again, as agents for houses dealing in slaves. Lewis Tappan was in New York trying to save his mercantile business from disaster. The Africans themselves, whose fate was to be decided here, waited in Westville, all attempts at getting some of them as spectators at the trial having failed. Baldwin, studying the audience, saw a larger number of Southrons and pro-slavery people than had appeared at either Hartford or New Haven. He saw also that the Chevalier de Argaiz had a Spanish delegation present to observe a high American court wrangle over justice to Negro slaves.

Chief Justice Taney opened the Court. Then Attorney General Gilpin presented the Government's argument in the case of Cinqué and other Africans captured in the schooner *Amistad*. For two hours he reviewed the case from its beginning to Judge Judson's hearing on board the *Amistad* to the appeal from the decision of the Circuit Court. In all his words, Adams could not detect one new bit of evidence or interpretation of law.

268

Gilpin reached his summary with still no deviation from the course Adams and Baldwin had anticipated.

"I contend," he said, "that the *Amistad* was a regularly documented Spanish schooner, employed in the coasting trade between the different ports of the Island of Cuba; that the passports of the passengers were regularly signed by the Governor General of Cuba, and prove beyond all controversy that the blacks were the property of Ruiz and Montes; that the Court, by the comity of nations, can not go behind or inquire into the validity of these documents."

While aroused spectators listened, he read again the laws and international agreements to support his last statement. Adams noted that he attempted no argument to show that the right of property remained unimpaired by the insurrection.

"I insist," Gilpin closed, "that all the Negroes ought to be restored to their owners, and that the Circuit Court erred in pronouncing the Negroes free."

Spectators boiled to take up his arguments, on one side or the other, but could show no more feeling than is revealed in a flushed face, a brightened eye. Adams and Baldwin felt some relief—no new argument had been introduced. The brief Baldwin had prepared covered adequately the points raised by Gilpin.

Baldwin spoke next, in behalf of the Africans, in a sound and eloquent but exceedingly mild and moderate argument. Adams, listening to him, wondered that his plea was not more impassioned. So mild and considered were his arguments that the spectators were lulled away from the excitement they had begun to generate.

Meticulously Baldwin developed the rights of the Africans. Then he analyzed the decision of the District and Circuit Courts, and commended their adherence to the principles of justice.

Adams admitted his reasoning was powerful—perhaps conclusive under better circumstances. But Adams was still apprehensive. There was strong prejudice in the Court

Chamber and abroad. There was an Executive influence operating upon the Court. He still feared the balance would turn against the Africans.

When he came to the insurrection itself, Baldwin firmly maintained the right of the Africans to self-emancipation, but he spoke in cautious terms to avoid exciting Southron passions and prejudices. He could not forget the Southrons on the bench, or those who shouted their pro-slavery feelings in House and Senate.

When he came to questioning the validity of the Governor General's *ladino* passports, Baldwin said little. Adams tried to get his attention, caught his eye, begged him to inject affidavits from Cinqué and Grabo, but Baldwin seemed to hold back.

Baldwin came quietly to the end of his speech—too quietly, Adams thought. The Court adjourned on a subdued note. Quietly the audience filed out, disappointed as if they had heard the lines of a great tragedy read in a montone.

The following morning, with increasing agitation of mind, now little short of agony, Adams rode in a hack to the Capitol, taking with him, in confused order, a number of books he might have use for. The very skeleton of his argument was not yet put together. He had spent precious time settling the affairs of Jeremy Leary out of deference to the family.

The largest audience yet to attend the trial wedged itself into the Court Room. Word had gone around that John Quincy Adams would on that day plead the cause of the *Amistad* Africans. Friends and foes of the blacks, friends and foes of Adams, crowded together in the small Court chamber. Adams was surprised to see how few women had braved weather and criticism to witness the trial. He was pleased to see Daniel Webster among the spectators.

Adams watched the Justices file in and take their chairs behind their mahogany desks: Chief Justice Taney ready to preside, Justices Story, Thompson, McLean, Baldwin, Wayne, Barbour and Catron in their places. Justice McKinley had not attended any of the *Amistad* hearings. Adams noted that his place was again vacant.

Judge Taney opened the Court, and then addressed Adams direct:

"The Court are ready to hear you."

Adams rose. The distress and agitation that had been increasing within him since the day he gave his promise to Tappan and Loring at Quincy remained until the moment he arose. Then it dropped away. He could feel that his spirit no longer sank at the thought of the task before him. With one grateful glance upward, he addressed the Judges.

"May it please your Honors:

"In a consideration of this case, I derive, in the distress I feel both for myself and my clients, consolation from two sources—first, that the rights of my clients to their lives and liberties have already been defended by my learned friend and colleague in so able and complete a manner as leaves me scarcely anything to say, and I feel that such full justice has been done to their interests that any fault or imperfection of mine will merely be attributed to its true cause—"

The eyes of the audience shifted from Adams to Baldwin, at a desk, a sheaf of papers before him. Had they been misled by his mildness? Had his plea been more telling than they had thought?

"Secondly, I derive consolation from the thought that this Court is a Court of JUSTICE. And in saying so very trivial a thing, I should not on any other occasion perhaps be warranted in asking the Court to consider what justice is. Justice, as defined in the Institutes of Justinian, nearly 2000 years ago, and as it is felt and understood by all who understand human rights is *the constant and perpetual will to secure to every one HIS OWN RIGHT.*"

He thundered the words into the ears of Judges and audience, then waited for their full effect. The words were burning, and it was apparent Adams had caught on fire with the righteousness of his cause.

"And in a Court of Justice, where there are two parties

present, justice demands that the rights of each party should be allowed to himself, as well as that each party has a right, to be secured and protected by the Court. This observation is important, because I appear here on behalf of thirty-six individuals, the life and liberty of every one of whom depend on the decision of this Court."

Quietly, but with deep feeling, he showed how the Africans had been held in jail eighteen months on diverse charges, the four children on no charges at all. At this injustice his voice rose again. Counsel and witness, pro-slavery men and anti-slavery men examined each other's faces. Here was the impassioned plea the friends of the Africans had hoped for, their foes dreaded. The Spaniards stared uncomprehendingly at this Old Testament prophet, standing in too full a light. Agents of the Administration turned white in anger—

"When I say I derive consolation from the consideration that I stand before a Court of Justice, I am obliged to take this ground because, as I shall show, another Department of the Government of the United States has taken, with reference to this case, the ground of utter injustice—"

There, it was out—before the Supreme Court of the United States, to be repeated in newspapers throughout the land—the whole bitter criticism against the petty machinations of a little man to keep himself in the White House, of a group of little politicians and paid henchmen to keep themselves in power. The little man's day had passed, the movers were ready to take his belongings away, but the judgment he had thrown over a handful of men still hung over them.

". . . and these individuals for whom I appear stand before this Court, awaiting their fate from its decision, under the array of the whole Executive power of this nation against them, in addition to that of a foreign nation. I shall be obliged not only to investigate and submit to the censure of this Court the form and manner of proceedings of the Executive in this case, but the validity, and the motive of the

272

reasons assigned for its interference in this unusual manner in a suit between parties for their individual rights."

The spectators' vigil had not been in vain. They were to witness the trial of one President by another. They watched Attorney General Gilpin redden under the attack. As Van Buren's minion, his turn had come.

"Press not a falling man too far." Adams turned to Gilpin with these words from Shakespeare. He paused for the effect, and then addressed the Judges again.

"It is, therefore, peculiarly painful to me, under present circumstances, to be under the necessity of arraigning before this Court and before the civilized world the course of the existing Administration in this case. But I must do it. That Government is still in power, and thus subject to the control of the Court. The lives and liberties of all my clients are in its hands."

A rustle, a movement among the spectators, aroused the Judges to quick stern discipline. The course Adams had taken could stir the factions to outbreak. Seeming not to observe, the old man went on speaking as if the words were impelled from his throat. Quiet returned under the Judges' glare. Friend and foe were compelled to hear him out.

"And if I should pass over the course it has pursued, those who have not had an opportunity to examine the case and perhaps the Court itself might decide that nothing improper had been done, and that the parties I represent had not been wronged by the course pursued by the Executive. In making this charge, or arraignment, as defensive of the rights of my clients, I now proceed to an examination of the correspondence of the Secretary of State with the Ambassador of Her Catholic Majesty, the Queen of Spain, as officially communicated to Congress."

In the first hour of his argument, Adams had presented his most sensational statement. The effect had been as dramatic as any friend of the Africans could have desired. Then, sure that the attention of Judges and audience would not be

distracted, he went ahead with his arraignment of the Ad
ministration.

He charged the Executive of having, in all proceedings
regarding the case, substituted for *Justice, Sympathy—Sympathy* for the Spaniards, *Antipathy* for the Africans, *Sympathy* with the white, *Antipathy* to the black. He reminded his
hearers that the same spirit of sympathy and antipathy had
pervaded nearly the whole nation.

"I know of no law, but one which I am not at liberty to
argue before this Court, no law, statute or constitution, no
code, no treaty applicable to the proceedings of the Executive or the Judiciary, except that law—"

He pointed to the copy of the Declaration of Independence
hanging against one of the pillars of the Court Room.

"That law, two copies of which are ever before the eyes of
your Honors. I know of no other law that reaches the case of
my clients, but the law of Nature and of Nature's God on
which our fathers placed our own national existence. The
circumstances are so peculiar that no code or treaty has provided for such a case. That law, in its application to my
clients, I trust will be the law on which the case will be decided by this Court."

That law fixed in his hearers' minds, he took the Administration severely to task for interfering with the liberty of
free individuals. Then he summarized the course his argument would take.

"The whole of my argument to show that the appeal
should be dismissed is founded on an averment that the proceedings of the United States are all wrongful from the beginning. The first act, of seizing the vessel and these men by
an officer of the Navy, was wrong. The forcible arrest of
these men, or a part of them, on the soil of New York was
wrong. After the vessel was brought into the jurisdiction of
the District Court of Connecticut, the men were first seized
and imprisoned under a criminal process for murder and
piracy on the high seas. Then they were libelled by Lieutenant Gedney as property and salvage claimed on them, and

Fig. 11 Daguerreotype portrait of John Quincy Adams. (The Metropolitan Museum of Art. Gift of I. N. Phelps Stokes, Edward S. Hawes, Alice Mary Hawes, Marion Augusta Hawes, 1937.)

Fig. 12 Drawing of Grabo by William H. Townsend (1822–51).
(Courtesy of Yale University Library.)

under that process were taken into custody of the Marshal as property. Then they were claimed by Ruiz and Montes and again taken into custody by the Court."

After this summary, Adams began building his evidence to prove the Executive had tried to use pressure on the Judiciary. He read letters of assurance to the Chevalier de Argaiz from Forsyth, he cited the eagerness of the Executive to furnish counsel to the Spaniards while denying it to the Africans, he exposed the whole miserable dealings between Holabird and the White House. As final proof, he showed the *Grampus* waiting in New Haven Harbor under Executive order to return the Africans to Havana for Spanish justice.

For four and a half hours Adams spoke. Then, before he could advance more than half through his argument, the Court adjourned for the day. Looking at the departing spectators, Adams felt that he had not answered public expectation. On the other hand, he knew he had not entirely failed. The Administration would not find an easy answer to some of the questions he had raised.

That was Wednesday. It was Monday before Adams went before the Supreme Court again—after a recess in honor of Justice Barbour, who had died in his sleep Wednesday night. Justice Barbour. one of the Southron Judges whom the friends of the Africans feared, was by death removed from the conflict.

During his brief respite, Adams tried to work on his argument in the *Amistad* case, but his mind was too preoccupied with the transiency of life, and many petty things intervened. The Capitol was filled with office seekers and preferment seekers, fighting to have the spoils system of the Democratic Republicans become the spoils system of the Whigs. In a kind of desperation, Adams told them all to go away. His word would work harm rather than good. But when he went with his wife to the Capitol for services on Sunday, he found the seats filled with those who had come to beg favors. It was a time of greetings and farewells, but Adams was too concerned with his arguments for the Africans, too outraged at the Capitol beggars, to mingle long with the crowds.

Then he was in the Supreme Court Room again. He found the crowd smaller, his own vigor less. The weight of Justice Barbour's death lay heavy on Justices and audience, giving them a heavy sense of foreboding. Adams' mind was on him and on Jeremy Leary as he rose to speak.

For four more hours Adams spoke, analyzing again the major points of the case, emphasizing details Baldwin had touched on lightly. But he could hear his voice falling dead on the people. The burden suddenly seemed too heavy for lifting.

He had meant to develop fully as a parallel the case of the *Antelope*, but he suddenly realized that the time was too short for such a development that day—and that he was a tired old man. He had neither strength nor will to take the time of the Court a third day. What energy he had must be spent quickly.

Abruptly he changed from arguments that had grown flat from too frequent repetition and lowered his voice for a personal plea—a plea that soon turned into the valedictory of an old man who had fought a good fight.

"May it please your Honors:

"On the 7th of February, 1804, now more than thirty-seven years past, my name was entered, and yet stands recorded on both the rolls as one of the Attorneys and Counselors of this Court. Five years later I appeared for the last time before this Court in defense of the cause of justice. Very shortly afterwards, I was called to the discharge of other duties—first in distant lands, and in later years, within our own country, but in different departments of her Government.

"Little did I imagine that I should ever again be required to claim the right of appearing in the capacity of an officer of this Court; yet such has been the dictate of my destiny—and I appear again to plead the cause of justice, and now of

276

liberty and life, in behalf of my fellow men. I stand again, I trust for the last time, before the same Court—

"I stand before the same Court, but not before the same Judges—nor aided by the same associates—nor resisted by the same opponents. As I cast my eyes along those seats of honor and public trust, I seek in vain for those honored and honorable persons. Marshall, Cushing, Chase, Washington. Where are they? Where is that eloquent statesman and learned lawyer who was my associate? Where is my opposing counsel? Where is the clerk? the marshal? the criers of the Court? Alas! where is one of the very Judges of the Court, arbiters of life and death, before whom I commenced this anxious argument, even now prematurely closed? Where are they all? Gone! Gone! All gone—"

The sounds of a woman's sobbing filled the pause Adams left.

"Gone from the services which, in their day and generation, they faithfully rendered to their country. From the excellent characters which they sustained in life, so far as I have had the means of knowing, I humbly hope, and fondly trust that they have gone to receive the rewards of blessedness on high.

"In taking, then, my final leave of this Bar, and of this Honorable Court, I can only ejaculate a fervent petition to Heaven that every member of it may go to his final account with as little of earthly frailty to answer for as those illustrious dead, and that you may, every one, after the close of a long and virtuous career in this world, be received at the portals of the next with the approving sentence: *Well done, good and faithful servant; enter thou into the joy of thy Lord.*"

The old man bowed deeply to Judges and audience. Then, not waiting to hear the closing of the arguments, he went out of the Court chamber and walked slowly home.

For over a week Adams went through the confusion of Washington in inaugural time, taking his part in social meetings and affairs of the House of Representatives, but always with a sense of having failed to do his best for the Africans.

Then on the morning of March 9 he rose early and walked to the Capitol. He had been told that the opinion of the Court on the *Amistad* case would be delivered that morning.

Only a small group of people waited in the Court Room when Justice Story read the opinion. His voice was low, his words memorable in the story of human justice. It affirmed the decision of the District and Circuit Courts, except in regard to the Africans. It reversed the decision placing them at the disposal of the President of the United States to be

Roger S. Baldwin Esqr. New Haven

"Washington Tuesday 9. March 1841. noon

Dear Sir

The decision of the Supreme Court in the case of the Amistad has this moment been delivered by judge Story. The Captives are free.

The decision of the District Court placing them at the disposal of the President of the United States to be sent to Africa is reversed. They are to be discharged as free. The rest of the decision of the Courts below including Lieutenant Gedney's claim for salvage, affirmed.

I requested the Clerk Mr Carroll, to transmit the order of the Court to the Marshal as soon as possible — He says it cannot be issued till after the Court rises to. morrow.

Yours in great haste and great joy.

J Q Adams.

Letter from John Quincy Adams to Roger Sherman Baldwin announcing the Supreme Court decision. Reproduced with permission of Yale University Library.

278

sent to Africa, declaring them immediately free, and directed the Circuit Court to order them discharged at once from the custody of the United States Marshal.

Adams heard the words in humility, and bowed his head in thanksgiving. In all the South, slaves were being sold, separated from their families, beaten, degraded; in all the land two systems of justice prevailed—one for whites, another for blacks. Now, in this one case, justice had prevailed, humanity triumphed. Adams raised his head and held it high as he walked past pro-slavery men who hissed his name—walked in confidence that the time would come when Justice would not ask the color of a man's skin.

In the Chamber of the Committee on Manufactures, alone, away from the sounds of praise and censure, he wrote two letters: one to Baldwin, one to Tappan.

To Tappan he wrote:

"The Captives are free!

"The part of the Decree of the District Court, which placed them at the disposal of the President of the United States to be sent to *Africa* is reversed. They are to be discharged from the custody of the Marshal—*free*.

"The rest of the decision of the Courts below is affirmed.

"But Thanks— Thanks! In the name of humanity and of Justice to you!"

To Baldwin he wrote essentially the same, and added, "Yours in great haste and great joy."

XX

"FROM GREENLAND'S ICY MOUNTAINS"

With Adams' letter in his hand, Tappan knew no business important enough to keep him in New York. What business could be more important than releasing Cinqué and his companions from Westville, from the cruelty of Colonel Pendleton? What greater joy than to tell Cinqué that he was at last free, that no American jail could hold him longer?

He took the boat to New Haven and the cars to Hartford, where he applied to Judge Thompson for an order to discharge the Africans from the Marshal's custody. The following morning he was on his way to New Haven again. It was March 15, the feel of spring was in the air, Sleeping Giant Mountain was beginning to waken with color of earth and twig. Spring stirred the old man out of the gloominess of his own autumn. In the cars, rolling through pleasant Connecticut valleys, he was building a new way of life in Africa— building, and as he built, he hummed missionary tunes of his childhood.

In New Haven he hired a hack in front of the Tontine Hotel driven by a colored man, George Phillips. He called for Roger Sherman Baldwin and together they went to Westville. On the way, Phillips told of things he had seen at the County House while waiting in his hack stand. He had seen the barkeeper sell mead and rum to the Africans. Only the

Sunday before, he had seen Mrs. Pendleton whip Antonio severely for not brushing her child's shoes.

At Westville, Colonel Pendleton greeted them without cordiality and showed them to the school room, where the Africans were at Bible class.

"Cinqué," Tappan called softly.

Cinqué, who had been reading aloud, sprang from his place on the floor and ran to Tappan. He dropped to his knees and clasped Tappan's hand.

"Cinqué," Tappan said, showing him the order for their release, "you are free."

"Paper lie sometime," Cinqué said distrustfully.

"Not this time, Cinqué," Tappan and Baldwin reassured him. "You are free at last."

"Free," Cinqué shouted to the other Africans. "We are free."

He fell to the floor and embraced Tappan's feet. Grabo, Kimbo, Foone—all of them fell to their knees about the two men.

"We go home?" Cinqué asked.

Cinqué laughed like a happy child.

"We go home to Mani. Go home to friends—to Tafe. No more cold . . . no more whip." He changed to Mendi and soon had the others laughing with him.

James Covey shook hands with Tappan and Baldwin and offered to continue working with them as long as he was needed.

"When we go?" Cinqué demanded.

"Soon, soon," Tappan assured him. "When we can get a ship and prepare you for the voyage."

"Then we sail east," Cinqué said proudly.

Professor Day stepped forward.

"We must have a thanksgiving meeting for their deliverance," he said.

With his hand raised to mark time, he began singing a hymn. Like well-trained soldiers the Africans took their places facing him and sang Isaac Watts' words:

"When I can read my title clear
To mansions in the skies,
I'll bid farewell to every fear,
And wipe my weeping eyes. . . ."

Tappan and Baldwin joined in the singing and then each offered a prayer of thanksgiving. No matter how fervent their prayers, how responsive their singing, the Africans did not rise to the height of feeling Tappan had expected. In his own mind he knew what they felt. They had been promised freedom so often. After the meeting, Tappan would go, and they would belong to Colonel Pendleton again.

The meeting over, Professor Day stood among the Africans.

"I am convinced," he told Tappan, "that the shackles of paganism and Mohammedanism have been cast from these children and that they are in the full freedom of Christianity."

Tappan and Baldwin left the Africans to their prayers and lessons and returned to New Haven. There they called together as many friends of the Africans as they could to make plans for caring for the blacks until they could be returned to Africa.

The Farmington community had offered to house them—the men in barracks built for them on A. F. Williams' farm, the three little girls in the home of Edward Deming. Deming also offered to set up a school for them in the quarters above his store. But how long should they be kept?

"I am in favor," Lewis Tappan said, "of keeping them in America at least another year in order that they may be more thoroughly instructed in the Christian faith and way of life. Such insurance against a return to native customs and beliefs is necessary. We must grapple their hearts to God. We must also prepare preachers and teachers to go with them to Africa. The name of Christ must be writ large to shine in the darkness of Africa."

After the meeting, the friends of the Africans went through New Haven raising money to outfit them for their stay in Farmington. The friends in Farmington had offered to house them; but food and clothing still had to be furnished. Before nightfall they had raised enough money to buy mittens and socks, and, for each, two yards of "Lion's Skin" to wrap around their underclothes for the journey to Farmington.

The problem of Antonio and the three little girls had not yet been settled. Tappan went before the Judge of the Probate Court and had Amos Townsend named as guardian of the little girls. He was a bachelor, Cashier of the New Haven Bank, and faithful in his efforts for the Africans; hardly qualifications for the guardianship of the little girls, in the eyes of New Haven critics.

Tappan went to see Antonio and found him working in the tavern that was a part of the County House. The favor of Lieutenant Meade and the Spaniards denied him, Antonio had lost his arrogance toward the Africans and their friends. He knew now that he had played the wrong side, and lost. In desperation, he threw himself on the mercy of this strange kind man.

"The decree says you are to be returned to Havana," Tappan told him. "Do you want to go?"

"No, no," Antonio cried. "I want to stay here—with you. Mrs. Pendleton beat me last Sunday. I don't want to go back to Havana and be beaten. I don't want to be a slave." He pointed to the "F" Jacinto and Vicente had branded in his flesh.

"Will you trust me?" Tappan asked.

"Yes, yes."

"Tomorrow afternoon I am going with Cinqué and the other people on the cars to Farmington. The next morning I will take the *Barber Hill* here in New Haven Harbor to New York. If you are on that boat, I will help you and see that you arrive in New York among friends."

Antonio begged to be taken to Farmington, but Tappan

283

was firm. "I can help you only when you have escaped the control of Pendleton and Wilcox."

Then Tappan, accompanied by Townsend and James Covey, went to the quarters of Colonel Pendleton to demand custody of the three girls. Mrs. Pendleton admitted them and let them speak to Marghru, Teme, and Kene. When they knew they were to be taken from this, the only home they had known in America, they began crying and begging to stay with Mrs. Pendleton and Miss Pendleton.

At this point Colonel Pendleton came blustering in. Tappan showed them the writ from the Probate Judge naming Townsend their guardian, and announced they would take the girls away.

"I refuse to deliver them up," Pendleton shouted. "They shall never leave my house with my consent."

"They are free—"

"Free to go with such peculiar friends as you are—free to become the wards of an old bachelor—free to be subjected to the brutality of Cinqué. The devil knows what will happen to them if they go with you."

Tappan, even-tempered under the attack, stood his ground, still holding the writ for Pendleton to read.

"We demand the right to have Cinqué talk to them."

"I deny any of you the right to talk to them," Pendleton shouted back.

Finding both writ and argument futile, convinced that Colonel Pendleton did intend to make slaves of the girls, Tappan went to the New Haven County Court and filed a petition for release of the girls on *habeas corpus* proceeding.

From the high seriousness of the Supreme Court of the United States the case of the *Amistad* Africans suddenly became an *opera bouffe* in the New Haven County Court, with Colonel Pendleton as the chief clown, with editors from rival New Haven papers to spur both sides in bitter fight. Wearily, friends of the Africans rallied themselves for one more legal battle.

284

The case was brought to trial at three o'clock in the afternoon, with C. A. Ingersoll as counsel for Colonel Pendleton.
Word had spread quickly; every person in New Haven able
to leave bed or business crowded into the court chamber of
the State House. Yale students gathered on the Green and
hissed Lewis Tappan when he entered the Court.

Colonel Pendleton and Mrs. Pendleton and Miss Pendleton, with the little Pendletons and Marghru, Teme, and
Kene, made a grand entrance. Colonel Pendleton smiled
broadly and winked at his friends, his lady bowed and smiled
as if she had achieved a personal triumph. Across the room
from them, Tappan and Townsend frowned at the display.
With them were two Abolitionist ladies, their elongated
faces severe, their habits dull gray, waiting to take charge of
the girls when custody was awarded to Townsend.

Baldwin, opening for the friends of the Africans, proposed
that they should have free and uninterrupted communication with the girls in order to ascertain whether they remained with the Pendletons through choice or through
constraint, and to explain the motives of Townsend in re-
moving them from Colonel Pendleton.

His request granted, Cinqué and James Covey were
brought to the stand. Over the objections of Ingersoll, Baldwin instructed Covey to ask Cinqué to explain their motives
to the girls.

Cinqué began calmly to speak of the generosity of the
friends of the Africans and of their self-denying efforts in
obtaining their freedom. As his soul warmed in retrospect of
the past two years, his eyes blazed, his voice rose, his gestures
became passionate. Eloquently he tried to convince the girls
that Colonel Pendleton was their enemy, Mr. Tappan their
friend.

When he had finished, Kin-na and Professor Day were
called to add to his explanations.

"Do you want to stay with Colonel Pendleton or go with
Mr. Townsend?" Baldwin asked.

Marghru began to cry wildly.

285

"We are afraid to go with Mr. Townsend," she wailed.

"Why?"

"A white man told us we would be whipped and sold as slaves."

Colonel Pendleton reddened under the gaze of the audience. "Well, I never," Mrs. Pendleton hissed.

When Marghru had quieted somewhat, Mr. Ingersoll went to considerable pains to show that Mrs. Pendleton had been a mother to the girls, Miss Pendleton a sister. He tried to show that no moral hurt had come to them under his care. They had been kept entirely in the family quarters, away from the public part of the house and the saloon.

"Mrs. Pendleton has given them excellent training in housework," he added.

This statement brought a laugh from the audience. Baldwin struck while the temper was right.

"Mrs. Baldwin has indeed trained them in housework—to be slaves for her and her family, to be whipped, beaten into submission. Colonel Pendleton has had his gain from these unfortunates as well. Until he was forced to stop, he exhibited these very people as cannibals, and pocketed the money. He had wax figures made of them and has sent them to exhibits about the country. For all this, there has been no accounting. Now Colonel Pendleton no doubt wants to keep these children for his own personal gain—"

Before Baldwin stopped speaking, it was apparent the argument was over. Too many among the spectators had paid their shillings to see the Africans. Too many of them had seen Colonel Pendleton and his lady laying on the lash.

When the Judge ruled that the girls should be removed from the custody of Colonel Pendleton, Townsend and the two Abolitionist ladies took them in charge, and pulled them from the State House through a mob of hissing Yale students to a waiting carriage. The girls screamed and fought against going.

When they reached the carriage, Marghru jerked away and ran for the only sanctuary she knew—the county jail. Across the Village Green she ran, her skirts flying, her terrified screams rousing people from shops and houses. Close on her heels were Townsend and the two Abolitionist ladies. Behind them came Colonel Pendleton, puffing and swearing. Her steps were swift, but they caught her at the edge of the Green, when only Church Street separated her from the County House.

They dragged her screaming back to the carriage and drove immediately to the cars, where the other Africans were waiting to be taken to Farmington. From the State House, from the streets, residents of New Haven came to the cars to witness the last act of the drama in New Haven.

Before the train could pull out, Colonel Pendleton found Simeon Jocelyn in the crowd and tried to give him fifty dollars for the Africans. Jocelyn refused it as conscience money. Colonel Pendleton, determined to right himself with the village, gave the fifty dollars to the Burying Ground Committee.

At last the Africans were united in the cars and on their way to Farmington. Many of their friends rode with them.

"We are all happy now," Fuleh told them. "You want to do us good and we want to do you good."

The friends made plans for the meeting to be held in the First Church of Farmington when they arrived. They would talk *God palaver* with the Africans, raise money for missions, recruit missionaries to return with them to Africa.

A thought continued to bother them. The African names were heathen names. They would sound harsh and ungodly in a New England church.

"A diluted gospel is another gospel," they reasoned among themselves. "We should not dilute the gospel by baptizing in heathen names."

So, as they rode in the cars to Farmington, they gave Christian names to the Mendis. The leader, they agreed, should retain the name the Spaniards had given him—Joseph Cinqué. Through the car they went, giving new names, trying to familiarize the Africans with them. Marghru became

Sarah Kinson, Kin-na became Lewis Johnson, Ka-le became George Lewis. Konoma received his name, Henry Cowles, from a prominent man in Farmington. In the same manner, Faquanah became Alexander Posey. Teme became Maria, and Kene, Charlotte, for the two Abolitionist ladies.

It was dark when they reached the church in Farmington. A congregation was already in meeting, their hymns and prayers mingling in the fresh spring air.

Professor Day led the Africans to the front of the church to the pews reserved for them. Whites stared hard at their black faces, their bizarre dress. Mothers held tightly to their babies—making sure they would never become tempting morsels for the tattooed cannibals.

With the Africans among them, the missionary zeal rose higher and louder in prayer and song. Lewis Tappan spoke, describing the missions that would be set on African soil, the missions that would span dark Africa like a bright ribbon. Cinqué spoke, pleading with them to send missionaries. The little girls sang a hymn to show how quickly black people could adapt themselves to Christianity.

Then the whole congregation came to their feet as Simeon Jocelyn led them in singing:

> "From Greenland's icy mountains,
> From India's coral strand,
> Where Africa's sunny fountains
> Roll down their golden sand;
> From many an ancient river,
> From many a palmy plain,
> They call us to deliver
> Their land from Error's chain."

While they sang, men and women who had never been outside a New England village dedicated themselves to work and die on the African Slave Coast. . . .

The following morning, Lewis Tappan was on the *Barber Hill* bound for New York. Antonio was not on board. Had

288

he chosen to return to Havana after all? Tappan did not believe so. No doubt Colonel Pendleton had prevented his escape. Perhaps another trip to New Haven on his behalf would be necessary.

Tappan had been in his office in New York only a few hours when a colored messenger came to tell him that a Negro boy named Antonio was on board a ship in New York Harbor and asking for him. Tappan started immediately toward the docks, but on the way decided to work through others—to obliterate the trail as he went. He went to the home of a colored friend, a member of the Committee on Vigilance, and explained the circumstances.

"We must get Antonio hidden away immediately," Tappan told him. "The Spaniards will not let him get far ahead of them."

"Once we get him in the Underground, they'll never catch him again."

When Tappan returned to his office, United States Marshal Wilcox and Señor Vega were waiting in the warehouse.

"Where is Antonio?" Wilcox demanded.

"I do not know where he is," Tappan said.

"You know he escaped from New Haven?"

"Yes, but when or how, I do not know."

"He escaped on a vessel for New York. He must be in New York now. Do you know where?"

Tappan truthfully swore that he had not seen Antonio, did not know the name of the vessel he was on, or his destination.

Señor Vega had held his tongue long enough.

"This will be paid for," he threatened. "The Chevalier de Argaiz has written to your Secretary of State, Daniel Webster. He has demanded that Antonio be restored to Spanish custody in Havana. He is holding your Government wholly responsible."

"We must find him," Wilcox urged. "We are responsible—"

"You must search New York very carefully," Tappan told

289

them, without humor. "You might find him. Now, if you will excuse me—"

They went their way knowing that Antonio was beyond their reach. He was no doubt already on the long journey to Canada, stopping at hidden stations in attics and cellars, handed forward by people who loved justice and hated the whole system of slavery.

From that day, Antonio, as such, was never heard of again.

XXI

MERICA MEN

Farmington, Connecticut, a New England village with white houses set among green fields, with the high-spired church the center of life, with homes of leading citizens serving as stations on the Underground Railroad, seemed to the friends of the Africans the best possible place to keep them for the year of education and religious training. The entire village would be a school for the blacks—an object lesson in Christian principles and New England morality.

The Africans worked, talked, laughed with the villagers, but they were not happy. They had been promised their freedom; they had been told they could return to Africa. Now there was talk of another year in America, another long New England winter. They were no longer in jail, but they had less freedom than they had ever had under Colonel Pendleton at Westville. There they could sometimes buy a glass of wine or refill their snuff boxes. At Farmington, the catechists employed to teach them, all the villagers as well, kept them from the tavern at Elm Tree Inn, watched them day and night to see that they did not deviate from the straight and narrow road to a Puritan heaven—to keep them from returning to their pagan African ways, to close their lips on Mohammedan prayers. Sometimes they were asked to sing a Mendi song to please a curious audience, but, if at night, their longing for home broke into a Mendi chant, the catechists were there immediately to lead them in singing a Christian hymn.

Cinqué was more resentful than the others. Through two years of voyaging, mutiny, prison he had been their leader. Through two years he had helped them overcome a despair his white benefactors could never understand—they who had never been enslaved in chains, who had never felt the slaver's scourge. Now he could see his leadership slipping from him— his place usurped by two colored catechists and a gray-bearded God.

"We want to go home," he said daily to the catechists.

"By and by," they answered.

Their schedule was rigorous. Every day they worked in the fields, recited lessons, met for long prayers and hymn singing. Evenings and Sundays they were placed on exhibit in churches in New England and New York, where they read the Bible, spelled English words, sang Mendi songs approved by James Covey—all this to raise money to take them back to Africa and to establish a mission there.

One trip took them to New York City, where they were shown at the Broadway Tabernacle, tickets fifty cents each. In the evening they went to the Colored Baptist Church in Pearl Street. The sight of hundreds of friendly black faces gave them a sense of belonging, of being less a show, and stirred them to put on a good demonstration of their accomplishments.

"How do you know you have a soul?" the colored pastor asked Cinqué.

Cinqué took a Bible and held it up dramatically.

"This book tells me I have a soul that will live ever, ever, everlastingly eternal."

Then the pastor called on Kin-na to address the congregation.

"You are black," he said, "and so am I. You have souls, and so have I. Jesus died for us all. God has made us of one blood.

If we love Him, when we die we shall go to heaven. If we are wicked, we shall go down to hell."

His words brought forth a burst of "Amen." "That's right, brother." "Praise His holy name." The congregation was suddenly fired with evangelistic spirit.

The pastor, quick to detect fervor in his congregation, shouted, "Let us give them the right hand of fellowship."

Someone started singing "We're Marching through Emmanuel's Land." Colored brothers and sisters shook their hands, embraced them. The meeting that had been orderly broke into a shouting and crying outburst of love for God, love for the Africans, sympathy for the unfortunate strangers. This was a warm, fervent religion, much more to the Africans' taste than the cold cheerlessness of New England churches.

When the wave of emotion had passed, the Africans begged to stay with their new-found friends until they could go home. But the Mendian Committee, shocked by the savage outburst of their charges, sent them back to Farmington without delay.

Meanwhile, members of the Committee were pushing forward their plans to send them back to Africa with their teachers. Refusing to accept donations from missionary societies in any way supported by slaveholders, shunning the American Colonization Society because of its Southron support, they had to raise the money from individual donations, exhibitions, and abolitionist groups.

Money was almost a secondary problem, transportation being a chief consideration. They were afraid to send the Africans back in a private vessel, afraid they might be captured by Spaniards and returned to Havana. How pleased the Spaniards would be, they thought, to lead Cinqué in chains through the streets of Havana.

They applied for aid to John Tyler, who had become President on the death of Harrison, beseeching him to send them in a vessel of the African Squadron, the Squadron the

United States had at last sent to help in patrolling the Slave Coast. But Tyler, a Virginian, was slow and cautious, afraid of pro-slavery reaction. He held their requests so long that they soon despaired of help from him.

The British Government having shown itself friendly in the case, Lewis Tappan began negotiations to have the Africans declared British subjects. The Spaniards would not dare touch them if they had British passports. He found the British willing, but the process required a minimum residence of sixty days in Jamaica—time they did not care to lose.

In July, Tappan went to visit the Africans in Farmington and found them listless, dejected.

"We want to go home," Cinqué told him. "We do not want to wait winter in Farmington."

Tappan had a conference with the teachers. They agreed that it would be better to start the Africans home, regardless of risks. Some of them might not stand another severe New England winter. As for teaching them, instruction could be given on the way to Africa.

William Raymond and his wife had agreed to accompany them as missionaries. So had James Steele, a fiery young man who had been involved in a lynching at Oberlin and had then turned to religion. They were all preachers, all Abolitionists who had fought the battle against slavery as far south as Philadelphia. Henry and Tamar Wilson had also agreed to go. They were the colored catechists who had been assigned to give religious instruction at Farmington.

In August, Lewis Tappan received a message to come to Farmington at once. Foone had drowned in Pitkin's Basin while swimming with some of the other Africans. He was to be buried in Riverside Cemetery at Farmington, and Tappan was wanted to speak at his grave. When he arrived in Farmington he learned that a decent funeral had been planned for Foone, and that a stonecutter was already at work on a white marble marker for his grave. Sadly Lewis Tappan spoke his words, sadly the white friends in Farmington laid him in the grave.

His death raised new problems for the Mendian Committee.

"I believe he was a suicide," Henry Wilson told Tappan. "So do the people here who know the circumstances."

"Why?"

"Before he went to the Basin to swim, he said, 'Foone very homesick. Foone die and see his mother.' He was an expert swimmer and there was no reason for him to drown unless he wanted to."

Suicide or not, his death decided the Committee in favor of sending the Mendians—the thirty-five left—to Sierra Leone before the first snowfall.

Despairing of help from the United States Government, the Committee engaged the *Gentleman* to take the Africans to Sierra Leone. Anchoring her near Staten Island, they began storing her holds with farming implements, clothing, books, food—all the necessities they could foresee for running a mission one year.

On November 17 the Africans went to the First Church in Farmington for their farewell meeting. The time had been advertised, and the church was filled with their friends. Dr. Hawes preached on the text, *"and hath made of one blood all nations of men, for to dwell on the face of the earth."* Then all together they sang "From Greenland's Icy Mountains." There were no dry eyes in the church, of either white or black. Then the Africans and their white friends went to the basin, where a canal boat waited to take them to New Haven. It was a time of gift giving, with the Africans receiving clothing, rugs, jewelry, money.

In New York they were taken to the Broadway Tabernacle for another farewell service. Again the church was filled, while hundreds waited outside to get a glimpse of the Africans and missionaries as they arrived.

Simeon Jocelyn spoke for the Mendian Committee, recounting the strange story of the *Amistad* and stating their plans for the Mendi mission. Kin-na spoke in English, proving himself an apt pupil. Marghru read the CXXX Psalm. Then they all sang a Mendi song, a song that made them weep with its intense longing for home. Cinqué gave a short sermon in Mendi. As he talked, the Mendians responded animatedly in the manner of the congregation of the Colored Baptist Church—too animatedly for the taste of the white audience.

Time came for the meeting to end—for the Mendis' last performance for their American friends. Some of their friends had thought they should end by singing "Auld Lang Syne." The missionaries had objected strenuously to the use of a secular song, and insisted that they close with "When I Can Read My Title Clear." A compromise arrived at, the Mendis, thirty-five of them including the children, sang:

> "When I can read my title clear
> To mansions in the skies,
> I'll bid farewell to every fear,
> And wipe my weeping eyes. . . ."

They sang the words to the tune of "Auld Lang Syne."

At sunset on November 26, 1841, a steamboat towed the *Gentleman* to Quarantine near Staten Island.

"Red sky tonight," the sailors said. "Fair breeze for Africa tomorrow."

On the way down to Quarantine, the Mendians assembled in the cabin of the *Gentleman* with Lewis Tappan, Simeon Jocelyn, Joshua Leavitt, Amos Townsend, and A. F. Williams. They prayed, sang hymns, asked for each other God's blessings a thousand times over.

Lewis Tappan stood before them to make the farewell speech. He spoke again of all the sad experiences they had gone through. He spoke again of the faith their friends in America had in them.

"You go back to Africa to establish a mission, to teach your people that God is good. We have given you much to begin with. The cargo of this vessel is for that purpose. You will preach the Gospel to all nations. At the same time you

296

will teach them English and a trade. You have missionaries to help you." With his hand he indicated Mr. and Mrs. Raymond, James Steele, Henry and Tamar Wilson. Mrs. Raymond carried an infant in her arms. "They will be in a strange land. You will have to protect them, guide them. If God be for you, who can be against you?"

"If we stop at Sierra Leone and not go right to Mendi," Cinqué asked, "what will the English Governor and officers do?"

"They have directions to help you the same as if you were in an English ship."

"Well, we thank you for that."

"We have made the best provisions we could for you until you reach Mendi."

"When we get to Mendi, if any harm comes to Mr. Raymond and the teachers, you look to me."

Tappan shook Cinqué's hand on this assumption of responsibility.

"We will get a place for Mrs. Raymond and the girls," Cinqué continued. "Then all go home and see father and mother and bring them to live with teachers, and Cinqué will be Governor."

Then Kin-na spoke.

"We do as Cinqué say. We all do as he say. Me little—Cinqué big. Cinqué he know. Cinqué he great man. He get us all free. He President!"

"Yes," the others chanted, "Cinqué the President of the poor."

The whites were beginning to feel embarrassment, uneasiness when Cinqué bowed his head.

"Our Father, Who art in Heaven," he began.

The whites were astonished at his expression, gestures; they were struck by his pathos, his tenderness, his powerful eloquence. Surely he would be a good leader of his people; surely he would never abuse the advantage given him.

The towboat being ready to cast off, they all went on deck for the last farewell. The Africans and their teachers stood

297

together and sang once more "From Greenland's Icy Mountains." James Covey stood with them, ready to accompany them. Near them were Lewis Tappan and Simeon Jocelyn, both with tears on cheeks and beard.

Cinqué stood with his face to the sunset, his skin black and shining against the purple eastern sky. The sense of drama still held him. With one hand upraised, he spoke the thanks of the Africans for all their American friends had done for them.

"Merica men are good; Merica men are kind. We thank God for Mr. Tappan. We thank God for Merica men. Merica men, we thank you."

The American missionaries drew closer together, their faces calm, resolved, benevolent, trusting in God yet touched with the pathos of parting from friends, from home. Around them huddled the Mendis, happy to be going home at last, weeping at leaving their friends behind.

Tappan and Jocelyn shook hands around again and descended to the boat. "No doubt they will be safe enough," they reassured each other. "It is incredible that God should have brought them so far to let them be destroyed now."

As they pulled toward Manhattan, they watched darkness enfold the *Gentleman*—their hope for an enlightened Africa. . . .

For two weeks the *Gentleman* beat her way through storms and rough seas—so rough the Africans were forced to stay below deck and the missionaries were unable to give instruction or hold religious services. After they were into the Middle Passage they ran into severe squalls. Once they hit a wave strong enough to throw the Africans to the deck and splash water over them. Their confidence in the missionaries, never strong, began to break. They also began to mistrust the Captain. Would he take them home?

With Grabo and Kimbo to help him, Cinqué went through the hold examining the merchandise their friends had provided for them. It was a fine cargo. Could the Captain not get more gold selling it and them to slavers?

Then they struck warm, calm waters. Spirits rose immediately. By day the Africans watched the sun and knew they were sailing east; by night the missionaries taught them to read the stars for directions. At night the course still lay east. Ahead of them, not many days away, lay Africa—home. They were content to work long hours at their lessons.

Then one morning they awoke to find that their direction had changed—from east to south. Alarmed, they went to Mr. Raymond.

"We do not go to Africa?" they asked.

"Not at the moment," he replied. "It is necessary for us to go to the Cape Verde Islands for fresh water. Our supply has become foul."

But Cinqué was not willing to accept that explanation.

"We do not trust the Captain," he said. "We think he is a very bad man. We think he will take us to other shores. Will he sell us and the colored teachers? The Captain would give you a barrel of money for us."

Mr. Raymond laughed at the fears they had built up. James Covey spoke to them of the goodness of the Captain and the missionaries. Still Cinqué was not convinced.

"The Captain said this was a temperance ship," he worried.

"Yes."

"I can show you rum."

"Where?" Mr. Raymond asked unbelievingly.

Cinqué led them to a hold opposite those in which the mission supplies were stored. There Mr. Raymond counted a hundred barrels of rum. Surprised, concerned, he called the other missionaries. The Captain had deceived them. How could they preach temperance when they carried rum to Africa? How could they be sure the Captain would not return with a slave cargo?

"You do not trust the Captain?" Cinqué asked.

"We must trust him."

"Then why do we not sail for Africa?"

"I have explained that we must get water."

In spite of Mr. Raymond's reassurances, uneasiness persisted among the Africans. Their uneasiness increased when they came to Santiago in the Cape Verde Islands. There they saw slavers—American, Spanish, Portuguese—riding at anchor in the harbor, waiting for the dash to the Slave Coast and a full cargo. The Africans prepared for another fight for freedom.

The *Gentleman* anchored in Porto Prayo Harbor and a swarm of native boats came out to trade fruit and chickens. The sight of so many dark, friendly faces made the Africans forget their fears for the moment.

Cinqué and Kimbo went to the hold and brought up a load of mission supplies—axes, hammers, cloth—and were already negotiating with the natives when Mr. Raymond discovered them.

"What are you doing with those things?" Mr. Raymond demanded.

"Trading for fruit."

"They are not your things. Who gave you permission to trade them?"

"No one. They belong to me. I am the Governor, and Mr. Tappan said he gave all things to me. I made a promise."

"You misunderstood him," Mr. Raymond insisted. "All the things in the hold are for the mission. I am in charge. Nothing is yours unless I choose to give it to you."

"Mr. Tappan gave me all things," Cinqué shouted angrily. "I am Governor of Mendi and Merica men. Mr. Tappan said so."

Mr. Raymond jerked some tools away from Cinqué and sent him below.

"You will see who is in charge," he told him.

All that day they lay in the harbor while the crew brought casks of fresh water on board. The missionaries kept close watch on the Africans, especially on Cinqué, who sulked alone in his bunk. Mr. Raymond went ashore and traded for fruit for them. He gave them a good meal and led them in hymns and prayers. Still there was uneasiness, mistrust on both sides.

"Mr. Raymond no do what Mr. Tappan say," Cinqué kept insisting sullenly.

Grabo slipped past the missionaries during prayers and traded his coat for three chickens, a defiance that angered the missionaries and cheered the Africans.

The strife continued after they had pulled anchor and started east again for Sierra Leone. Mr. Raymond, trying to restore confidence, increased the hours for prayer and hymn singing. But something had been lost. Mr. Raymond feared it was faith.

When they came at last in sight of the Sierra Leone Mountains, the Africans recognized them and knew they were indeed approaching home. They laughed, played, sang Mendi songs, and tumbled about the deck like so many children. They were suddenly friendly, affectionate with the missionaries.

"I am very glad today," they said repeatedly to Mr. Raymond.

Burnah touched him on the arm.

"In Merica," he said, "I cried every day to see my mother. Now I am here, I don't want to look back."

XXII

AFRICA'S GOLDEN SAND

On January 15, 1842, the *Gentleman* anchored at Freetown at the mouth of the Sierra Leone River. Officials of the British Government provided a building for housing the Mendians and unloaded their supplies, admitted duty free—in every way tried to aid them in their return home. The three white missionaries accepted hospitality in the homes of American residents of Freetown. Henry and Tamar Wilson, disturbed over the conflicts on board the *Gentleman,* distrusting the ability of the whites to adjust themselves to work among colored people, decided to part company with them on landing. After a farewell prayer on board ship, they went on to Liberia to find mission work in Monrovia.

Mr. Raymond had planned a triumphant entry into Freetown. When he saw, from the harbor, the few wooden buildings, residences of officials and merchants, and the hundreds of grass huts crowded together without design, his plans altered somewhat. But there must still be a show. He and Mrs. Raymond would lead the way, the Africans would march in a column of twos behind them, all singing "From Greenland's Icy Mountains."

Resolutely they pitched the tune and started the march to the Governor's residence. But they were soon surrounded by hundreds of Mendis—some of them recaptured from slavers, some who had come to Freetown to trade. Most of them wore country clothes, a cloth tied around the waist and hanging

302

down before and behind. A few had blue and white cotton robes draped around their shoulders. The *Amistad* Africans, eager to find friends and relatives among them, began throwing off their clothes to show their *grisgris* marks, to reveal their tribal tattooes. Horrified, the missionaries huddled them together, reminded them sharply of the promises they had made in America. They pulled their clothes on again and, with still a veneer of civilization, marched on to Freetown, surrounded by a mob of shouting Africans.

At the house assigned them as their temporary dwelling, Mr. Raymond found that some of the *Amistad* Africans had deserted already—among them Grabo, who was eager to get back to his camwood and ivory trade, and Kimbo, who had some carousing to do in Campbell Town, the colored quarter. Saddened by their desertion, disillusioned by his first hours in Africa, Mr. Raymond decided to let the others mingle freely with the Mendians outside the compound. The bands forged in Farmington would hold, he had to believe.

Among them they found many friends and relatives, and learned that the three years of their absence had been hard in Mendi. There had been a bitter war between the Mendis and Timmannees—a war that laid waste to hundreds of villages and ended in slavery for men, women, children on both sides. The only winner had been the slave trader.

Among them Cinqué found his sister's husband. Solemnly they advanced to each other and cracked fingers.

"Where is my father?" Cinqué asked.

"Gone on the war road."

"Tafe?"

"Gone on the war road."

"My children?"

"The same."

For the first time since Havana, Cinqué wept. He had returned from slavery; his family had been sold into it. They might be dead in the Middle Passage, or toiling their lives out on a sugar cane plantation. He went to Mr. Raymond and told him what he had learned.

"I must go to Mani," he said. "I must see the place of my father."

"Not yet," Mr. Raymond told him sadly.

Mr. Raymond was concerned over what report to send to America by the Captain of the *Gentleman*. Should he tell the truth about the defections of the Africans? He could hear how the enemies of the African race would rejoice. He could see how the newspapers would throw reproach on the Abolitionists. It was a bitter choice to make, but he truthfully set down all the disillusioning things that had happened.

On February 4, a small exploring party set out in an ordinary whaleboat for Kaw-mendi, seeking a place for a mission station, for it was clear their whole purpose would be lost if they remained longer at Freetown. Among them were Mr. Steele, the only white man, James Covey, Cinqué, and Burnah.

They stopped at York, a Methodist mission station for liberated Africans, at the Banana Islands, where Thomas Caulker, Chief of the Sherbro Bulloms, had his residence, and at Sherbro Island, where the first settlement of the American Colonization Society had languished for a year and died, a victim of wily native chiefs. They heard that Don Pedro Blanco's factory had been destroyed by the British, that a famous slave trader named Canot now followed peaceful pursuits at Cape Mount.

At Yingin on Sherbro Island Burnah found his sister, who told him that his mother was living at a village up the Jong River, on their way to Kaw-mendi.

When they arrived at the village, early in the morning, friends of Burnah told him his mother had gone into the bush for firewood. They sent a messenger for her and sat down to wait—Steele in a chair with his notebook open, Burnah and Cinqué on a native bench under some orange trees.

After an hour of waiting, they heard someone sigh deeply

at the other side of a house near them, and then a heavy crash from the fall of the bundle of wood his mother had brought on her head. Burnah heard but did not move. Then his mother came slowly around the house with her hands raised as high as her face, her open palms presented. Tears streamed down her furrowed face, she moaned piteously, she trembled as if she had been frightened by a returned spirit.

She did not approach him directly, but walked around nearly to the opposite side from which she had come, continually weeping and moaning and uttering short exclamations. Burnah did not move from his seat, but sat petrified by the intensity of his feelings. His head was on his hand, his elbow on his knee. Tears fell, and he gave an occasional sigh.

The mother at last faced her son. He was indeed still alive and now before her. Her maternal feelings seemed to rush upon her like a torrent. She plunged at full length on the sand at his feet, and embraced his ankles. She seemed in perfect agony, and rolled from side to side, still uttering her mournful cries. The struggle was long, and Steele turned away, unwilling to watch longer the show of feelings, unrestrained by art or refinement. After a considerable time the mother rose and embraced her son, and, at some length, went through the Mendi ceremony of rubbing the palms of their right hands together, repeating again and again, "Welcome!"

Cinqué, deeply stirred by this scene, determined to go beyond Kaw-mendi to visit his village of Mani, to see if he could find some remembrance of his father and Tafe. But Mr. Steele would not permit him to go.

They took their boat up a branch of the Jong River to Kaw-mendi, where the famous chief Charles Tucker lived. It was Steele's plan to pay Tucker a reasonable fee for bringing in their supplies and setting up a mission station at Kaw-mendi. But Charles Tucker was a wily chief and a greedy one, skilled in speaking English and bargaining with white men. He set his price—enough rum and tobacco to drain the missionaries of all their resources. He entertained them well, killing a goat one day, a sheep another, a pig the third, but he was uninterested in the stated purposes of the missionaries. He had been too long engaged in the slave trade and had received too much gold by it to wish white men to stop it.

By the end of the third day it was clear that they could not expect immediately to settle at Kaw-mendi. Dejectedly, Steele bade Charles Tucker farewell and went back to Freetown.

There they found a sad state of affairs. All of the Africans except ten had deserted Mr. Raymond. To hold those, he had moved to York and taken over the empty buildings of the Wesleyan mission. Their only hope now was to settle on Sherbro Island and maintain limited operations until more missionaries could come from America.

One morning, without warning, Cinqué was gone. He had taken his trunk of clothes and the rug given him in Farmington. He had also taken a gold ring belonging to Marghru.

"He has played us false," the missionaries said to the other Africans. To themselves they questioned how one could expect more of a child of the jungle. They consoled themselves with stories of Africans who, after years of education and training in England, returned to their old pagan ways when they came back to the missions in Africa. They consoled themselves with the thought that the natural heart is selfish, that in America Cinqué had received too many favors. They justified their own behavior to each other, but they knew secretly that the bonds broken at Porto Prayo had never been mended.

Leaving Sherbro Island, Cinqué struck through jungle and upland to Mani, dodging the fighting, asking always for news of his village and people. Then he stood one day where Mani had been. Burnt spots marked the sites of palaver hall and houses. A year's growth had pushed the jungle across the rice fields. A ghostly silence made him turn away. It was

Fig. 13 Drawing of Marqu (Marghru) by William H. Townsend
(1822–51). (Courtesy of Yale University Library.)

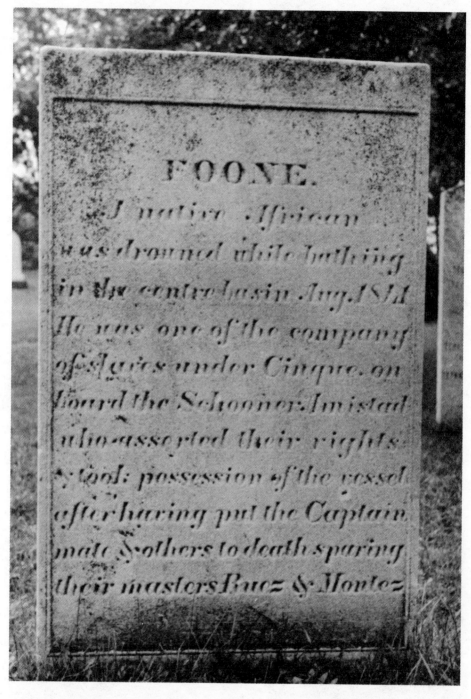

Fig. 14 Stone tablet marking Foone's grave in Riverside Cemetery, Farmington, Connecticut. (Courtesy of Mrs. Robert R. Kalogeros.)

true: his family and friends were dead, or they had gone on the war road.

On the way back to Sherbro, Cinqué got drunk on palm wine, blasphemed the missionaries and the white man's God. He took the long route, to pass by Birmaja's village, to take revenge on the man who had stolen him from Mani. Revenge was also denied him. From stragglers along the way he learned that Birmaja also had gone on the war road. To relieve his grief, his loneliness, he joined a group of Mendians who lived by banditry on native trails.

One morning Cinqué came to Bonthe, where the missionaries had located their Sherbro Island station. He was followed by a woman wearing only a breechclout and Marghru's gold ring. He had discarded his American clothes and wrapped himself in a blue cotton robe. They could hardly have distinguished him from the hundreds of other blacks who came and went at the mission station.

"This is Tafe," he explained, speaking of the woman.

At first the missionaries thought he had found his wife. But he told them of his sad trip to Mani. On the return, among the people along the road, he had found this woman named Tafe and had decided to marry her.

"We cannot permit this," Mr. Raymond said angrily. "I must speak plainly to you of your wickedness. You are dishonest. You took Marghru's ring and other things that did not belong to you. You are licentious—drunken. You can not be head man any more."

"Mr. Tappan say Cinqué Governor of his people."

"You can not be head man any more, no matter what Mr. Tappan said. If you stay, you must work as a laborer on the farm. I cannot permit you to marry this woman. I will not give you an allowance for her. You must throw off your evil ways and return to God."

He might as well have commanded the Sherbro mud to become white sand.

For a few days Cinqué and Tafe lived outside the mission station—long enough for the missionaries to see that he had allied himself to a selfish grasping woman. She convinced him that there was no money to be made working on the mission station at small wages, that their future lay in trading. All they needed was a stock of goods for a beginning.

They wheedled clothes and money from the Mendis who had remained faithful to the mission. They threatened Marghru, Teme, and Kene with Bun-du, the rite of circumcision. This was a fearful threat for girls who had been so long in America. They had heard tales of the horrors that took place in the special house outside the village. They had seen young girls, younger than themselves, naked and oiled, marched through town accompanied by singing and dancing women. The missionaries prevented the ceremony, but the frightened girls had already given Cinqué and Tafe most of their gifts and clothes from America.

One day, without bidding the missionaries good-bye, Cinqué and Tafe took their trading goods by boat and carrier to the Kaw-mendi country. There they soon established a profitable trade with Charles Tucker.

Soon the stories came back. Cinqué had collected a band of Mendi stragglers on the coast opposite Sherbro. His establishment exceeded in extent and splendor that of Charles Tucker. His growing strength led to conflict with other chiefs, to building fortifications for protection, to taking and selling slaves to pay for all the things he wanted. Stories drifted back that he was living like a white trader, like Pedro Blanco, profiting by his experience in New England, buying goods and power with the gold of the slave trade. . . .

How to unravel the skein farther?

For forty years the American Missionary Association, the name adopted by the Mendian Committee, maintained missions among the Mendis. The station on Sherbro Island became a shelter for Mendis, a grave for white men who were God-impelled into its hot unhealthy climate. Though a third of those who went out died, the missionaries built church and schools and farms at Bonthe. Still eager to reach into the interior, they built a larger station at Kaw-mendi.

But it was a hard life for these Americans. Fever and dysentery sapped their strength. Ignorance and superstition gave way too slowly to Christianity and education. They watched the *Amistad* Africans serve faithfully awhile and then turn to paganism and disappear into the jungle.

Of all the group, Marghru proved most faithful. She returned to the United States and studied at Oberlin College. Then she went back to Africa and became principal of the mission school at Bonthe.

At last the struggle became too great. The American Missionary Association had to turn its stations and work over to another group, the United Brethren in Christ. But that was not the end of the American Missionary Association. Disillusioned over their results in Africa, they found new directions in the American South, in educating Southern Negroes suddenly freed by the Civil War. There they built schools and colleges for Southern Negroes. Howard, Hampton, Fisk, Atlanta, Talladega, Tillotson, Tougaloo, among many others, owe their beginnings to the American Missionary Association and to a handful of Mendi Negroes.

And Cinqué?

Cinqué prospered long on the training white men had given him. He became one of the principal rulers among his people. He made Cinqué a name feared by Timmannees and Bullomes, and far into the Mandingo country.

But there was something else the white man had given him during the long waiting in New Haven and Farmington.

When he was an old man and death was near, he thought of how Tuar and Foone had died and been buried in the faith of the white man. He thought of how he had once committed himself to that faith. He thought of how white men of that faith had been his friends and protectors a part of his journey.

In 1879, he crossed again to Sherbro and to the little mission at Bonthe, accompanied only by the men who rowed his canoe of cotton-silk wood. There he spoke to the Reverend Albert P. Miller, a young man just out from America, one of the last representatives of the American Missionary Association in Africa. Slowly he told the long story of his journey from Mani to Mani, of the wonderful things done for him by Merica men.

"Cinqué come to die," he ended his story simply.

He had not come too soon. Within a week he was dead, the last of all those on the *Amistad*.

In the little cemetery back of the mission, among the graves of the white missionaries, they dug a grave for him. Then on a hot afternoon the Mendis of the mission gathered around his grave for the Reverend Miller's sermon and the burial rite. Quietly they stood while his coffin was lowered, quietly they listened while he sprinkled in a little dirt and intoned "Ashes to ashes, dust to dust. . . ."

Then, in the ceremony the missionaries had not taken from them, they slowly circled his grave, each casting his stone, each chanting:

"Walky good, hear!"

Afterword

From the moment I first heard of Cinqué and the *Amistad* mutiny I was fascinated by the dramatic possibilities of the story. A preliminary research convinced me that it was a story I should tell. Once committed to the project, I found myself running down every last detail of information, in a search that took me from Hartford, Connecticut, to Washington, D. C., to Nashville, Tennessee.

When the facts were all assembled, I still had to decide how they should be presented. The choices soon narrowed to two: one, a completely factual treatment with the inclusion of pertinent documents and footnoted references; the other, a dramatic telling. I have chosen the latter.

The whole story is based on Government documents, court records, official and personal correspondence, diaries, and newspaper accounts. My typescript copies of these have become a part of the *Amistad* collection of the New Haven Colony Historical Society Library. The factual background can be documented in every important detail.

To tell the story dramatically, I had to create some dialogue and furnish some settings. Most of the dialogue is taken from court records or paraphrased from diaries and letters. The method is best illustrated in the use I have made of the diary of John Quincy Adams. The remainder of the dialogue, used chiefly for transition, I have tried to make as near the record as possible.

A full list of acknowledgments is impossible; however, of the following some special mention must be made:

New Haven Colony Historical Society, for the portrait of
Cinqué painted by Nathaniel Jocelyn, for the anonymous
painting of the schooner *Amistad,* and for much assistance
in materials on New Haven and the *Amistad* story; Library of the Supreme Court of the United States, for a
full record of the various trials of the *Amistad* Africans;
Library of Congress, for special permission to use the
Lewis Tappan diaries and letters; Yale University Library, for the use of the Roger Sherman Baldwin papers,
and the nine pencil sketches of *Amistad* Africans made
by William Townsend; American Missionary Association,
for copies of letters and reports from the Mendi mission
stations.

WILLIAM A. OWENS.

Rockland Road,
Sparkill, New York.

CHRONOLOGY

April–June 1839 Cinqué captured and bought by Blanco at Lomboko, then sold to Alvarez (CHAPTER 1). Cinqué taken on Portuguese slave ship *Tecora* from Africa to Cuba (CHAPTER 2).

June 1839 Cinqué and others, mostly Mendis, bought by Ruiz in Havana (CHAPTER 3). The schooner *Amistad* leaves Havana for Guanaja with 53 slaves, accompanied by their owners, Ruiz and Montes (CHAPTER 4).

July 1839 Mutiny on *Amistad* led by Cinqué; Africans kill captain and take control of the ship (CHAPTER 4).

July–August 1839 Cinqué's orders to steer ship for Africa evaded by Montes; vessel sighted and hailed off American coast (CHAPTER 5).

August 1839 *Amistad* captured by the brig *Washington* off Long Island; Africans detained and taken with vessel to New London. (CHAPTER 6). Judicial hearing held on *Washington*, Judge Judson presiding; Africans held for Circuit Court and imprisoned in New Haven jail (CHAPTERS 8–9).

September 1839 Committee of Friends of the *Amistad* Africans formed by Tappan and others (CHAPTER 10). Circuit Court meets in Hartford to consider *Amistad* case, Judge Thompson presiding; all matters connected with case referred to District Court (CHAPTER 12).

October 1839 Communication established with Africans by Professor J. W. Gibbs through Mendi interpreter James Covey; provision made for their instruction in English and religion (CHAPTER 13). Ruiz and Montez sued in New York by Cinqué, Fuleh, and Foone on charges of assault and false imprisonment (CHAPTER 14).

November 1839 District Court meets in Hartford to determine disposition of Africans, Judge Judson presiding; case postponed (CHAPTER 15).

January 1840 District Court reconvenes in New Haven, Judge Judson presiding; Judson's ruling that Africans be delivered to President for return to Africa appealed by government to Circuit Court (CHAPTER 16).

August 1840 Africans taken to Westville (CHAPTER 17).

September 1840 Circuit Court Judge Thompson upholds District Court; government appeals decision to Supreme Court (CHAPTER 17).

October 1840 John Quincy Adams engaged to argue case for Africans in Supreme Court (CHAPTER 18).

February–March 1841 *Amistad* case heard by Supreme Court, Baldwin and Adams arguing on behalf of Africans; Court orders that Africans be immediately freed (CHAPTER 19).

March–November 1841 Freed Africans go to Farmington for further instruction; Mendian Committee plans African mission (CHAPTER 20).

November 1841 Surviving Africans leave for Africa aboard the ship *Gentleman*, accompanied by missionaries (CHAPTER 21).

January 1842 Africans arrive in Sierra Leone; mission encounters difficulties (CHAPTER 22).

INDEX

McIntosh, Francis, 113-15
McKinley, Justice, 270-71
McLean, Justice John, 260, 270
Madden, Dr. Richard, 218-20; as member of Court of Mixed Commission in Havana, 45-48, 157-58; discusses case with Tappan, 214-16; meets Africans, 217; testifies that Africans are *bozales*, 223-25
Mandingo (people), 145, 309
Mani (Mendi village), 4, 7, 25, 28, 39, 128, 231, 306
Marghru, 52, 55, 65, 101, 104, 169, 171, 174, 176, 183, 296, 306; as servant in Pendleton home, 246; custody of granted to Townsend, 286; named Sarah Kinson, 288; reluctant to leave Pendletons, 284-87; threatened by Cinqué with *Bun-du*, 308; years later studies at Oberlin and becomes principal of Bonthe mission school, 309
Martínez, Pedro (House of), 224; in African slave trade, 17-18, 37, 44; protected by Spanish government, 36
Maum, 65
Meade, Lieutenant, 106, 124-27, 135, 161, 163, 222; at New London hearing, 128, 130-32; claims salvage rights, 134, 175, 218-20, 232, 235; in capture of *Amistad*, 96-97, 100, 102-4; sues Tappan for slander, 188, 221; to testify against Africans in Havana, 228, 230
Mendi (country), 4, 40, 49, 194, 226, 303
Mendi (language), 145, 154, 156, 193-98
Mendi (people), 10-11, 13-14, 41, 78, 81, 88, 291, 303; customs, 27-29, 43, 157, 190, 305, 310; dances, 45, 89-90, 200-201. *See also* Bun-du, Grisgris, Mani, Ngil-li, *Poro, Wuja*
Mendian Committee, 293, 295, 308. *See also* Committee of Friends of the *Amistad* Africans
Methodists, 21, 304, 306
Middle Passage; *see Tecora,* Slave trade
Miller, Reverend Albert P., 310

Misericordia (Havana slave mart), 43-45, 47-50, 131, 224
Montes, Pedro, 51, 220, 228, 233, 237, 268; battles mutineers, 66-68; charged with assault and battery by Africans, 203-13; evades Cinqué's orders, 77-91; on board the *Amistad* off Cuba, 56-59, 61-62; ordered to steer ship to Africa, 72-76; rescued by Lt. Meade, 96-97, 102-4; tries to regain possession of captives, 126-32, 134-36, 161-63, 165, 167-68, 175, 177-79
Moru: flogged, 61

New England Anti-Slavery Society, 107-8
New Haven, Connecticut, 137; Africans in jail in, 138-44, 198-202; District Court meets in, 231-35, 237-38
New London, Connecticut, 103, 124; hearing on board the *Washington,* 125-35
New London *Gazette,* 125, 136, 149, 180
New York *Evening Post,* 152-53, 210
New York *Sun,* 136, 138, 148-49, 157
Ngil-li (Mendi deity), 11, 156, 188

Paine, Lieutenant, 229, 235, 237
Paulding, Secretary of the Navy James K., 229
Pendleton, Colonel and Mrs., 146, 154-55, 169-71, 173, 176, 189, 190-92, 243, 280-81, 283; as jailers of Africans, 138-44, 198-202, 244, 246, 253-54; Cinqué complains of their treatment, 261-62; refuse to give up African girls, 284-87
Pennsylvania Freeman, The, 107, 118, 120, 153
Pennsylvania Hall, 107, 118-20
Phillips, George, 280
Phrenology, 192-93
Pieh: flogged, 61
Poro (Mendi boys' initiation rite), 13, 19, 28-29, 68, 88, 100
Portugal: in illicit slave trade, 16, 24, 37, 300

Posey, Alexander; *see* Faquanah

Purroy, Attorney: represents Ruiz and Montes, 205-6, 212, 220

Raymond, William, 294, 297, 302-3; difficulties begin with returning Mendis, 299-301; disillusioned by defections from mission group, 304, 306-7

Ruiz, José (Pepe), 220, 228, 233, 237, 243, 268; battles mutineers, 65-68; charged with assault and battery by Africans, 203-13; on board the *Amistad*, off Cuba, 56-60, 62; on voyage to New York, 72-73, 75-81, 86-91; purchases Cinqué and others, 48-51; rescued by Lieutenant Meade, 96-97, 102-4; tries to regain possession of captives, 126-32, 134-36, 161-63, 165, 167-68, 175, 177-79

St. Louis *Observer*, 115-16

Sedgwick, Theodore, 152-53, 174, 204, 212, 242-43; argues for Africans in Circuit Court, 178-79; argues for Africans in District Court, 223; discusses case against Ruiz and Montes, 207-9; dropped from case, 247, 251; letter to Van Buren, 167-68

Seme: killed in mutiny, 65-66

Senegambia, 178

Sessi, 65; at helm of *Amistad*, 71, 74, 79, 81, 87

Sheffield, James, 126-27, 129, 133, 136, 138; lithograph from sketch of Cinqué widely circulated, 146-47

Sherbro Island, 306-8

Sierra Leone, 16, 65, 216-17, 224; arrival of Mendis in, 301-3; as refuge for rescued slaves, 18, 33-35, 195-96

Slave trade: by Portuguese, 16, 24, 37, 300; by Spanish, 17-21, 25, 35-36, 45-46, 182, 195-97, 300; in Africa, 5-22, 303, 306, 308; in Cuba, 38-52; the Middle Passage, 23-37; United States complicity in, 35, 195-97, 300. *See also* England

Slavery: in Cuba, 33, 40, 43-45, 47-50, 164, 185, 196; in the United States,

Slavery—*Continued*
106, 108-9, 129, 149, 161, 175, 182. *See also* Abolitionists

Spain: decrees prohibition of slave trade, 179; in illicit slave trade, 17-21, 25, 35-36, 45-46, 182, 195-97, 300; relations with United States, 177-78, 222-23, 235, 237-38; treaties with England on abolition of slave trade, 36, 45-46, 235, 243, 259, 261; Treaty of 1795, 161-66, 168. *See also* Argaiz, Calderón de la Barca, Vega

Staples, Seth P., Jr., 152, 174, 204, 242-43; argues for Africans in Circuit Court, 184-86; asks to be relieved from case, 247, 250-51; discusses case against Ruiz and Montes, 207-9; letter to Van Buren, 167-68

Steele, James, 294, 297; seeks unsuccessfully to locate mission at Kawmendi, 304-6

Stephenson, Ambassador Andrew, 216

Stewart, Margaret Monroe, 257-58

Story, Justice, 260, 270; reads Supreme Court opinion freeing Africans, 278

Supreme Court, 260; government appeals Circuit Court decision to, 245-46; hearing on case, 266-77; orders that Africans be freed, 278-79

Swift, Mayor John, 119

Talladega College, 309

Taney, Chief Justice, 260, 266, 270-71

Tappan, Arthur, 148

Tappan, Senator Benjamin, 219, 242

Tappan, Lewis, 252, 268, 294, 298, 300-301; at Circuit Court trial, 172, 175-76, 178, 187; at District Court trial, 220, 231, 235; confers with Baldwin, 154, 174, 203, 210-11, 217-19, 227, 242-43, 245-49; discusses case with Madden, 214-16, 225; engages Adams, 249-51; has Townsend named guardian for girls, 283-85; letter from Adams to, 279; meets with Africans, 154-55, 173-74, 188, 226, 238-41, 280-81; meets with Vega, 207-9; organizes committee to aid Africans, 147-51; plans African

320